Peter Vine

Seychelles

France Albert René,
President of Seychelles.

FOREWORD

Over the years, many authors have written about Seychelles. For those of us who have been born here, grown up in the islands, experiencing the great changes and challenges in our lives, and observing the rapid progress as our young nation develops, there is a deep and special interest in everything that is written about our country. Many tourists come here to visit our superb beaches or to gaze in awe at our unique and fascinating wildlife but there is much more to Seychelles than these aspects. Our history itself makes unusual reading. Islands scattered over a vast area of the Indian Ocean, many with plentiful fresh-water and abundant food supplies, yet lacking any permanent human settlement until 1770 when the first French colonists and African slaves arrived here. They were greeted by islands whose animals and plants had been unaffected by Man. Gradually, and in the face of much hardship and suffering, they created their settlements and placed their signatures upon the landscape.

Today, Seychelles is an independent, non-aligned nation whose ethnically varied population live in peace and harmony, creating an example to other nations for whom racial differences create weakness and divisions rather than strength and unity. This is not to say it has always been thus. The deprivation of freedom suffered by African slaves brought here by early settlers has been lightly commented upon by many writers of Seychelles history, almost as if these people had no objection to the degradation and torment they must have suffered. For many years, during its colonial phase, 'democracy' in Seychelles ignored the majority of its population, conveniently limiting the franchise to land-owners. Today, however, all adult Seychellois enjoy the vote and experience equality of opportunity. The struggle to achieve this, while protecting the interests of all Seychellois living in the islands, has been led by the Seychelles People's United Party whose successor, the Seychelles People's Progressive Front is today spearheading the country's rapid development.

The author of this new book on Seychelles, Dr Peter Vine, has portrayed much of our history in a new, refreshing and balanced manner, helping the reader to appreciate the events which form our past. At the same time, he has focussed on the present, describing our magnificient natural history, revealing and reviewing our modern progress. We welcome this eclectic view of Seychelles and are confident that the reader will find here much of interest and hopefully feel encouraged to discover more about this young, energetic and vibrant nation.

James A. Michel
MINISTER FOR EDUCATION
INFORMATION AND YOUTH

Artwork and Design Copyright Immel © 1989

Text: Copyright Peter J. Vine © 1989

Editor: Paula Casey

Design: Henry J. Sharpe, with jacket design by Jane Stark,
Connemara Graphics

Printed by: Dai Nippon Printing Co., Hong Kong

Typeset by: Datapage International, Dublin

Photographers:　Peter J. Vine
　　　　　　　　　Susanna Harrison
　　　　　　　　　Dr Mike Hill
　　　　　　　　　Guy de Moussac
　　　　　　　　　Jacques Fauquet
　　　　　　　　　Francis Marsac

Black and white postcards provided by Indian Ocean Studies Centre.

Other Contributors: Paula Casey contributed to the Natural History Section of this book.

Other Titles by the same author and publisher include:

The Red Sea
Red Sea Safety Guide
Red Sea Invertebrates
Red Sea Explorers
Pearls in Arabian Waters: The Heritage of Bahrain
Jewels of the Kingdom: The Heritage of Jordan
Arab Gold: Heritage of the UAE
The Heritage of Qatar
The Heritage of Kuwait
New Guide to Bahrain

ISBN 0 907 151 40X

British Library Cataloguing in Publication Data
Vine, Peter, 1945–
　　Seychelles.
　　1. Seychelles Islands.
　　I. Title
　　969'6

IMMEL PUBLISHING
Ely House
37 Dover Street,
London W1X 3RB, UK.
Tel. 01 491 1799　Tlx 296582 ELTOUP
　　01 409 1343　Fax 01 409 1525

CONTENTS

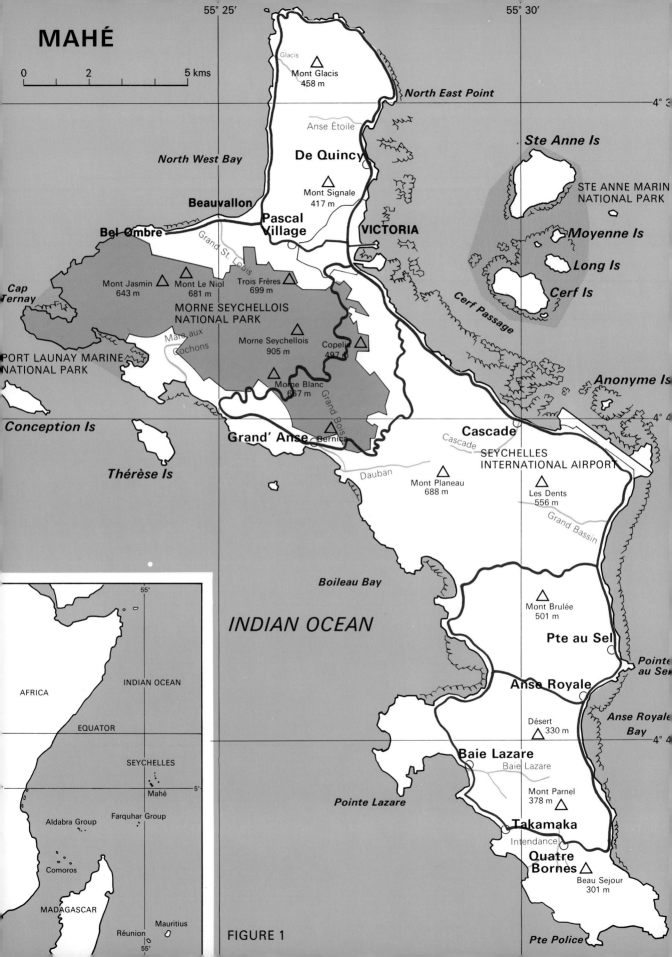

MAHÉ

0   2   5 kms

Mont Glacis
458 m

North East Point

De Quincy

North West Bay

Ste Anne Is

STE ANNE MARINE
NATIONAL PARK

Mont Signale
417 m

Beauvallon

Pascal
Village

Moyenne Is

Bel Ombre

VICTORIA

Long Is

Grand St. Louis

Cap
Ternay

Mont Jasmin
643 m

Mont Le Niol
681 m

Trois Frères
699 m

Cerf Is

Cerf Passage

MORNE SEYCHELLOIS
NATIONAL PARK

Mare aux
Cochons

Morne Seychellois
905 m

Copelia
497 m

Anonyme Is

PORT LAUNAY MARINE
NATIONAL PARK

Morne Blanc
667 m

Grand Bois

Conception Is

Grand' Anse

Bernica

Cascade

Cascade

Thérèse Is

Dauban

SEYCHELLES
INTERNATIONAL AIRPORT

Mont Planeau
688 m

Les Dents
556 m

Grand Bassin

Boileau Bay

INDIAN OCEAN

Mont Brulée
501 m

Pte au Sel

Pointe
au Sel

Anse Royale

Anse Royale
Bay

Désert
330 m

Baie Lazare

Baie Lazare

Pointe Lazare

Mont Parnel
378 m

Takamaka

Intendance

Quatre
Bornes

Beau Sejour
301 m

Pte Police

FIGURE 1

AFRICA

INDIAN OCEAN

EQUATOR

SEYCHELLES

Mahé

Farquhar Group

Aldabra Group

Comoros

MADAGASCAR

Réunion

Mauritius

55°

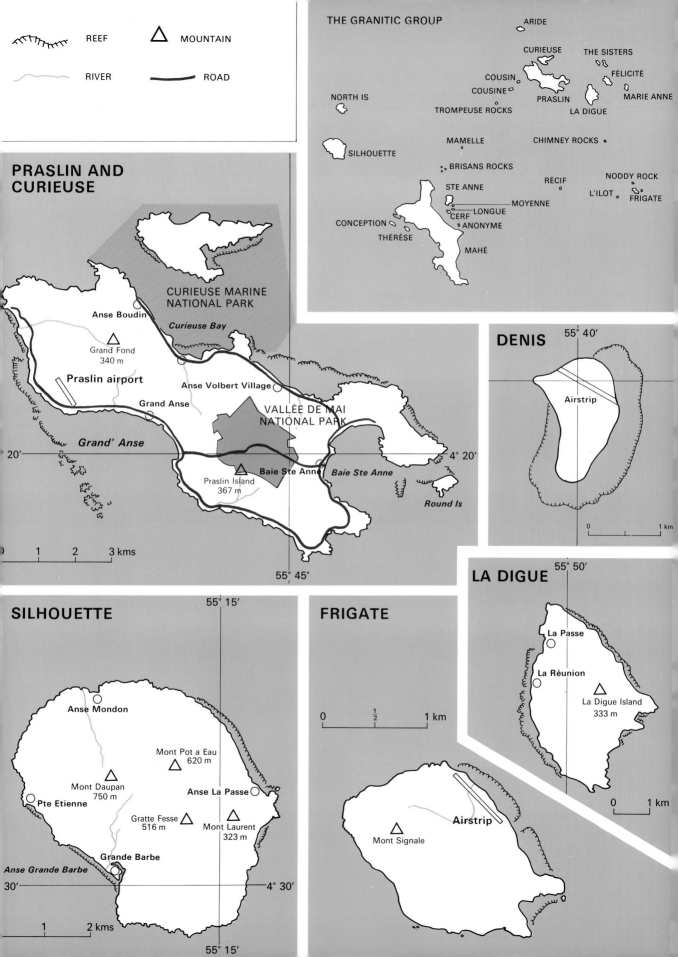

Legend

- REEF
- RIVER
- MOUNTAIN △
- ROAD

PRASLIN AND CURIEUSE

- CURIEUSE MARINE NATIONAL PARK
- Anse Boudin
- Curieuse Bay
- △ Grand Fond 340 m
- Praslin airport
- Anse Volbert Village
- Grand Anse
- Grand' Anse
- VALLÉE DE MAI NATIONAL PARK
- 20′
- △ Praslin Island 367 m
- Baie Ste Anne
- Baie Ste Anne
- 4° 20′
- Round Is
- 55° 45′
- 0 1 2 3 kms

THE GRANITIC GROUP

- ARIDE
- CURIEUSE
- THE SISTERS
- COUSIN
- FÉLICITÉ
- COUSINE
- NORTH IS
- PRASLIN
- MARIE ANNE
- TROMPEUSE ROCKS
- LA DIGUE
- SILHOUETTE
- MAMELLE
- CHIMNEY ROCKS
- BRISANS ROCKS
- RÉCIF
- NODDY ROCK
- STE ANNE
- L'ILOT
- MOYENNE
- FRIGATE
- LONGUE
- CONCEPTION
- CERF
- ANONYME
- THÉRÈSE
- MAHÉ

DENIS

- 55° 40′
- Airstrip
- 0 1 km

LA DIGUE

- 55° 50′
- La Passe
- La Réunion
- △ La Digue Island 333 m
- 0 1 km

SILHOUETTE

- 55° 15′
- Anse Mondon
- △ Mont Pot a Eau 620 m
- △ Mont Daupan 750 m
- Anse La Passe
- Pte Etienne
- Gratte Fesse △ 516 m
- △ Mont Laurent 323 m
- Grande Barbe
- Anse Grande Barbe
- 30′
- 4° 30′
- 1 2 kms
- 55° 15′

FRIGATE

- 0 ½ 1 km
- Airstrip
- △ Mont Signale

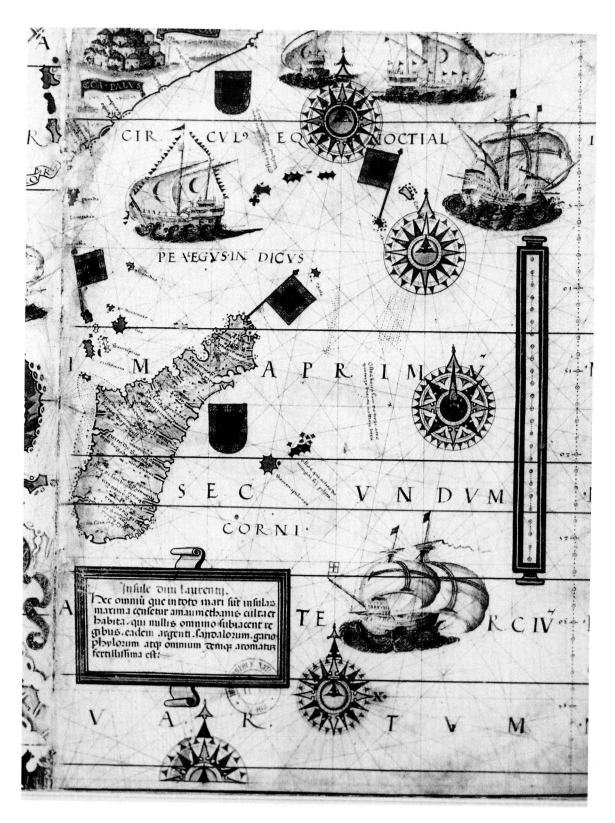

THE PAST

Discovery and Settlement

I found it difficult to escape the feeling that my return visit to Seychelles was, in many senses, a journey into the past. Despite the fact that my mode of travel, on board a bright, new, Air Seychelles plane had, if anything a taste of the future, thoughts of my destination evoked memories of earlier days spent exploring its coastal waters and diving its coral-reefs. It was something more than just my personal experiences however which seemed to be dragging me into a time capsule. These isolated tropical islands resemble an open-air museum, inhabited by plants and animals, themselves living reminders of how this part of the globe appeared long before *Homo sapiens* emerged onto the world-stage. Such endemic species have been preserved, to a greater or lesser extent, by the very isolation of their environment, surrounded by the vast expanses of the Indian Ocean. Scientists affirm that the Seychelles represent a unique remnant of that early mega-continent which comprised Africa, Madagascar, and India. When the Earth's crustal plates began to crack and the continent of India moved slowly away from Africa, the present day granitic islands of Seychelles remained, sandwiched for a while, between the ancient Indian subcontinent and modern Malagassy (Madagascar). A second break released "India" to gradually drift further eastwards and, as it did so, Seychelles were left behind, rather like crumbs falling to the ground as one breaks a biscuit. In the course of time, and by that I refer to many millions of years, the plate on which the Seychelles are situated, continued its gradual slide away from Africa thus creating the fascinating spectacle of mountainous, granitic, verdant islands in the midst of a tropical ocean dominated by coral-reefs and low, coconut fringed sand-cays. And on this anomalous archipelago, terrestrial and fresh-water species, whose forebears hailed from the continents of Africa and India remained undisturbed by Man until his first settlement there less than two hundred and fifty years ago! Recent evidence to emerge from study of amphibians in Seychelles indicates that the islands were never completely submerged by sea-water since their original break-away from the major continental land-masses. Thus, when (and if) early Arab navigators caught sight of them, Seychelles were still completely uninhabited by Man and its wildlife remained totally unaware of the danger posed by this most predatory of beasts.

There is a certain amount of controversy regarding how much knowledge the early Arab navigators had of Seychelles. In his interesting study, Plants and Man on the Seychelles Coast, Jonathan Sauer quotes personal correspondence from Paul Wheatley who wrote:

"*I have often reflected that in the pre-European historic period the Seychelles were remarkably unnoticed. I don't remember ever having*

Opposite

Portuguese chart dated 1519, showing presence of Seychelles. (National Archive Centre).

9

come across a recognisable reference to them in the rutters of the Chinese or Arab pilots, some of whom left rather detailed accounts of their voyages in the Indian Ocean."

Others are convinced that the 12th century Arab navigators who referred to Zarin Islands were in fact reporting on visits made to Seychelles. Of particular interest in this regard are the Arabic manuscripts translated in 1718 by Abbe Renaudot and published as "The Voyage of Two Muhammedans in the Indian Ocean". The first of these is thought to be by an Arab merchant and written in 851 AD; the second refers to the earlier work and is accredited to Abu Zeid al Hussain (c.915 A.D.). The writers make clear reference to what are undoubtedly the Maldives and to the "High Islands beyond" which have been interpreted as Seychelles.

One piece of evidence supporting the view that Arabs knew of Seychelles is the fact that Coco de Mer nuts were already a prized possession in the Maldives and in India long before the first Europeans 'discovered' the islands. The nuts, extremely dense, usually sink when placed in sea-water so it is argued that they must have been carried there by sailors making chance landings on Seychelles (from whence the Coco de Mer nuts must have originated). Additional evidence for earlier visits to Seychelles were reviewed by botanist and conservationist John Procter (1984) when he wrote of the occurrence among the islands of four supposedly 'native' species; i.e. *Casuarina equisetifolia*; *Tacca leonopetaloides*; *Terminalia catappa* and *Adenanthera pavonina*. Procter commented as follows:

Seven circles and oblongs of stone were found covered by dead leaves. Each was oriented towards the north, either by alignment of its long axis, or by placement of a head-stone at the northern side (Vine).

"These four species may antedate the modern colonisation of the Seychelles and I suggest that they did not arrive by 'natural' means. I also suggest that the supposed arrival of coco de mer (Lodoicea) nuts in the Maldives on ocean currents is a myth. The routes and means of transport

of the successive non-African colonists of Madagascar are not known. I suggest that these people may have used Seychelles as at least a temporary staging post, and brought with them seeds or tubers of Adenathera, Casuarina, Tacca, Terminalia and perhaps others (bananas?) not now found wild in the Seychelles...."

Paula Vine, standing on beach-rock at Anse Lascars (Silhouette) indicates the tangled vegetation amongst which were rediscovered, in 1987, a number of early "Arab graves". (Vine).

Others claim that the occasional hollow or partially rotted and thus lightened nut is indeed buoyant and able to float for considerable distances. It was these nuts, borne upon ocean currents, they claim, that Maldivians had collected. The Arabs probably spent little time in Seychelles however for they were more interested in reaching larger land-masses such as Madagascar, East Africa or indeed India and points east. However, the paucity of evidence proving that they actually landed on Seychelles is not really surprising since, if they did so, they would have been intent on collecting fresh-water and fresh-meat, but would not have been inclined to stay long since there were no people with whom they could trade. The pilot whom Vasco da Gama collected from an Indian vessel at Malindi on his first voyage to India may well have known of the risk to navigation posed by the Seychelles Bank and its associated reefs and islands since he directed the Portuguese vessel to head north for several days before cutting a route to the east.

Having been informed by many people that the so-called Arab graves on Silhouette had all been destroyed and that this possible link between Man and the pre-settlement period of Seychelles no longer existed, I was more than somewhat surprised on my visit to Silhouette island, in August 1987, to discover that Arab-type graves are still in existence there, above the beach at Anse Lascar. Each grave, consisting of a carefully constructed circle or oblong of stones, had a head-stone on the north pointing side, probably orienting the graves towards Mecca. The graves may be those of Moslem sailors from India who arrived on board European vessels, or they may pre-date this period.

Wreckage from a Portuguese vessel
which foundered in the Amirantes
during the mid sixteenth century.
(courtesy of National Museum.
photo: Vine).

To the best of my knowledge the site has not been investigated by
archaeologists. Hopefully a study of these re-discovered graves will
finally solve the mysterious identity of these early visitors to Silhouette.
Exploring the area of coast-line where the graves are situated, I had the
distinct impression that other ancient sites exist here and that perhaps
Silhouette island was the first of the Seychelles islands to be occupied,
possibly long before Europeans arrived; but wait, I am rushing ahead
of the story!

"Welcome to Seychelles. We are pleased that you have come back.
If there is anything which I can do to assist in your research please let
me know." I was sitting in the office of the acting Director of Tourism
on Mahe. "Captain Ferrari is in England this week so I am standing in
for him", my host explained; "We call it 'double-jobbing', my other hat
is Director of Port and Maritime Services. In case you need to contact
me, here's my card". I looked down at the name—Andrade, Sam
Andrade. Bells rang as I gazed across the desk at this descendant of one
of the first Portuguese commanders to have sailed extensively throughout the Indian Ocean. Once more my thoughts flowed towards the past
and to that eventful period of history, during the early sixteenth century, when the Portuguese navy invaded the Indian Ocean and set out
to corner the market in exotic goods and spices from India and China.
After the first rounding of the Cape of Good Hope by Bartholomew
Diaz and the subsequent epic voyages of discovery in the Indian Ocean
by Vasco da Gama, indigenous sailors who had plied the ocean in
pursuit of lucrative trading between East Africa, Madagascar, India,
China and Arabia were faced with the direct threat of competition
from sleek Portuguese caravels intent on crushing the monopoly on
European spice-markets hitherto controlled by merchants of Suez,
Cairo and Alexandria. Soon after Vasco da Gama's first voyage into
the Indian Ocean an expedition was mounted under the leadership of
John de Nova. They left Lisbon in 1501 AD with four ships and 400
men, discovering Ascension Island before sailing into the Indian
Ocean, towards India. On their passage eastwards they encountered
Farquhar or Jean de Nova island in the Amirantes. This pre-dates by
a few months the second voyage of Vasco da Gama during which he
took a short cut from Mozambique to India and in so doing sighted an
island at 4 degrees south, henceforth referred to as 'Almirante'. The
Portuguese were thus the first European navigators to make clear reference to islands under the present jurisdiction of Seychelles. Antonio
Galvano referred to this early discovery by Vasco da Gama when he
wrote his volume on navigational discoveries in 1555 (republished by
Richard Haklyut). The Portuguese were not slow in making charts of
their discoveries. The first map showing Seychelles was drawn by Al-
berto Cantino in 1501; Nicolas Caneiro's map of 1502 is a copy of this,
whereas Pedro Reinel's map, drawn a few years later, shows the Mahe
group as the "Seven Sisters".

Into this melee, at the beginning of the sixteenth century sailed such
famous commanders as Alfonso d'Albuquerque, founder of Portugal's
Eastern "Empire"; Joao de Castro, who carried out an early voyage up
the Red Sea; and Antonio Galvao, a distinguished navigator and captain. By the second decade of the century Portugal's presence in the
Indian Ocean was firmly established and its King was intent on consolidating control of his far flung colonies. To this end, in early April

1515, a fleet of vessels had left Portugal to carry the new Governor General of India, Lopo Soares de Albergaria, to India. Commander of this important mission was one, Fernao Peres de Andrade: his instructions were to deliver the governor to India and from there to 'discover China' and establish a Portuguese embassy there. While the details of his successful mission are not directly relevant to the history of Seychelles it is perhaps worth noting that Commander Andrade proved himself as both superb commander and diplomat; after fourteen months in China he set sail towards home with his squadron in 1518. Barros describes Andrade thus: *'very prosperous in honour and wealth, things rarely secured together'*. In July 1520 Commander Andrade arrived back in Lisbon and was able to recount the details of his exciting voyage to the King and Queen who were truly fascinated to learn about China. Fernao Peres de Andrade hailed from a sea-faring Portuguese family and it was not therefore surprising that his brother, Simao de Andrade also captained a Portuguese vessel in the Indian Ocean and was attracted to the notion of settling down in the region. Indeed, in a letter dated 10th August 1518, he had written to the King of Portugal seeking to be appointed as commander of one of the Portuguese fortresses at Malacca, Goa, or Hormuz. The request was in fact turned down and Simao Andrade was despatched on a new voyage to China. On board with him was Francisco Rodrigues the famous cartographer whose navigational book on the Red Sea and charts of lands encountered during his voyages provide us with a detailed picture of Portuguese knowledge of the Indian Ocean at this time. A chart drawn by him around 1512 shows the Seychelles in a reasonably accurate position. And so my mind raced over the incredible link between the gentleman who sat before me, still imbued with a love of the sea and deeply involved in development of maritime facilities of Seychelles, and the important role his sea-faring ancestors played in the early exploration of the Indian Ocean.

Flask and congealed debris from ship-wreck at Boudeuse Cay. Underwater exploration of old Portuguese wrecks in Seychelles waters has resulted in recovery of bronze cannons, copper ingots and other interesting finds. (Vine).

Such meetings in Seychelles are by no means as uncommon as one might imagine. Given the fact that the entire population of the country has been established over the short space of about two hundred years, it is a relatively simple task to trace the ancestry of many Seychellois to personalities involved in events which took place in the Indian Ocean during the mid-eighteenth century or before. Although they were not settled for more than two hundred and fifty years after their presence became known to the great European colonial nations of Portugal, France, Spain and Britain, there was plenty of activity in the general region, with many Europeans venturing into the area, either as sailors, buccaneers, military personnel, administrators, traders, planters, or just plain settlers in search of an escape from the turmoil affecting their own lands.

The British lagged somewhat behind the Portuguese in the race to establish a maritime trade with India, but by the beginning of the seventeenth century their determination to win a share of the huge profits being made by their rivals led to the creation of the East Indies Company and to a series of trading voyages to settlements of the Indian Ocean. The company's fourth voyage sailed from Woolwich on March 14th 1608. At a cost of £1,250 a 400 ton sailing vessel, the "Union" had been purchased by the company and a second vessel: the "Ascension", which had successfully completed two previous Indian Ocean expeditions, was acquired from its owners for the princely sum

A view, from Mahe, of Ste Anne Marine Park area with Praslin and La Digue in the background. It was among these sheltered waters that the first English ships anchored in Seychelles in 1610 A.D. (Vine).

of £485 17 shillings and six pence! The Company had appointed Alexander Sharpeigh as Commander of the mission and its instructions to him were relatively explicit, even if they did gloss over the enormous problems inevitably associated with such a lengthy voyage. Their ultimate objective was to reach India and to load-up at either Surat or Laribandar.

Following an eventful passage down through the Atlantic, around Cape of Good Hope, and into the Indian Ocean during which the ships lost contact with each other, the Ascension finally struck out from the East African coast and headed north-eastwards. On January 19th 1609, the British ship encountered a group of mountainous verdant islands which, based on their inadequate charts, they mistakenly identified as the Amirantes.

Our knowledge of all that happened on the voyage and of this early chance encounter with the main group of granitic Seychelles islands comes from the detailed journal of a British mariner, brought up in Lyme Regis, who had been engaged as "Chief Factor" of the mission:- John Jourdain. His log of the voyage provides us with the first eye-witness account of how the granitic Seychelles islands appeared before they were settled or exploited by Man.

"Jan. 19. 1609....Aboute nine in the morninge wee descryed heigh land, which bare of us E. & by S. At three in the afternoone wee sawe other ilands, which wee made to bee four ilands, and in the eveninge they bare of us N. & by East some five leagues of. And wee stoode with a slacke saile all night untill towards the morninge, and then wee stoode in for the land to seeke water and other refreshinge. At noone per observacion 4 d. 20m.

Jan. 20..... In the morninge, beeinge neere the land, wee slacked our saile and tooke out our skiffe to goe sowndinge before the shipp, and to seeke a good place to anker in. Soe they came to a small iland, (North

Island) *beeing neerest unto us, which lyeth aboute twoe leagues to the north of the heigh iland,* (Silhouette Island), *where they landed in a faire sandy cove, where wee might have ankored very well; butt because our men made noe signe of any water wee ankored not. Soe the boate re-tourned and brought soe many land tortells as they could well carrie. Soe wee stoode alonge towards the other ilands. The tortells were good meate, as good as fresh beefe, but after two or three meales our men would not eate them, because they did looke soe uglie before they weare boyled; and soe greate that eight of them did almost lade our skiffe. Goinge alonge by the ilands we found ten and twelve fathome within a league of the ilands; and two leagues of wee had twenty and thirty fathome faire shoaldinge. This eveninge we thought to have ankored at an iland which laye E.N.E. of us, which seemed to be a very fruitfull place and likelye of water but beinge neere night, and perceyveinge some shoalds and rocks neere the land, and other ilands ahead of us, wee brought our tacks aboard and stoode to the offinge N.E. & by N., hopinge the next daie to finde good ankoringe at the other ilands which wee sawe further to the E.N.E. of us.* (Praslin and neighbouring islands.) *But in our course there was a small iland* (Mamelle) *which laye aboute two leagues of the shoare, which we could not double but weare faine to goe betwixt the ilands and it, haveinge faire shoaldinge 15 and 20 fathome. This small iland is noe other than a rocke, alias ilheo. And being passed this rocke, wee stoode upon a tacke untill midnight, and then with a slacke saile wee stoode for the eastermost ilands with a fresh gale. Wee stoode W. & by N. and W.N.W., for soe wee had brought the body of the ilands of us; haveing seene this daie above thirty ilands, little and greate, faire shoalding round aboute them, I meane to the northward of them. The distance from the southernmost of these ilands to the norther of those wee sawe maye bee neere twenty leagues, close one by another.*

Jan. 21....In the morninge wee stoode in for the land, sending the skiffe before the shipp to sound, as alsoe to find a good place to anker in. Soe aboute nine in the forenoone wee came to anker in 15 fathome water, within halfe a mile of the land. But wee found it full of small rocks; wherefore we wayed and went further in, where we found cleare grownd and better rideinge; where we found very good water in dyvers places, but noe signe of any people that ever had bene there. (It has been concluded by Sir William Wharton who examined the course details, that they came to anchor in the shelter of St Anne Island, not far from Seychelles current major harbour of Victoria.) *It is a very good roade betwixt twoe ilands, aboute a mile and a halfe distant from iland to iland; and thre lyeth, betwixt the E.S.E. and S.E. & by E., other three ilands* (Cerf, Long and Moyenne Islands) *aboute three leagues of from the place where wee ankored; soe that wee weare in a manner land locked, except towards the E.N.E. and E. To knowe the place where wee ankored, there is a small iland* (Mamelle) *which lyeth next hand north from the roade aboute two leagues; and there is a rock or ilheo* (The Brisans) *lyinge betweene the iland where wee ride and the foresaid iland, the roade beinge to the southwards of that. To the W.N.W. there is a very high iland some 10 leagues of which was the first iland which wee descryed.* (Silhouette) *We ankored in 12 fathome water. The roade is in 4d. 10m. to the south-ward* (actually it is 4deg. 35min. S.)

Jan. 22...Finding a rowlinge to sea to come in out of the E.N.E., wee warped in aboute two cables length farther and anchored in 13 fathome water, very good ground and within a pistoll shott of the shoare; where

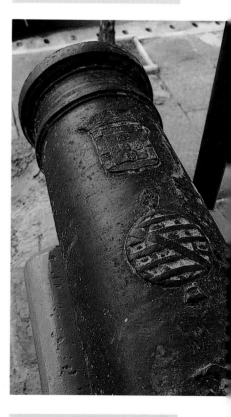

Portuguese cannon outside National Museum, Victoria. (Harrison).

wee ride as in a pond from the 22th to the 30th ditto; in which time wee watred and wooded at our pleasure with much ease; where wee found many coker nutts, both ripe and greene, of all sorts, and much fishe and fowle and tortells (but our men would not eate any of them, but the tortells wee could kill with staves at our pleasure) and manye scates with other fishe. As alsoe aboute the rivers there are many allagartes (crocodiles which, although no longer present in Seychelles, have been confirmed as earlier inhabitants of the group both from fossil finds, and by several other observers such as Abbe Rochon who wrote as follows: "...in 1769, when I spent a month here in order to determine its position with the utmost exactness, Secheyles and the adjacent isles were inhabited only by monstrous crocodiles".); *our men fishinge for scates tooke one of them and drewe him aland alive with a rope fastened within his gills. On one of these ilands, within two miles where wee roade, there is as good tymber as ever I sawe of length and bignes, and a very firme timber. You shall have many trees of 60 and 70 feete without sprigge except at the topp, very bigge and straight as an arrowe. It is a very good refreshing place for wood, water, coker nutts, fish and fowle, without any feare or danger, except the allagartes; for you cannot descerne that ever any people had bene there before us."*

John Jourdain was not the only scribe on board and the vessel's bosun later wrote of his visit to what they had christened the "Desolate Islands" as follows:

"These ilands are at the least some twelve or thirteene in number, and ought very diligently to be sought of them that shall travaile hereafter, because of the good refreshing that is upon them. Water is there in great abundance, also great store of coco-nuts, great store of fresh fish, and likelwise store of turtle doves, which are so tame that one man may take with his hand twenty dozen in a day; also great store of palmeto trees. So that these ilands seemed to us an earthly Paradise".

Author studies skull of Seychelles crocodile, greatly feared by early settlers, but now extinct. (Harrison).

Another sailor on board, William Revett, wrote his own account of the voyage which included a corroborative description of their arrival at Seychelles. He sums up their experiences as follows:

"...*Here wee ryd to water, wood and refreshe our selves untill the primo February; dewringe which tyme noe occurrent happened worthy the relatinge. Only wee fownde heere good store of cocos, some fresh fyshe (wherof most part were skates), lande turtles of so huge a bidgnes which men will thinke incredible; of which our company had small luste to eate of, beinge such huge defourmed creatures and footed with five clawes lyke a beare. Wee kylled also many doves with poles of wood, which was a a sygne of the small frequentation of this place; yet for those which are forced and stand in neede of water and such things as afforenamed it is an excellent place and comfortabell, in regard of the securety and good wateringe place wee fownd there, facill to bee fetched aboard; as also heere groweth such goodly shipp tymber as the lyke or better cannot bee seene, both for hayght, strayghtnes and bidgnes. Thus much I thought good to wryte touchinge these ilandes.*"

These written accounts of Seychelles in 1609, by members of the Ascension's crew, provide valuable confirmation that at this time there was no visible sign that Man had ever settled on the islands. As Indian Ocean trading picked-up however, and navigation between Africa, Arabia, India and China increased, it was inevitable that even the most isolated archipelagoes should be discovered by European sailors and eventually charted. More than a hundred and fifty years passed however before Seychelles were seriously colonised. In the meantime they remained relatively undisturbed. Several Portuguese vessels, sailing through the region, had already run aground and wrecked on corals-reefs of the Amirantes. The recent advent of SCUBA diving has encouraged the search for and exploration of early shipwrecks in Seychelles waters. A Portuguese vessel, measuring 46 metres in length and constructed from 10cm. thick planking, foundered at Boudeuse Cay in about 1550. Artifacts raised from the ship include eleven bronze cannons, a copper coin with the royal crest of Portugal, numerous fragments of the vessel itself showing long copper nails used in its construction, and a vase bearing the head of Vasco da Gama. In addition, amber beads, copper ingots and Mediterranean red coral were recovered. Cannons displayed at Victoria's National Museum were discovered in 1971 and are of the Falconet or Swivel Gun variety and represented something of a development on early fifteenth century cannons. They are particularly well preserved and carry the Royal Coat of Arms of Portugal together with the emblem of King Manoel I.

In many ways it is surprising that the British did not take more note of the enthusiastic accounts written by John Jourdaine and his colleagues following their brief visit to the islands. The only explanation can be that there were much larger prizes to be won and the low-lying coral reefs and cays of the Amirantes represented such a potential hazard to navigation, that sailing vessels often kept clear of them rather than risk being wrecked on uncharted shoals. This natural seclusion suited one group of mariners ideally however. Here was the perfect setting for large sailing boats to secret themselves; for their crews to

Model of Pirate ship in National Museum. (Vine)

relax with plenty of food and fresh water; and for their carpenters to obtain wood suitable for repairs to hull or spars. To pirates of the sixteenth, seventeenth and early eighteenth centuries the granite islands of Seychelles became a base to which they repeatedly returned following forays to attack richly laden merchant ships plying the increasingly well established Indian Ocean trade routes.

Understandably, written records of their activities are sparse. On the other hand, there is ample evidence of their depredations on Western shipping and several of the pirates attained a notoriety they found hard to live down, even when, in later years, they sought to retire from their illegitimate activities. Two of the most notorious were the French pirate Olivier le Vasseur, nicknamed "La Buze" (the Buzzard) and his British counterpart, John Taylor (a former lieutenant in the Royal Navy!). In 1721 this pair sailed into Seychelles in their vessels, "Le Victorieux" and "Defense". Working in tandem they became a lethal force, capable of attacking even the strongest of war-ships. In fact, they took a large Portuguese vessel, the "Vierge du Cap", as she was departing from St. Denis in Reunion (known at that time as Bourbon Island). The Portuguese ship had a rich cargo on board and this was now divided between "La Buze" and Taylor. What happened to the "treasure" has intrigued bounty hunters ever since. Le Vasseur is believed to have sailed back to Mahe and deposited his treasure in a cave there and in the following year, 1722, he decided to retire from piracy and settle down at one of the new French colonies. For a brief while he led a respectable existence at Ste. Marie and he was even offered an amnesty by the King of France. Since this involved a return of all his ill-gotten booty "La Buze" was either unwilling, or perhaps by that stage unable, to fulfill conditions of the pardon. He did his best to drift into obscurity and in 1730 was to be found earning his living as a pilot in the Bay of Antongil, Madagascar (Malagassy). Inevitably however he was eventually recognised as the redoubtable "Buzzard", and escaped capture by returning to his old trade, taking command of the "Victorieux". "La Buze" became such a thorn in the side of colonists of Indian Ocean territories that the French navy was under instructions to make every effort to put an end to his disruptive piracy. His last great battle took place off Madagascar's Fort Dauphin when the French vessel Medusa, commanded by Captain L'Ermitte effectively rebutted the pirates' attack and, after hanging all the members of the pirate crew, dragged their leader, the dreaded "La Buze", securely bound in chains, back to Isle Bourbon (Reunion), to be ceremoniously hanged there on 17th July 1730. On mounting the scaffold he is reputed to have flung a scrap of paper to the assembled onlookers, shouting: '*My treasure, to he who can understand*'.

Thus begins the long saga of Mahe's treasure hunters, a story which continues to this day, as one after another optimistic adventurer attempts to unlock the clues reported to have been written on that elusive scrap of paper. Whatever about the real facts behind all this, those who wish to dabble in the atmosphere of hunting for pirate's loot have only to visit the beach at Bel Ombre, next to the new Corsair restaurant, where the extensive workings of Grenadier Guardsman retired, Reginald Cruise-Wilkins, are still very much in evidence. He commenced his work in 1949 after raising funds in Kenya and gaining support from the Seychelles Government. He had been drawn to investigate the shoreline at Bel Ombre on hearing of an earlier discovery, made by a Mrs Savy who lived nearby, of a number of carvings which were revealed on the rocks after a cyclone in 1923. Shapes depicted on the boulders appeared to include dogs, horses, snakes, a young woman, a tortoise, hearts, an urn, a man's head and a large staring eye. These clues were invoked to link the site with one of the new breed of "pirates" known as Corsairs, who were in effect commissioned by the French Government to harangue British vessels sailing through these waters. The corsair in question, was Bernadin Nageon de L'Estang, "Butin" for short who, based at Mauritius, had repeatedly run the British blockade of that harbour in order to slip away into the expansive tropical ocean and attack ships of the new East Indies Company. "Butin", one of the

While most signs of pirates' early settlements on Frigate island have been destroyed, there remains strong evidence that pirates did indeed use this verdant island as a convenient base. This old "pirate's wall" however almost certainly post-dates their presence.

more successful brigands, before his death, left some clues as to the whereabouts of part of his loot. When the 1923 cyclone revealed the carvings at Bel Ombre a French notary heard of Mrs Savy's discovery and showed her his copies of the old corsair's will and letters referring to his buried treasure. On exploring the area close to the engraved rocks they discovered two coffins containing the remains of what they presumed to be pirates, since the skeletons still had ear-rings, and a third skeleton was buried without a coffin. Despite considerable searching they could find nothing else. Cruise-Wilkins spent more than twenty-five years trying to sort-out what it all meant. The hunt is by no means over however for his two sons have recently taken up the challenge.

Sceptics may be forgiven for taking all this with a pinch of salt, and for perhaps doubting that there is any evidence of pirates using Seychelles as a base; or of burying treasure there. They would be wrong however to be completely dismissive for there are many scraps of evidence which, put together, do create a reasonably substantive body of information in support of some of Seychelles islands providing a home from home for lawless Europeans who sailed under the skull and crossbones. One of the most convincing is the findings by early settlers on Frigate island. When a distinguished member of Mauritius' Natural History Society, Elisee Lienard, visited Frigate in 1833 she wrote as follows:-

"...I was shown a hole, dug sometime before my arrival, where was found a large box filled with crockery from various countries, Dutch pikes, knives, battleaxes, broadswords and Spanish piastres, the whole almost completely eroded by time.

"Further away, opposite a desert cove, I was led to the ruins of a house, which the pirates had built at this place. Foundations in coral and cut stones showed that this construction consisted of a long square. Not far from there, are also other traces of buildings covered with earth and thick growth of lianas and thickets; it is there that was discovered, in 1812, a crossbelt and a shoulder-strap in gold. On a rock lying in front of the cove (Anse au Parc), one can distinguish, without being able to decipher it, an inscription which appears to have been cut in the stone by means of a chisel...

"In another part of the island called Grande-Anse, were also discovered the remains of buildings, iron earthed up canon balls, a fifteen foot deep well, whose side was lined with lead, and on the side, a stone which had been used as a filter. The first inhabitants to visit the island, report that they found in another place, called Anse Lesage, a very tall mast in teak wood, whose base lay on a well made masonry platform; they also saw the remains of a blacksmith's shop, a lead channel which conveyed water to the settlement from a nearby spring, and on a height, to the left, three tombs made in coral on which were laid copper sword hilts; all around was a large quantity of bones.

"...The oldest inhabitants of the Seychelles relate that on their arrival the pirates had been gone for a long time, they had lived on Fregate for several years, and that several ships had been the victims of their depredations; that finally, fearing to be discovered in their den they had decided to leave the island taking with them a very large treasure. They also say these ruffians hid part of their treasure but having been caught some time later, they all received the punishment they deserved for their crimes,

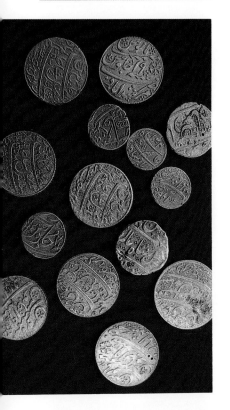

Arab coins uncovered on beach. Courtesy of National Archive Centre. (Harrison).

except only one who was spared on account of his youth.

"It is to him that these curious details are owed; on his death bed he gave one of his friends a note which contained an indication and description of the place where the treasure had been hidden. I have seen this note, and after reading it, I had no doubts about the authenticity of the preceding facts, as everything concurs to give them an unquestionable air of truth. Searches at the places pointed out have been without success; but Spanish piastres and other coins called cruzados have been found on the shore where they had been cast by the sea; I saw several of these coins, that sand and coral had cemented together to such an extent that they could not be separated. With calm weather, one can distinguish, half a mile from land, the debris of a large ship which lies at the bottom of the sea."

Place names may also provide clues to locations worth investigating for buried treasure. At the south end of Mahe lies the bay called Anse Forbans or Pirates Bay, perhaps this was an anchorage or rendezvous point for pirates during the NE monsoons. In his early attempt at a written history of Seychelles, John Bradley, provides a somewhat colourful, if not imaginative, account of piratical goings-on in Seychelles. A short extract is quoted below:-

"Some of these pirates brought with them the unfortunate ladies they had captured. Their fleets laden with plunder sailed to Seychelles to divide the booty. On shore they pitched their tents, landed puncheons of wine, and broached the barrels of rum they brought ashore. They indulged in orgies of drunkenness and rapine. Here they divided up their booty, and the gulls at that time must often have been startled at the brutal crimes they saw committed.

On Frigate Island a resident guided the author to an outcrop of white marble which he was convinced provided some clue to the pirates' supposedly buried treasure. (Vine).

"It was quite natural that some of the ill gotten treasure, pieces of eight, gold ingots, diamonds, gold ornaments which formed part of the booty, was hidden in the neighbourhood. The owners may have been afterwards killed in a fight, or lost at sea, and the treasures remain hidden to this day".

The era of Corsairs or Privateers continued in the Indian Ocean for some time after Seychelles were settled. For the most part they were , in effect, sailing as mercenary forces of their own nations. When it came to a battle, they hoisted their national colours and the most honourable of them returned to port with prizes, which they declared to their government before being awarded a share of the proceeds. Hodoul, one such honourable corsair based in Seychelles, harried the British quite effectively. Widely regarded as a brave navigator and clever tactician, honouring the articles of warfare then in force, he always returned to port with his captives in order that local French government representatives could adjudicate dispersal of the proceeds.

Despite their slow beginnings, and notwithstanding opposition from first Portuguese and then French and Dutch forces, the British toe-hold on the Indian Ocean showed signs of transforming into a half-Nelson. In 1730 a French vessel, "Le Lys" had sighted Farquhar ("Juan de Nova" or "Jean de Nove") and islands of the southern Amirantes including Alphonse, Saint-Francoise and Bijoutier. Alerted to the possibility that such islands could provide a permanent base for the British, and one from which they might mount attacks on the rapidly growing French "colonies" at Bourbon (Reunion) and Ile de France (Mauritius), Governor General, Mahe de la Bourdonnais, decided to forestall any such action and to survey the area where "Jean de Nove" had been sighted with a view to verifying their position and taking possession of any habitable islands for France. Thus, on 10th August 1742, Captain Lazare Picault was despatched from Ile de France on the tartane, "Elisabeth", together with a small, fifty ton vessel, "Le Charle". Their brief was simple: to investigate what islands lay to the north ("...*pour la decouverte et verification des isles ou bancqs de Cordouat, Angassay, Bancq de Nazaret, Jean de Nove, et autres isles et bancqs circonvoisin....*") and to seek suitable sites for colonisation. Despite the activities of pirates and other Europeans who had been sailing these waters for almost two hundred and fifty years, the real position and nature of Seychelles granitic islands was not widely known. Even Captain Lazarre Picault was pretty much in the dark, and it was ten weeks before he sighted the group, whereupon he mistook it for the Amirantes (29*th October, ship's journal* "...*Ce matin sur les huit heures, nous avons eu connaissance d'une grande isle tres platte qui ne peut etre que Jean de Nove qui nous restoit de l'E. au N.N.E., du compas distence de cinq lieus....*").

Returning from an armed sortie through southern Mahe's dense jungle, Lazarre's sailors reported enthusiastically about the quantity of birds (including parrots and many new species); turtles; land tortoises; timber suitable for making masts; coconut trees (whose nuts they collected) and last but not least, large crocodiles. Having arrived towards the tail end of the SE monsoon season, the southerly winds made their anchorage quite uncomfortable and potentially dangerous: the bay where they were alleged to have landed to go ashore, on the south-west coast of Mahe, still bears the name, Baie Lazare. The vessels explored islands of the group (named by Picault as "Isles de la Bourdonnais") until November 26th when they set-off back to Mauritius with a cargo of six hundred coconuts and three hundred land tortoises. The Governor General, although pleased with the ships' discoveries, was not impressed by Picault's confusing charts and sent him back to the islands to make a second investigation in 1743.

This time Picault, again sailing in the Elisabeth of 'Compagnie des Indies', took with him a skilled cartographer who produced some excellent maps of "Ile d'Abondance" (renamed as Mahe in honour of Mahe La Bourdonnais) and its surrounding islands. Records of the voyage indicate that he left Mauritius on October 7th 1743, with a south-easterly wind blowing; on April 16th the "Trois Freres ou Amirantes" was sighted; and on 28th May 1744 they landed at Frigate Island on which turtles were noted. Two days later, on May 30th, dropping anchor in what is today Victoria harbour off the east coast of Mahe, they remained there for two weeks, until June 15th, probably not too far away from where the Ascension had ridden, one hundred and thirty five years before. On June 9th, the expedition explored St Anne island and the next day visited Praslin ("Isle de Palme"), which they continued to study on the twelfth and thirteenth of June; marvelling at its water-falls, rivers, beautiful trees, and majestic mountains. Interestingly enough, the nearby island of Curieuse, was christened "Isle Rouge" because of the red exposed earth on its mountain-side—a feature sometimes attributed to poor land management but clearly, in this case, a natural aspect of the island.

Picault's investigations, on this voyage, were much more thorough and his assessment of the islands as sites for a French colony was

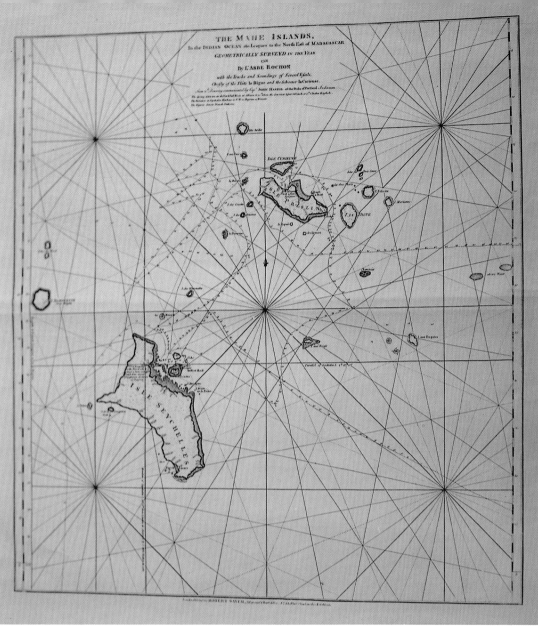

THE MAHÉ ISLANDS,
In the INDIAN OCEAN 160 Leagues to the North East of MADAGASCAR.
GEOMETRICALLY SURVEYD IN THE YEAR
1769
By L'ABBÉ ROCHON
with the Tracks and Soundings of Several Vessels.
Chiefly of the Flûte la Digue and the Schooner la Curieuse.

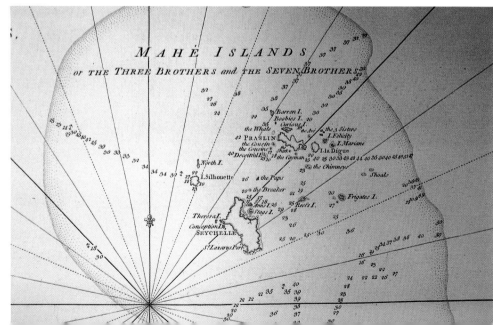

MAHÉ ISLANDS
or THE THREE BROTHERS and THE SEVEN BROTHERS

positive, (although it included a warning about the large crocodiles along the coast). There were suitable sites, he stated, for at least 300 fine "habitations"; plenty of timber, giant tortoises, and fish; and he could see no difficulty in growing sugar cane and rice.

By this time however, La Bourdonnais had other problems to consider. War between Britain and France had just broken out and it became more imperative than ever that France should assert itself in the struggle for control of the Indian and Coromandel coasts. In 1741 La Bourdonnais had led a French expedition to the Indian coast, landing at Pondicherry: now he returned there and attacked Madras, which he successfully captured. Despite his military success in India however, there were powerful political forces working against him, and by the time he returned to Ile de France, in 1746, he found he had been replaced by Barthelemy David, a former Governor of Senegal. Greatly upset by the injustice of such a move he decided to return to Paris to plead his case with the King. His opponents were however quick to move and only ten days after his homecoming, on 2nd March 1748, he was arrested and sent to the Bastille where he died just five years later, in 1753, at the age of fifty. While imprisoned in that most notorious of French institutions, he committed to writing, drawn in blood on his own handkerchief, all that he could remember about the Indian Ocean and the islands whose exploration he had supported; the largest of which still bore his name.

After Mahe La Bourdonnais left on his ill-fated mission to France (1746), the governorship of Ile de France entered a rather unstable phase involving a series of administrators. Barthelemy David was replaced on 9th April, 1753 by Lozier-Bouvet who held office for almost three years, before relinquishing his position, on January 3rd 1756, to Rene Magnon. Magnon, governing for almost four years, until 8th November 1759 when he was replaced by Desforges Boucher, brought to the attention of the French Government the poor state of affairs in 'Compagnie des Indies'. He also highlighted the efforts of Pierre Poivre who had recognised the potential of the French Indian Ocean colonies to grow spices for the European market. Poivre is credited with having introduced cinnamon, pepper, nutmeg, cloves and several fruit trees to Mauritius.

The prospect of British vessels taking possession of Indian Ocean islands once again reared its ugly head and Renee Magnon studied with renewed interest charts and written reports Lazare Picault had brought back under instructions of the sadly deceased ex-governor, Mahe la Bourdonnais. A new expedition was organised under Corneille Nicolas Morphey, a fine seaman and navigator, with an Irish father (who had escaped the British by sailing to France in 1690), and a mother who was the daughter of a sea-faring Breton. Nicolas Morphey was instructed to sail to the islands Lazare had visited, and to take formal possession of them in the name of the King of France. Such a task required an air of formality and as much pomp and ceremony as could be mustered by the crew of an eighteenth century sailing vessel after a voyage of a thousand miles or so. To this end, and in order to leave behind firm evidence of their declaration, Morphey was given a slab of engraved stone which displayed the Fleur de Lis of France, surrounded by the cordon of the Holy Ghost(Saint Esprit) and surmounted by the crown of Louis XV. The expedition, comprising the frigate, "Le Cerf", and a smaller boat: "St Benoit", arrived at the

anchorage of what is today Port Victoria on November 1st 1756. The formal Act of Possession was then read out:

"In consequence of orders given by Monsieur Magnon, Director and Commandant General of the Islands of France and Bourbon on 6th. September of the present year, in the harbour of an island of about twenty leagues in circumference situated 4 deg. 34′ Latitude and 52 deg. 30′ Longitude to the east of the meridian of Paris. Having further discovered on the 9th of the same month seven islands to the East.

"Judging that these islands would be useful to the state, we have placed in a block of masonry, facing the entry to the port, the Stone of Possession, ("Pierre de Possession"). Further we have raised a mast above the stone and hoisted the flag of the King of France. We have saluted same by three salves and cried "Long Live the King" and further we have fired nine guns in honour of same from my ship.

"This Act of Possession has been carried out by the order of M. Magnon, Director and Commandant of the Islands of France and Bourbon, and we have taken possession of the said islands and of its port in the name of the King, and the "Compagnie des Indies", under the name Sechelles.

"As witness in date this 1st November 1756 we have signed same as a valuable proof of our rights.

"Signed: Morphey, Hery, Prejan, de Kneister, Erant, Barre."

Stone of Possession, National Museum, Victoria. This is the country's oldest monument and originally stood on the hillside inside the grounds of State House, below Chevalier de Quincy's tomb. The stone was erected by Captain Morphey on November 1st 1756, signifying he had taken possession of Mahe and seven other islands towards the east, on behalf of the King of France. He named them SECHELLES in honour of Vicompte Moreau de Sechelles, Controller General of France at that time. The Ceremony of Capitulation was held at the same site in 1794, when De Quincy was forced to recognise British influence. The stone was almost lost in 1894 removed by a visiting French General to present it to the Paris Museum. Upon his arrival at Aden a telegram awaited him, demanding its prompt return. (Harrison).

The famous Stone of Possession thus became, barring shipwrecks, (and perhaps the Arab graves on Silhouette) Seychelles' oldest artefact. It is to be seen in the Museum of Victoria, and it also records the name change which Captain Morphey was requested to make. The islands were renamed SECHELLES in honour of Viscount Moreau de Sechelles, Controller General of France at that time. The village of Sechelles from which the French aristocrat drew his formal title is still to be found in the commune of Cuvilly, between Paris and Lille where an eighteenth century castle is preserved.

Apart from the Stone of Possession, another permanent memento of Morphey's visit is the island he named after his boat, "Le Cerf".

In his report of the voyage he commented that the southwest coast of Mahe was fringed with coconuts, grown he presumed from nuts cast up by the sea since they were not found more than twenty paces inshore. As for the huge bay forming Mahe's north-eastern coastline, it was lined with an impenetrably dense jungle of mangroves.

Despite their formal declaration of possession, and all the pomp accompanying it, there were no witnesses other than the islands' undoubtably impressed wildlife! The French were aware that swift action was necessary in order to consolidate their position, but exploration was suspended during the Seven Years War (1756–1763) and the British-French Colonial War (1754/5–1763). Robert Clive's victory at Plessey in 1757 effectively put an end to French plans for colonisation of India. Following the Peace of Paris in 1763 a triumph for Britain, the French position on its remaining Indian Ocean territories began to look more tenuous. They held onto Seychelles however for a further twenty years during which period English naval vessels became increasingly frequent visitors. They, in turn, were harried by French Corsairs.

In 1768 an expedition, led by Nicolas Marion-Dufresne and equipped with a schooner, "La Curieuse" and a supply boat, "La Digue" visited Seychelles. Dufresne renamed Isle des Palme, Praslin, after Gabriel de Choiseul, the Duke of Praslin (then Minister of Marine in France), and the islands of Curieuse and La Digue were named after their two vessels. Dufresne commented on the verdant vegetation of the islands; on the variety of palm trees including the strange Coco de Mer; and on the huge crocodiles which he claimed were up to six metres in length. For many years the Coco de Mer had been a legend in the east. Various writers have claimed that any of this fascinating tree's heavy double nuts found there must have drifted by sea and, while this is not disproven, there are others who suggest that, since a fresh Coco de Mer seed sinks, this is virtually impossible. Such sceptics speculate that knowledge of the nut in the East derived from vessels which had, from time to time, over the centuries, found Praslin by chance and collected some of the nuts. Indeed, the nut was held in such high esteem by Maldivian kings, that they sent missions to search for the land where the nut grew. For the most part they were certainly unsuccessful but, perhaps, some of them did locate the islands: any such visit, in search of the legendary nut, would have predated their "discovery" in 1609, by the crew of the "Ascension". One thing is certain, when Dufresne saw the Coco de Mer on Praslin in 1768, he and his crew already knew how highly prized and valuable the nuts were in India. Captain Duchemin on the "La Digue" promptly filled his hold with Coco de Mer nuts for sale in the east. Unfortunately, the expedition became suddenly pre-occupied with the unique plant and failed to make many more general ecological observations. It was a lost opportunity for, shortly afterwards, permanent settlers arrived and the islands would never again display such wildly beautiful, undisturbed environments. Europe, at this time was experiencing the application of science to engineering development: 1769 saw Watt announce his invention of the steam engine while Cugnot unveiled his steam car. The Indian ocean colonies however were still run on slave-power!

Brayer du Barre, a colourful but sadly irresponsible character, instigated the first true settlement in Seychelles. On arriving in Mauritius in 1770, (following three and a half profitable years as official receiver of the Lotterie de l'Ecole Royal Militaire in Rouen) he had planned to engage in the slave trade or, perhaps more accurately, to take some quick profits from pirating. Through his friendship with Governor Desroche and Pierre Poivre, he gained support for the construction of three vessels; the Duc de Praslin, the Thelemaque and the Compte de St Florentin. During the construction, he heard from the Governor and Poivre of their intention to create plantation settlements in Seychelles. After persuading his compatriots to grant him an exclusive concession for Ste. Anne Island, Du Barre altered his plans and set about establishing his own estates in Seychelles. Early records of the colony have much to say about Brayer du Barre, partially because he himself seems to have spent the majority of his time writing to Governor Desroche, various ministers in France, and even the King himself requesting more help in the form of land, slaves, guards, wine, brandy, money etc., and partially because he turned out to be a dishonest conman responsible for the extreme suffering experienced by the first colonists. In many ways it is remarkable that du Barre's name is so closely linked to the early history of Seychelles since he never actually stayed there, but carried out most of his plotting, persuading, and pleading for his far-flung business venture from the relative comfort of Mauritius.

Du Barre's hopeful but woefully misled colonists arrived in Seychelles on board the newly built "Thelemaque" on 27th August 1770. Also on board were several people appointed by Governor Desroche and Marine Superintendant of the Islands, Pierre Poivre, to oversee development of the colony, and M. de Launay in overall charge. Others who arrived on this first immigration to Seychelles were, Mr Anseleme, Mr Berville, Dr Bernard Drieux, Mr Lavigne (carpenter), Jean Jacques, Mr Michel, Jean Marie Fustell, Charles Aumont, Joseph Bonneavoine, Jean Thomas Gorineau, Louis Verdiere, Claude Gevart and a Mr La Rue. They were accompanied by seven slaves: Miguel (in charge); Fernande; Ignace; Jouan; Le Villers; Matadoo and Matatan; five laborers from the Malabar coast of India: Charvy, Moulia, Meinatte, Corinthe and Domingue and one negress by the name of Marie. Du Barre himself had remained behind in Mauritius and was anxious to receive news of his enterprise. This long-awaited information duly arrived in the form of reports from the captains of two vessels, L'Heure du Berger and L'Etoile du Matin, which had visited the colony about five months after it had been established, in January 1771. After loading, between them, a cargo of 710 land tortoises, 140 goats and 50 "fowls", they had sailed to Mauritius where Du Barre eagerly listened to their enthusiastic reports about the new settlement and plantations. Greatly buoyed by the news, he wrote to Duc de Praslin, French Minister of the Colonies, with an account of their progress.

Bust and explanatory plaque commemorating Pierre Poivre, the true founder of the first French settlements in Seychelles. (Vine).

"....M. de Launay (the Commandant) has had houses and stores built....rice and maize are flourishing perfectly, as well as manioc and all kinds of vegetables. The seeds from the Ile de France, especially the coffee, have surpassed all expectations."

From his friend Poivre, who had provided both the seedlings and know-how for the initial plantation, du Barre sought permission for a second, larger settlement on the main island of Mahe itself. Keen to see his long-held dream of spice gardens in the new French Colony come to fruition, Poivre agreed and sent a workforce of forty people together with cows, poultry, seeds and other provisions on board L'Etoile du Matin, arriving in Seychelles on 30th October 1771. Also on board was Nicolas Benoit Gillot who had been given the tasks of selecting a site on Mahe for du Barre's new settlement, and of locating a suitable place for Poivre's precious spice plantation. Gillot and de Launay seem to have aggravated each other from the beginning—certainly de Launay was peremptorily dismissive towards the new arrival. Gillot brought with him news that further supplies for the colony were on their way, on board "La Marianne", but de Launay showed no pleasure at this information. '*What we need*', he insisted, '*is more black slaves to work the land. They can be quite well maintained on a staple diet of maize*'. A few days after his arrival at Ste. Anne, Gillot took a boat across to Mahe and began his exploration and land-clearing operations, lasting from November 1st 1771 to 15th February 1772.

This first settlement on Mahe was established on the coast facing Ste. Anne and Cerf islands, close to the mouth of the Rochon river, in the region of Mont Fleuri just south of Victoria's new harbour. Due to lack of sufficient supplies for maintainance of the workforce while they were in the process of setting themselves up, the experiment was abandoned within three months of its initiation. The workers were subsequently transferred to Ste Anne where they replaced many of the sick and dejected first settlers sent back to Mauritius without being able to realise their ambitions. The collapse of Brayer du Barre's ill-planned Mahe settlement was the first major blow to his plans, from then on it was a downhill slide.

Several French vessels visited Seychelles in 1773. The renowned navigator, Captain de la Perouze, in charge of the "La Seine" filed an extremely negative report on the management of the colony. He stated that, instead of creating profitable plantations, the settlers were slaughtering land tortoises and turtles for food, and many workers showed signs of serious malnutrition. Another vessel to call that year was "L'Etoile", under command of Denis de Trobriand—this visit is of particular interest since it marks the discovery and naming of Ile Denis or Denis Island. De Trobriand had departed from the main anchorage of Mahe on Wednesday, August 11th 1773, bound for Pondicherry, and at 4-30pm on the same day the mast-head lookout spied an island where all their charts, both old and recent, indicated neither dangerous reefs or islands. They could still sight Praslin from the crow's nest, so took bearings on it and prepared to approach early on the following day.

Since early descriptions of Seychelles islands, prior to their first settlement, are relatively scarce, and of great importance in generating an image of the environment before Man placed his unmistakable signature on the landscape, Trobriand's account of this most enchanting island is quoted below:

"....L'Isle a environ 1/3 de lieue de largeur; le sol m'a paru excellent, nous avons trouve dans le milieu une terre noire coupee de racines et couverte de feuilles, cette terre n'a pas moins d'un pied d'epaisseur; quelques parties de l'isle sont coupees par des especes de praieries dont l'herbe parait tres bonne quelqu'autres petites portions sont d'une terre assez seche melee de sable: Environ la moitie de la surface de l'Isle et couverte d'assez gros arbres mais dont le bois m'a semble etre trop gras et trop spongieux pour etre propre a la construction des vaisseaux.

"La cote nous a paru fertile en corail d'un tres beau rouge, elle est fort poissonneuse et l'Isle est generalement couverte de tortues de terre et de mer, de vache marines et d'oiseaux, dont plusieurs especes inconnues a ceux de nous qui avons fait des campagnes rares. Ces oiseaux etaient si peu accoutumes a voir des hommes que nous en avons pris une tres grande quantite dans les arbres et que nous en avons tue autant que nous avons voulu avec des Batons......

"Nous n'avons trouve sur cette isle aucun vestige qui nous annoncent qu'il y est passe des hommes. En consequence nous en avons pris possession Au nom du Roi de France, en y aborant son pavillon, y plantant un poteau a ses armes, au pied duquel nous avons enfoui une bouteille contenant l'acte de prise de possession sous le nom de L'Isle Denis sous le Ministere de M. de Boine, le nom du Vaisseau, celui de son etat-major, la date de sa decouverte avec sa Latitude et Longitude: 3deg.49' et 53deg.27'."

When I visited Denis Island in 1987, its owners Mr and Mrs Pierre Burkhardt, were still hoping that one day they would find that famous 214 year old bottle buried with the Act of Possession. The character of L'Isle Denis has changed somewhat since Denis Trobriand's first landing. Between 1929 and 1941, 16,195 tons of guano were exported from the island, and extensive plantations established there. Today however it has regained much of its peaceful seclusion and its bird-life has reverted to that fearless nature described, and so sadly abused, by its early explorers. We must return however to those critical first years of Seychelles' colonisation. What of Brayer du Barre's settlement on Ste Anne?

The replacement of Desroche and Poivre in Ile de France with D'Azac de Ternay and Maillard Dumesle effectively removed du Barre's support. On hearing of the plight of the Ste Anne settlers, D'Azac de Ternay revoked du Barre's permit to colonise either Ste Anne or Mahe and, despite a great deal of argument from the group's first coloniser, all his settlers were removed from Ste Anne on board

Pierre Burkhardt, owner of Denis Island, points out areas of interest from the top of the island's historical lighthouse. (Vine).

"La Belle Poule" in 1773. This was not however a complete break for settlement on the islands. By the end of 1772 Nicolas Gillot had returned to Seychelles and started the task of creating Mahe's first Spice Garden, the Jardin du Roi at Anse Royale on the east coast of Mahe. This was the site he had chosen on his first voyage in 1771 and, following his return to Mauritius on "La Marianne" in April 1772, he described his findings as follows:

"The part approximately to the south-south-east is the one which has been chosen for the Jardin du Roi; it may have one league or more in width and nearly one in depth. The soil there is black and deep, the bottom is sandy. It has a very large swamp which is passable everywhere and two fine rivers. At the back of this garden is a fine hill wide and gentle which leads to a small, well wooded, plateau which I believe to be more than two leagues in circuit whose soil is excellent and fairly well watered. This cove is named the Anse Royale and has in its reef a very fine channel and a 'barachouas' sheltered from the north-west winds.

"The Jardin du Roi is situated at the Anse Royale, it has a square surface of fifty gaulettes of fifteen feet each, this surface is divided into four square of twenty five gaulettes each, with in between a cross-shaped space of the thickness of two gaulettes of standing trees. Two of these squares will be cleared, with the reserve of soft-bark trees spaced at twenty feet; the two others will be cleared entirely. All the squares will be planted all round with a single row of banana trees, the first will be planted with banana trees spaced at fifteen feet and planted in quincunx, the third with 'nouroc' (Indian Coral Tree) or spiny wood also in quincunx and the fourth with only its row of banana trees all round. This work will be done, as it is stated, for the months of June and July."

Poivre, who had for many years set his heart on breaking the Dutch monopoly of European spice markets by growing such spices in French colonies was, by 1771, beginning to doubt whether Mauritius was the right place for such a development. His results with a large consignment of nutmeg and clove seedlings brought from the Moluccas in 1770 had been singularly disappointing since most of the plants had died. Disconcerted but not defeated, he organised a second trip to Geby island from where he had obtained the other seedlings. This time, however, he decided to split his options and he sent the newly acquired nutmeg, cloves and pepper seedlings to Reunion, Seychelles and Cayenne. They were dispatched (together with some Ceylonese Cinnamon) to the new "Jardin du Roi" on July 1st 1772, accompanied by Gillot; Pierre Hangard (a retired military officer of the French East Indies Company); and a small group of "the King's blacks". Hangard is widely regarded as the first true settler to live in Seychelles by his own choice; to work there for a lengthy period and then to retire and die on Mahe (in 1807). Rue Hangard in Victoria is named in his honour.

The fortunes of Gillot's Spice Garden were little better than du Barre's efforts on Ste Anne or the short-lived Rochon river settlement. Gillot received very little help or support from what remained of the Ste Anne settlement and, back in Mauritius, Brayer du Barre was still doing his best to scotch attempts by Gillot and Hangard to make progress with the colony's development. For fifteen months Gillot and his workers survived on a diet consisting of little more than maize: several of his labourers took, quite literally, to the hills, in an attempt to escape their masters. Later the spice gardens were raided for food by run-away slaves. In 1775 Gillot returned to Mauritius to seek renewed support for his venture and Hangard was placed in charge during his absence. By this time the grandiose scheme, so enthusiastically expounded by Gillot two years earlier, had been abandoned. Records indicate that the gardens comprised five nutmeg trees, four cinnamon trees, one clove tree and forty pepper plants! Not much reward for the effort and suffering which had gone into the project. Gillot's arrival in Mauritius was greeted, not by Desroche and Poivre, visionary creators of the project, but by the new administrators, de Ternay and Maillard Dumesle whose interest in growing spices ranked far down on their list of priorities. Gillot pleaded that he had lost much of his own time and money in trying to set up "Le Jardin Roi" and that he had received almost no help from the authorities. His arguments fell on unsympathetic ears however and in 1777 the French administration in Mauritius cutting loose from the project altogether, withdrew the slaves they had allotted to the spice-garden, and told Gillott he could take full possession of it. It was too late however for Gillott to muster the same degree of energy and enthusiasm with which he had begun his work, and after three more years of fruitless effort the garden had for all intents and purposes disappeared. Gillot was forced to abandon the project altogether when it was purposely set on fire (see below). In the longer term this first agricultural effort on Mahe was not quite the total disaster which its brief history suggests. The Cinnamon imported from Ceylon had its seeds spread by birds (especially the introduced Indian Mynah) and in the course of time became the second most important crop in Seychelles! In 1937 over seventy tons of cinnamon leaf oil were exported.

A measure of how Land Tortoises were hunted to virtual extinction within a few years of the first settlement in Seychelles is provided by records of Brayer du Barre's early dealings. A list signed by him of cargoes brought back to L'Isle de France in 1771–73 is reproduced on page 33.

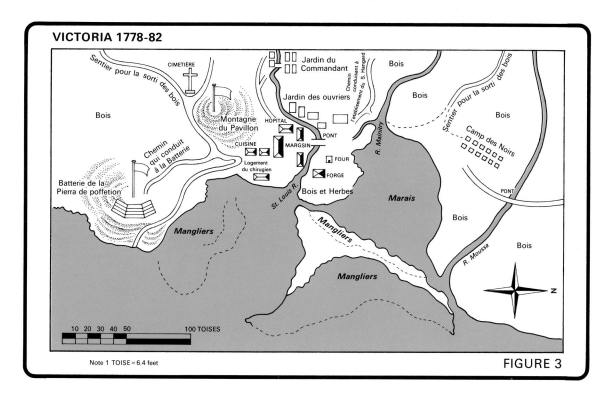

VICTORIA 1778-82

Note 1 TOISE = 6.4 feet

FIGURE 3

**List of Supplies Brought from the Settlement of
Seychelles by the King's Vessels, as follows:**

Vessel(voyage)	Tortoises	Goats	Chickens
L'Heure du Berger	360	80	25
L'Etoile du Matin(1)	350	60	25
L'Etoile du Matin(2)	450	100	45
La Marianne	1,500(inc.turtles)	130	80
Le Necessaire	900	60	25
La Belle Poule	200	—	—
Total	3,760	430	200

Signed: Brayer du Barre.

Brayer du Barre really fell into ill-favour when it transpired that he was responsible for the rumour that there was silver to be mined on Ste. Anne island; a story with no foundation. He was exiled from Mauritius, but not before accusing everyone and his brother of having plotted against him. His erstwhile supervisor in Seychelles, De Launay, was admonished for allowing all the valuable fruit trees to die while his people busied themselves with collecting sea shells.

It was around this time that an increasing number of English vessels began sailing through Seychelles waters and frequently raided Praslin for coco de mer. Their crews also set fire to forests on some islands, causing untold damage to the natural timber stocks.

33

When war again broke out between France and Britain in 1778 it became imperative for the French to protect their Indian Ocean colonies. This military concern was met in the same year by arrival at Mahe of the royal corvette, L'Helene, carrying Lieutenant de Romainville together with fifteen soldiers. Thus began the period of formal French Government administration of Seychelles as a military garrison. By this time French interests in Seychelles had changed from aspirations to establish agricultural projects there to a desire to satisfy the more immediate needs of the Indian Ocean colonies by providing a source of fresh meat in the form of tortoises and turtles, timber for building and repair of vessels; and as a military base designed to prevent settlement by their British adversaries. Indeed, it was this rivalry which led to the final demise of "Le Jardin du Roi" since, in May 1780, a ship presumed to be British was sighted approaching the relatively defenseless colony. Rather than allow their enemies to acquire their hard won spice plants, what remained of the garden was set on fire. When the ship finally reached the anchorage it turned out to be a French slave-boat from Madagascar with a human cargo on board! She had arrived to load up with wood, tortoises and water but, fearing that the English may have already taken possession of the French outpost, had raised the Union Jack, to be on the safe-side!

Mahe's natural resources of timber, tortoises, turtles and coconuts were there for the taking and it is not surprising that the island's settlers concentrated on these for their income. Gillot, De Launay and Hangard were awarded land concessions by De Romainville who only remained for a relatively brief period before he fell ill and returned to Mauritius where he died in 1781.

Romainville was replaced by Berthelot de la Coste who had very little time for the place, nor belief in its future prospects. His report on the islands, dated 26th September 1781 is a litany of negative opinions together with a few interesting observations. Among other things, he noted that the few remaining "caimans or crocodiles" took refuge in coastal caverns along the west coast, but, by this time, they showed considerable fear of Man and were no longer regarded as dangerous since they would flee on being approached. He stated that timber resources suitable for ship construction were limited; the soil was gravelly and sterile; it was too hot; and the whole place was of little future use except as a supply port for passing ships. The settlers however held a different view and were less than enamoured by their governor's ineffective stance and complete lack of control. Eventually, in 1783, he was dismissed from his post by Francoise de Souillac, then Governor of Ile de France. His temporary replacement, pending the arrival of Louis de Malavois in 1788, was Gillot. By 1786, when the colony was visited by Saulx de Rosnevet the total military population of Mahe and Ste. Anne only comprised 24 personnel, i.e. one Commander, one Sergeant, one Corporal; nine Fusiliers and twelve black slaves including some women. The civilian population comprised four whites and one free negro plus a total of 122 slaves. On Praslin there was one planter with approximately twelve slaves. Rosnevet had few hopes for agricultural development on the islands but he was impressed by the possibility for cutting and planting timber and he also observed that a herd of around sixty cattle had been running free on Mahe for two years and was on the increase. Apart from building houses and creating small agricultural areas to serve their immediate needs, the settlers were primarily engaged in cutting timber and dragging it down the hill-sides so that it could be loaded aboard ships bound for Mauritius (whose natural timber resources had already been indiscriminately felled and severely depleted). Takamaka (*Calophyllum inophyllum*)—that wonderful tree whose spreading branches still create shady arbours along the fringe of some of Seychelles most scenic beaches—was a prime target since its wood was suitable for boat construction. It was especially useful for curved members of a vessel's framework, including the ribs. Other trees had different qualities: the "False Gaiac" (*Intsia bijuga*), so named because of its resemblance to a South American tree (*Guaiacum offininale*), was used, along with 'Bois de Table' (*Heritiera littoralis*) for planking while the main spars were constructed from 'Bois de Natte' (*Mimusops sechallarum*) whose trunks were reported to exceed 30 metres in height and two metres in diameter!

It was just at this time, when settlers like Gillot and Hangard were realising that the island's natural resources required organised management, that the colony received an effective Commandant: Jean Baptiste Philogene de Malavois whose talents included engineering; agriculture and a good knowledge of geography. Malavois' arrival proved to be the best thing to have happened to Seychelles since the Declaration of Possession had been read out thirty years earlier. Shortly after his arrival he made a series of decrees designed to bring a state of order into the colony's affairs. As the islands' first management plan, they displayed a great deal of insight and common sense. The major points are listed on page 36.

These instructions also served to provide the framework by which de Malavois could preserve the Pas Geometriques (or Cinquante Pas du Roi)—a hundred metre or so wide strip of ground (extending inland from high-water mark) on which no development was to take place except for defence installations and access routes. This relatively densely wooded perimeter was intended as a natural barrier to invading forces and as a source of wood for visiting vessels. It was a device which had successfully preserved the coastal plain of Mauritius but had less impact in Seychelles.

Overall, however, Malavois' plan began to work, establishing a lasting pattern for land-use and settlement in Seychelles. The colony is indeed fortunate that it had such an intelligent administrator so early in its history. Malavois advised on agricultural development, approving wet rice cultivation along coastal marshlands but not supporting dry rice and maize planting in the uplands. Original settlers were granted 108 "arpents" equivalent to 112 acres, while freed slaves received 28 acres. In 1786 twenty tons of paddy rice and forty tons of maize were produced. Where upland soils became rapidly exhausted, he reccommended cultivation of ground-covering plants such as sweet potatoes and cassava (manioc). He was somewhat distressed by the islanders' indifference to growing vegetables and fruit trees introduced from Mauritius, but was pleased to report that bananas, sugarcane, cotton, tobacco and pineapples thrived. Advocating a controlled exploitation of timber resources, he applied for a work-force to implement this proposal.

Above all, Malavois was optimistic about the future of Seychelles and wrote a series of nine comprehensive reports on the the islands and opportunities which he felt they presented to industrious settlers. There were plans announced for placing settlers on Cerf, Silhouette, Frigate,

DECREES ISSUED BY DE MALAVOIS
November 5th 1788

1. *No person until further notice to capture tortoises, hawksbill turtles, or to cut down firewood.*

2. *Green turtles may be captured for personal use only and they may only gather coconuts growing on their own property.*

3. *No inhabitant of the Colony is allowed to carry on commerce in the above articles without a licence.*

4. *Commerce in firewood and timber is forbidden. Only the necessary timber to build and repair houses will be allowed to be cut down.*

5. *No concessions will be issued for the adjacent islands until all concessions on Mahe are disposed of.*

6. *The French flag will be flown at Praslin, and guarded by a "picquet" in charge of a corporal. The guard will be relieved once or twice per month.*

7. *No unmarried man will be granted a concession.*

8. *No concession will be valid unless duly signed and the titles certified as correct by the Commandant of the Colony.*

9. *Those who have obtained two or more concessions, will now be only allowed one concession, and must declare to M. de Malavois the concession which they have opted for. Boundary lines and title will then be drawn-up.*

10. *Concessions will only be made in future to Creoles from Ile de France and from Seychelles, providing they are married; and to children of colonists; or to people whose principle occupation is that of seamen or agriculturist.*

11. *In places where a settler does not have sufficient wood available on his concession, M. de Malavois will mark out an area where the necessary wood may be cut, either for fire or for building purposes.*

12. *In order to avoid any similar problems arising in future, M.de Malavois will henceforth define how much land each settler may be allotted, and what quantity of woodland he is entitled to own. He will also take steps to ensure that inhabitants conform with his instructions in this regard.*

13. *All lands not conceded are the property of the King. Coconuts, Hawksbill turtles, or any other commodity collected from such lands will be auctioned off.*

14. *It is forbidden for any planter to sell or cede his property without the permission of the Commandant, and if he leaves the islands without presenting to us a solvent purchaser the State will repossess the property.*

North, La Digue, Praslin and Curieuse. In passing, it is worth noting that Malavois recorded the destruction, by fires lit by slaves, of large amounts of natural forest on Cerf and Long Islands. In his biological observations he made many interesting comments. Of Bird Island, then known as L'Isle aux Vache Marines he commented: *"On voit sur celle-ci des vaches marines."* He also commented on "Vache marines" occuring at L'Islot aux Vaches de Mer, L'isle aux Recifs and at Frigate Island. The habitats described for these creatures, and indeed the suggestion that they may have been seen above water, on rocks, indicates that there may have been a degree of confusion at this time between seals or sea-lions and sea-cows or dugongs. It remains unclear as to which were present on or around the islands mentioned by Malavois. Neither occur there regularly today, although it remains likely that dugongs are present in Seychelles waters.

De Malavois set out the available knowledge on turtles and tortoises together with reccommendations for their preservation: the Giant Land Tortoises had been severely depleted during the first few years of colonisation and he realised he was fighting a rear-guard action on their behalf. In his memo dated March 25th 1787 he wrote that it would be extremely difficult to gather more than six or eight thousand tortoises on all the islands. "*The true cause of the devastation of their population*", he wrote, "*is the number of cargoes of land tortoises which have been taken from the islands, both legally and illegally, particularly in recent years. A calculation made with the assistance of M.Gillot has convinced both of us that, under his command alone, i.e. during the last four years, 13,000 Land Tortoises, have been removed or consumed by vessels calling at Seychelles. Le Sieur de St. Pe captain arrived with permission to hunt tortoises in Seychelles on behalf of the King and on two voyages he removed more than 4,000 Land Tortoises which were shipped to Isle de France.....It is possible also that cats and rats which have multiplied in recent years, particularly on Praslin and Mahe have contributed to their downfall through predation on juveniles.*" Malavois also commented that French naval vessels calling at Seycelles regarded it as their right to take tortoises for the officers and crew and that each vessel took at least 60 tortoises per visit. He reckoned that over a three year period; i.e. 1784–1786, at least 3,000 tortoises were removed in this way. In view of the danger of their imminent extinction Malavois proposed that all the tortoises which could be found, especially on Mahe and Praslin but also on the outer islands, should be collected during a special expedition utilising a two or three hundred ton boat plus two good pirogues from Bourbon (Reunion) commencing in April, and transported to protected 'tortoise parks' on Ste Anne (upto 3,000 tortoises) and Cerf (upto 4,000).

On the subject of turtles Malavois was equally enlightened. "*La Tortue de Mer*", he wrote, "*devient de jour en jour plus rare dans les Isles Seychelles...*" He described how turtles were taken, either at night when they mounted beaches to deposit their eggs, or else in daytime when they recce beaches by swimming along the reef-edge. Malavois was without doubt an enlightened conservationist and his concern was both that of a pure lover of nature as well as a pragmatist who believed in careful management of renewable resources. In a bid to protect marine turtles from a similar fate to that suffered by land tortoises, he commented as follows:

"*...Mais pour conserver cette espece de tortue et pour etre a portee d'en peupler successivement le parc, il seroit convenable de defendre aux habitans, tres expressement et sans reserve, d'en fair la peche et de ne la permettre aux vaisseaux qu'avec l'agrement du Commandant qui n'y consentirait que lorsque le parc se trouveroit absolument depourvu.*" It was a manifesto for conservation which might have been written yesterday!

Among the land concessions granted under Malavois' instructions were the following: 28 acres to Louis and a similar plot to Annette, both freed slaves of Mr Hangard; plots of 112 acres to: the husband of Hangard's daughter, Jean Marie le Bleuge; Mr d'Offay (with wife and four children), Mr Hangard (who had three existing concessions confirmed), Sieur Savy (with wife and four children); Mr Quienet; Mr Lambert (already living at Praslin), and several others. A number of plots were marked out for future settlers who did indeed start to materialise. Sensing a need to provide spiritual as well as material guidance to his growing band of colonists and their slaves, Malavois wrote to the Governor of Ile de France, asking him to send a priest. It was a request which could not be met immediately since the Catholic church in Mauritius was itself short-handed. Soon after this the French Revolution intervened and placed a temporary halt on ecclesiastic development in Seychelles. That is not to say that the settlers were without religion. Far from it in fact. All Catholics, they had constructed their own church in honour of St Anthony of Padua and held their own services. Occasionally, a priest from a visiting vessel officiated and they were thus kept in touch with their religion.

A measure of the colony's growth during the final decade of the eighteenth century is provided by an 1803 census in which the following figures were given:—White population: 215 comprising 63 men, 45 women, 63 boys, 44 girls; coloured population: 86 (17 men, 20 women, 28 boys, 21 girls); slaves: 1,820 (959 men, 445 women, 254 boys, 162 girls). Seychelles' recorded history relies on the reporting of European writers while the silent majority are given little credit for their major contribution to settlement of Seychelles.

News of civil strife and political uprising in France, culminating in the Revolution of 1789, took some time to reach Seychelles. The new French democratic order, based on liberty and equality for all its people was accompanied by administrative chaos, upheavals, and excesses which led, ten years later, to the seizure of power by Napoleon and to the ensuing Napoleonic wars. The Indian Ocean colonies assimilated news of the revolution at home with tempered enthusiasm. The call for universal equality sounded like a cry for the abolition of slavery (which indeed it was), something the French planters could not concede. It would, they argued, be completely impossible to run the Indian Ocean colonies without slave-labour. While embracing the general thrust of their homeland's freedom movement, and in the process deposing the Governor General of Ile de France, Count de Conway, the new National Assembly in Mauritius passed a motion on 15th May 1791 that no discussion would be permitted on the question of slaves.

De Malavois' gallant efforts to inject a measure of organisation and control into development of Seychelles were effectively ended by an emissary from Ile de France bringing news of the new administration. The land-owning white inhabitants of the Seychelles voted unanimously, on June 19th 1790, to create a Permanent Colonial Assembly which would appoint an administrative committee responsible for running the affairs of the island. In the same year, De Malavois resigned but carried on living there as a private citizen until 1802.

De Malavois was succeeded as administrator, first by Caradec, and then, in 1791 by Nageon. In 1792 the Administrator appointed by the new government of Ile de France, Sieur Esnouf, arrived in the colony accompanied by Daniel Lescallier recently appointed by the French National Assembly to introduce the revised French constitution to its Indian Ocean colonies. Following a period of quarantine on Ste Anne, M. Esnouf moved to Mahe and attempted to institute the unpopular new procedures. To some extent, he had already been pre-empted by the islanders' local legislation, aimed at preventing further interference by officials imposed on them from Ile de France. Taking the matter further, their new Assembly passed a motion in the last days of 1790 in which they declared that they were severing their direct ties to any other French Colony and should henceforth be considered as responsible directly to France.

In 1792 Chevalier Jean-Baptiste Queau de Quinssy (later spelt "Quincy") arrived in Seychelles to replace Nageon as French Commandant of the Colony. He was forty-four years old and was to spend the rest of his life in the colony, dying on Mahe in 1827. It was De Quinssy who guided the colony through the last years of its French administration, through the uncertain years of the Napoleonic wars, when it was unclear whether Britain or France had control, and finally during the early years of British administration. Such a "high-wire" acrobatic act demanded nimble footwork and an instinct for self-preservation; talents he displayed throughout his chequered career.

During the latter part of the eighteenth century, many French vessels turned from their hitherto normal commercial trading between Indian ocean harbours to a policy of plundering any foreign boats, unfortunate enough to venture within their sight. Having lost hope of creating a French Colony out of India, and losing their West African base in Senegal, they had every reason to concentrate their attention on vessels of the British East India Company. These merchantmen, known as privateers or corsairs, formed their own private naval force to resist the spread of British colonisation, and among them were some fine seamen and brilliant strategists. One such was Robert Surcouf: born and brought-up in Saint Malo, he had run away to sea at the age of only thirteen, in 1786. After three years spent sailing the Atlantic and Indian oceans, he arrived at Ile de France from where he made voyages to Madagascar, India and beyond. By the time he was twenty, in 1793, he had command of his own vessel: "Le Creole" and, ignoring the new French ban on slave-trading (passed in 1794), he undertook some illicit raids on the East African coast. His initial application for a letter of authorisation from the French Government to become a privateer was turned down but it was not long before he took-up arms against the English and in so doing earned himself a fearful reputation as one of their most dangerous and courageous opponents.

In the meantime, Commandant de Quinssy was doing his best to hold the Seychelles together as a colony. While fully supporting the privateers' fight against the British, he was also wary of Seychelles being used, too openly, as their base. It was inevitable that sooner or later the English would retaliate and there would be no chance to defend the colony against the fire-power of one or two Men o' War and the ensuing invasion.

On May 16th 1794 a force of four large British naval Men o' War: the 50 gun "Centurion", 44 gun "Resistance", 36 gun "Princess", and the 32 gun "Orpheus" sailed into Victoria harbour from the anchorage at Ste Anne where they had spent the previous night. They were accompanied by two captive vessels: a Danish boat, "Theodore Elisabeth" and the French craft: "Dugay Trouin". That very morning the brig "Olivette", captained by Corsair Jean-Francois Hodoul, had arrived in Port Victoria and had communicated to De Quinssy, when he visited the ship, that the boats seen lying off Ste. Anne, flying French flags, were actually English. Hodoul had entered Port Victoria ahead of the British fleet and had on board four hundred slaves. Before Hodoul had the chance to run his vessel ashore, it was boarded by English sailors and placed under arrest. A first-hand account of what followed is

The peaceful setting of De Quincy's tomb on a small hillock in State House Gardens. (Vine).

reproduced on page 42 in a translation of de Quinssy's letter to the Commandant at Ile de France to whom he owed an explanation for his apparent surrender and capitulation of 'Sechelles' to the British. As his letter, and the British ultimatum (see below) explain, Commander Newcombe left him with little option other than to comply.

Text of order to surrender issued by Commander Henry Newcombe.

BY HENRY NEWCOMBE ESQ. CAPTAIN OF HIS BRITANNIC MAJESTY'S SHIP "ORPHEUS" AND SENIOR OFFICER OF HIS BRITANNIC MAJESTY'S SHIPS EMPLOYED ON A PARTICULAR SERVICE ETC.

I DO IN HIS BRITANNIC MAJESTY'S NAME DEMAND AN INSTANT SURRENDER OF THE ISLANDS OF MAHE AND ITS DEPENDENCIES, WITH EVERYTHING IN AND BELONGING THERETO.

I GIVE YOU ONE HOUR FROM THE DELIVERY OF THIS MESSAGE TO DECIDE. IF ANY RESISTANCE IS MADE YOU MUST ABIDE BY THE CONSEQUENCES THEREOF.

GIVEN UNDER MY HAND, ON BOARD OF HIS BRITANNIC MAJESTY'S SHIP "ORPHEUS" THE 16TH DAY OF MAY 1794.

SIGNED: HENRY Y. NEWCOMBE

The corsair Surcouf dropped anchor in Seychelles on 15th September, 1795 in his relatively small 18 ton vessel, the "Modeste". Intending to take on board a cargo of land-turtles and rice from the new plantations, he spent three peaceful weeks in the general vicinity and recruited several seamen from the islands. In the early afternoon of October 7th however this tranquility was shattered by a cry from the lookout on Ste. Anne bringing news that two large English Men of War were tacking up the passage, towards the anchorage. Surcouf heaved anchor and made good his escape from the naval vessels by sailing through some dangerous uncharted waters on a north-easterly course from the site where the Ennerdale later sank, past Mamelle island, Blanchisseuse rocks, Trompeuse rocks and eventually out into open ocean, beyond Praslin. The British were forced to give-up the chase for fear of running aground, but they reported the incident and plans were laid to oust the privateers from these waters. Increasingly, Seychellois colonists were themselves becoming involved in these battles. The recent loss of Hodoul's vessel, 'L'Olivette' had been a temporary set-back but other boats were fitted out to continue the fight. These Seychelles-based privateers, including the vessels: Dugay-Trouin, Le Courrier des Sechelles, L'Emilie, La Rosalie, Le Syrus and La Nymphe, were a

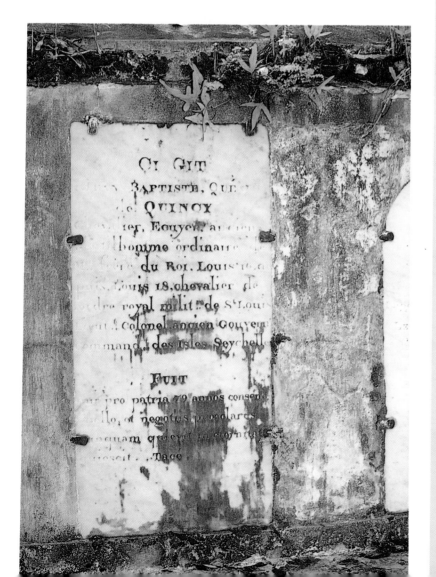

Plaque at tomb of Jean Baptiste Queau de Quincy, first Governor of Seychelles. The tomb is situated within the grounds of State House, Victoria. (Vine).

DESPATCH BY CHEVALIER QUEAU DE QUINSSY
1794

To the Commandant, Ile de France:

Citizen,

I received information on May 16th at about 5 a.m. of the approach of 5 three-masters from the south. I was at that moment at the farm of Citizens Bonvalet and Wantzlǫben, where I had arrived the evening before to fulfil my official functions. I embarked at once, so as to reach the Establishment [Victoria] as rapidly as possible. I had given orders for two shots of cannon to be fired during my absence, so as to advise me of any naval vessels approaching. This signal was given at the moment of my arrival. The brig "l'Olivette" entered in the early morning...... I went on board and asked Captain Hodoul what his plans were in case the naval force turned out to be the enemy. He replied that he intended to run his vessel aground on the coral reefs as near as possible to the shore. I then went to the Establishment at 7 o'clock where I ordered alarm signals to be given, the flag to be hoisted and three cannon shots to be fired every four minutes, and also to beat the drums. I sent a circular around to warn the more distant inhabitants to come to the Establishment and also took all the precautions to which I had engaged myself as per circular letter of 5th December 1793, all in accordance with the modest means at my disposal. see Official report, No.1, attached.

*These five vessels, Citizens, which I made out to be warships, arrived in line on the Ste Anne anchorage, **flying the French flag and the 'Flamme nationale Francaise'**; but from their build, their sails and as they bore no badge of command on the leading vessel, I did not doubt that they were enemy vessels. I had one more general alarm beaten, sent the citizen settlers to the battery and gave them arms and ammunition. These vessels were out of reach of my guns. I then gave order to show my flag by firing one ball shot, hoping to get them to confirm their own colours. **But they continued showing the same flag.** At 9 a.m. there came from the frigate a ship's boat, unarmed with an officer. When this boat began to draw near, I sent out a boat to have a look at them and to return speedily if they recognised the enemy. The cutter passed alongside the l'Olivette, on board which were only Lascars. The English officer left a man on board and also left the **French national flag flying on this vessel**, which stopped me from opening fire. I then saw my boat landing together with the cutter with the English bearer of a flag of truce. When the boat had landed I had the English officer brought to me. He was accompanied by Citizen La Brache, a French prisoner, acting as interpreter. I asked him what the object of his mission was; he replied that his name was Gote and that he was a lieutenant on board the "Orpheus"; that the Commander Newcombe was in command of this division, consisting of the "Centurion" of 50 guns, the "Resistance" of 44 guns, the "Orpheus" of 34 guns and the "Princess Royal" of 36 guns. He told me that this division, on its sailing cruise near the Ile de France, had captured the Danish vessel "Theodore Elizabeth", on its way from Tranquebar to the Ile de France and also the vessel "Dugay Trouin", on board of which they had 200 casualties from the engagement of 5th June; that the number of Frenchmen sick and wounded was very considerable, and that this was their reason for their putting into port at Seychelles. He said that Captain Newcombe demanded that he be supplied with provisions for his division and the French sick. I replied that I could not render assistance to the enemy of the Republic, that it was astonishing he had not written to me and that I would communicate the object of his visit to the assembly of settlers. From Official report attached, no. 2, you will see, that he was arrested under the rather delicate circumstances.*

Captain H. Cormier Bellevant was then deputed to board Commander Newcombe's vessel and to treat with him in my name, and the name of the settlers about the interests of the island. He was charged to announce that, true to our country, we could not give him any assistance.

Commander Newcombe then declared his intention of forcibly taking the island and called upon me to surrender within one hour, otherwise he would use all means at his disposal. At about three o'clock the Lieutenant Gote returned with Captain H. Cormier Bellevant. This officer handed the surrender demand of the English commandant, a copy of which is attached (*No.3*).

I communicated this to the assembly of settlers who called upon me to surrender the place. I persisted that I was not willing to surrender until I was assured of a capitulation which left the honour of my nation and of the French flag beyond any reproach and further, before I was sure that the conservation of buildings, whether private or of the state and of the property of the Citizens, the settlers in this colony was inviolately guaranteed.

This capitulation was signed, as is attached: No. 4.

In consequence, Citizens, I surrendered the place on May 17th at 9-0 a.m. The English garrison did not debark, and the French flag was not struck till this hour, after three charges of gunfire with balls for each piece of artillery and after three charges of rifle-fire. My slender means, Citizens, did not allow me to hold out for more than 24 hours. I have surrendered to superior enemy forces. You know that Sechelles was without any garrison, that all the means of defence were 8 guns, four of which were eight-pounders, two six-pounders and two two-pounders, which I still have; two pieces of eight, meant for the second battery had not yet been mounted. We were still working to finish this battery.

I had 60 rifles and of 40 inhabitants about 20 are capable of carrying arms. The English forces consisted of 4 vessels carrying 166 cannons and about twelve to thirteen thousand men. The attached papers, Citizens, will prove to you my behaviour and I submit them for your judgement and for that of my co-citizens, whose high esteem I shall always consider it my duty and an honour to attain.

The grig "l'Olivette" was sent to Praslin on May 20th, to search for victuals and refreshments for the squadron. It was armed with 'pierries' and a good crew. It found at Praslin the brig "l'Utilite" which it did not take. The captain reported that he had found a poor fishing vessel; and the commandant did not show any interest, the brig not being in view of his squadron.

The English citizens had during their stay in the Establishment a guard of 30 men under a lieutenant. There was absolute tranquility, the property was respected in conformance with my capitulation.

I gave all my care to the conservation of the civic and state buildings and to the Spice-Garden. Nothing has suffered any damage. The gun-emplacements were either broken to pieces or taken away. The four pieces of eight were damaged, the two pieces of six were taken aboard and the two pieces of two remain with me on strength of the capitulation. Military stores, anchors and some ropes were taken away. You will see from the attached note No. 5, signed by Commandant Newcombe, that this gives me discharge. I am rendering account of the surplus of material in the warehouses, which I have conserved for the General Administrative Commissioners of the Ile de France.

During the stay of the enemy, Citizens, I had taken the precaution in two parts of the island to try and warn any settlers, who might come from either the Ile de France or from the African coast. I had asked the settlers to send out their pirogues. On the 26th May, at 1 p.m. I was informed of the appearance of a three-master near the North-Island, at about 8 miles distance. I asked Captain Hangard to send out his vessel. The sea was very strong, the weather bad and he could not venture out. Next morning, the 27th, the vessel found itself windwards of St. Anne. It was not possible to send out any vessel; the English having always two armed observation-cutters outside. **The English displayed, both on land, and on their vessels, the French national flag. The French vessel came to anchor at about midday, believing the vessels to be part of the expedition to Java.**

Thus, being near Ste. Anne, the French prisoners gave all possible signals to this vessel to make off. It turned towards the shore. The vessel "Resistance", which was appearing, fired a broadside which did not carry and then sent four armed cutters to chase the boat. It got under sail; at two o'clock the "Resistance" came up and fired several shots of cannon and the vessel struck colours at 5 p.m.; they then rejoined the squadron. This was the vessel "Deux Andres", Captain Hardy carrying 400 blacks. The English divided these blacks on their vessels; 200 of them remained aboard the "Deux Andres" and were carried to India or Ceylon.

On May 31st, in the evening, the English re-embarked the garrison they had in Sechelles.

On 1st June, at 6 a.m., the English division set sail for the Indies, consisting now of seven vessels. I knew that many of their French prisoners had escaped on rafts to the Sechelles and that many had hidden in the forests and among the mountains of Ste. Anne. The Commandant having wsarned me that he was leaving about forty sick and a surgical helper with rations for one day. I ordered the Citizen Collet, an officer from the vessel "Dugay Trouin", who had been disembarked as sick, to bring them food and all possible help. He established their number. I had a circular letter sent to the settlers to inform them of the departure of the squadron and asked them to report to the Establishment the French fugitives spread over the island and to assemble on June 6th for a General Assembly (copy attached as No. 6.)

On June 2, I was at Ste. Anne with the Citizens Collet and Ecroignard to take a roll-call of the men, to establish masses for them, to get to know their needs and to establish some order and a police service.

On 5th June the General assembly of the Colony was held......The critical position of this Colony, Citizens, which was called upon to feed 200 men, has required the measures we have taken to inform you of the events which took place on this island. The only means left were the Brig "L'Utility" at Praslin and the boat of Citizen Piquenard, beached on the muds at Sechelles. We have considered it indispensable to send them to you at the expense of the Republic and to embark as many as possible of the French prisoners, escaped from the English and to inform you of the forces and plans of the English and to leave to the Colonial Assembly and the General Administrators the question of settling the freights, the indemnities, damages and all other demands, that may be made by the owners, freighters or insurers of these vessels. I have let Captain Collet travel with these ships, as I am not a seaman and have to look after the provisioning of the 190 men on St. Anne.

I have noted, Citizens, during the stay of the English squadron at Sechelles, that it had left England on 25th November 1793 composed of the Orpheus, the Centurion, the Resistance and the Diomede....They have been at the Cape. At the end of March Commandant Newcombe received orders to cruise around the Cape and to intercept all that he could, of shipping on its way to the Ile de France.

Having learned from an American vessel (I read this in his log book) about the strength of our forces, the names, the quantities of men and guns of all our Corsairs, and that they had done great damage to English commerce; that the "Princess Royal" had been taken by corsairs and that the expedition from Java had already sailed, he decided to send the "Diomede" to Madras, ten days before his departure from the Cape, so as to cruise windwards of the Ile de France, in the hope of fighting the expedition to Java on its return and to take the prizes captured by our corsairs. Near Rodrigues he took the schooner of the Citizen Maragon, which he released, as he said, for reasons of humanity. They remarked here, Citizen, quite openly, that the squadron destined for India and for the attack on Ile de France, would be under command of Admiral Gardner, and would leave England in January. I have taken notes on the vessels, as much as I could procure, and also on the forces. They are attached hereto....

Commander Newcombe seems to have interested himself in the Sechelles; he told me on board his ship in the presence of Citizen Trehouart, that the harbour of this colony was very good, that the position on its route to the Indies was very advantageous; that the provisions, the turtles, the fish in their abundancy were a great source of help for the sick, that his crew had recovered in a few days time; that the timber, suitable for construction, the spices, the cotton, all made this country of great interest; that he compared it with Dominica in the Antilles; that the other islands of the archipelago offered the same resources and that he would do all in his power to induce the Council at Madras to take over these islands and that he might come here in October. I would believe, that if their forces do not arrive, they will come here when they cruise around the Ile de France.

I cannot press you sufficiently, Citizens, to send a vessel to take away the French prisoners who remained here. You will realise the urgency as this Colony has not got sufficient provisions. I cannot allow more than a pound of rice per man; sweet potatoes and pumpkins as a supplement; the rest of the ration has to be turtle meat and fish. Several are without clothing. Here there are neither shops nor warehouses. I try to assist the most needy. I have only nine sick patients in the hospital in Sechelles where they are well satisfied. I have only seven Blacks for the use of Government in case they are required. I have looked after them.

I cannot pass over in silence the zeal shown by several settlers. I reiterate the request for a vessel. The Citizen Ecroignard, who is charged with passing to you this parcel of dispatches, deserves well for his patriotism, his zeal etc.

I am, with the expression of my respectful and fraternal sentiments,

Your co-citizen,
N. Bte. Queau de Quinssy

considerable annoyance to the British. As is mentioned in De Quinssy's letter to Ile de France, they even succeeded in capture of the warship "Princess Royal" carrying 33 guns. This they accomplished by moving in close and engaging in hand to hand combat.

British interest in Seychelles stemmed more from a desire to put an end to the pillaging of their Indian Ocean fleet, than from aspirations to create another colony. Their resources were already quite stretched, and they could ill afford the men and supplies required to establish a permanent and effective administration on the islands, particularly when the colonists were not likely to welcome such a change. Thus, for several years they contented themselves with the knowledge that their ships could sail into the colony and demand fresh-water or other supplies. Frequently though, they were more concerned with flushing out the privateers than with any interference with the islanders themselves. De Quinssy continued to govern the colony and, so long as there was no English naval vessel in the harbour, he flew only the French flag. A description of Mahe in 1801, obtained from a reference in the National Archive, is reproduced below.

DESCRIPTION OF MAHE IN 1800–1801
Extracted from: "History of the Double Conspiracy"

"Since the year 1794 when the Colony of Sechelles had obtained from the English terms of surrender favourable to its trade, it had prospered exceedingly. Its population, which had consisted of only five or six families and about 200 negroes, had risen in 1801 to more than eighty families and nearly 2,000 negroes. This extraordinary prosperity was due to the facilities the settlers had for sailing to India and the coast of Africa under the special Sechelles flag which was a blue ensign on which were traced the words: "Sechelles: Capitulation".

"The soil of the Sechelles is sandy. The islands bristle with mountains and are largely covered with coconuts, palms, mango trees, palmettos, ebony, latenia, trees of "pomme de jacquots" and superb takamaka (sic) a kind of mahogany which is used for boat building, and from a single log of which they make pirogues (dug-outs) 24, 30, and 36 feet long by 5 or 6 feet wide.

"The islands produce rice, maize, pineapples, bananas, sweet potatoes, manioc (cassava) roots, lemons, nutmegs, cinnamon, vanilla pods, and principally very good cotton. They provide a great deal of fish and a prodigious quantity of hawksbill turtles and several other species of land and sea tortoises. The woods are full of birds such as egrets, turtle doves, widow birds (African swallows), 'poule bleues' and black and green parrots. These last are very common indeed. The air is healthy; the water abundant and good.

"There is, in the Sechelles, only one Commandant whose powers are very extensive although the establishment of this colony is under the Government of Mauritius. There is no minister of religion and no man of law; when there is some major dispute among the settlers, they have to plead in the Ile de France which is 390 leagues away. Several of the settlers have their own ships and engage in commerce and the slave trade.

"Poultry and pigs are raised in large numbers in Sechelles and are mostly used for revictualling ships which come in for rest and to buy tortoise-shell.

"The first navigators who called at these islands found them peopled by caymans or monstrous crocodiles. Although their numbers have been successfully diminished, they still do much damage there. Woe to men or beasts who let themselves be surprised by these redoubtable reptiles for they hurl themselves at their victim so quickly that it is difficult to escape.

"The waters are infested with sharks and torpedo-fish which can always be seen along the coasts. In 1801, one of the former was noticed; it often showed itself and passed for the hugest seen to date. The settlers of whom it was the terror gave it a length of 40 feet, but most likely that length was exaggerated.

"Mahe, the principal island of the Sechelles was discovered on 19th November 1742 [*author's note: this is of course incorrect, it was visited in that year by Lazare Picault but had already been "discovered" by the British in the early 1600's and most probably by Arab navigators before then.] *It is seven leagues long from North to South; four and a half wide from East to West; and about twenty two in circumference. The settlement is situated in 4deg. 39 min. of meridional latitude and 53 deg. 13 min of longitude taken from the Paris meridian. The port and roads of this island are open to vessels of all nations. It is very high and surrounded by reefs; but there is almost no means of defending it; a ship*

armed with four cannon could lay down the law.

"*The first settler in Sechelles established himself on the island of St. Anne which neighbours the east coast of Mahe. The man, whose name was Hangard, was still alive in 1801, but had completely lost his sight. He had worked as a sailor on a ship which called at the Sechelles. He asked to be put ashore on Ste. Anne island whose position seemed to him to be very favourable. He was given some negroes, some weapons and agricultural implements and all that could be necessary for him at the beginning of his stay in the colony. His properties, the most beautiful and the richest in these islands, were cultivated, in 1801, by more than two hundred negroes. The sale of tortoises had made a large contribution to the fortune of this old settler.*"

On July 11th 1801 the frigate "La Chiffon" arrived in port together with her human cargo of Jacobin deportees whom Napoleon had sent to Seychelles in reprisal for an attempt on his life. Included in the list of thirty-two prisoners were Jean Rossignol, Commander in Chief of the revolutionary army in the west, who had led the attack on the Bastille; the architect Jean Baptiste Lefranc who took part in the massacre of Louis XVI's guards; Louis Moreau, a leader of the September massacres; Jacques Saint-Amand, an actor who is reputed to have strangled a hundred Callotins, and Jean Baptiste Vanheck, a wealthy businessman who led a band of anarchists in an attack on the Convention. On arriving at Mahe the Chiffon's commander, Captain Guiyesse, enquired about another vessel engaged on a similar mission, "La Fleche" which had left France two months before him. She had not arrived and was presumed lost. Following lengthy discussions the ragged, undernourished detainees were permitted to land on Mahe, where they were to be housed at l'Etablissement (present day Victoria) under guardianship of a detachment of soldiers. "La Chiffon" remained at anchor while she carried out repairs and her crew rested following the long voyage. On August 20th, HMS Sybille sailed into

Quincy Street is named after the first Governor of Seychelles, Commandant Queau de Quinssy, later spelt "Quincy". Many of Victoria's street names recall its interesting multinational origins and important events in its brief history. (Vine).

47

the harbour and a fiercely fought sixteen minute naval action ensued, resulting in capture of the French boat with the loss of 35 dead and fifty wounded from a crew of 190. The battle against the English ship was in fact joined by a new shore-based gun-battery consisting of four big twelve pound cannons taken from "La Chiffon" and manned by her sailors: a state of affairs which caused considerable anger to Captain Macadam of the Sybille.

On the following morning Macadam met with Governor De Quinssy demanding an explanation. Had he not already capitulated to the British and was this not now an English colony? If so what was he doing providing facilities for a French naval vessel to not only attack him from the water, but also to mount an aggressive cross-fire from a shore battery? De Quinssy argued that it had been his concern to look after the colony and to maintain the peace. There was no escaping the fact that its colonists were French and owed their natural allegiance to that country. Was it not understandable and entirely honourable that they should fight for their survival? Macadam was singularly unimpressed but to some extent magnanimous in his victory. He demanded however that De Quinssy sign a new capitulation document. The wily diplomat agreed to this on condition that the guarantees inherent in the 1795 document still stood, and that, in future, Seychellois vessels would not be attacked by the English. The latter point was of great interest to De Quinssy, since it would enable his boats to pass through the British blockade of Mauritius. Macadam agreed to this providing the boats carried large flags on which the words: "Sechelles Capitulation" were clearly legible.

Captain Macadam left Mahe with HMS Sybill on September 3rd and he was hardly clear from sight before the overdue French boat, "La Fleche" arrived with her own allottment of deportees. In this second batch of thirty-seven prisoners were many well-known anarchists including Antoine Boniface who participated in the September 1792 massacres and whose wife is reputed to have drunk the blood of victims; Mathurin Bonin responsible for sending many people to the guillotine; Nicholas Paris, a shoemaker and assassin of prisoners at L'Abbaye; the fanatic Louis Monneuse responsible for the massacre of all prisoners at "La Force" and who personally presided over 171 killings, including that of Queen Marie Antoinette's friend, Princess de Lamballe; and Andre Corchant, known as "Le Bourreau de Lyon", who sent 1,684 inhabitants of Lyons to the guillotine without holding a single trial. They were rapidly disembarked to join their compatriots housed at Etablissement. Meanwhile, Captain Bonamy of "La Fleche" wasted no time in advising Governor De Quinssy that he had been sighted, and recently chased, by an English sloop. Two days prior to their arrival they had been in action with her, but had made good their escape. Early on September 5th the English frigate, HMS Victor, sailed towards the harbour. She was almost equal in size and strength to La Fleche and the ensuing battle was a particularly tough one, lasting more than two and a half hours. Eventually, however, the continual barrage of cannon balls crashing into the hull of La Fleche caused it to make water and the vessel began to sink. Rather than let her go down in the harbour, Captain Bonamy sailed her onto the reef and set the vessel ablaze before departing from his ship on board a pirogue sent out by De Quinssy. At a later meeting between commander of HMS Victor, Captain Collier and Captain Bonamy, the French commander was praised for his fierce fight. It was, Collier claimed, one of the hardest naval battles he had ever fought. Once more, De Quinssy found himself in conference with an English commander, seeking ratification of the terms under which Seychelles had capitulated. To the French Governor it had become as important to obtain reaffirmation of the negotiated protection of citizens and their property; as it was for the English to confirm that the colony would not raise arms against them.

Prior to his departure from Seychelles on September 20th, Captain Collier visited the French detainees held at Etablissement: with the addition of those from the late arriving "La Fleche", they now outnumbered the white settlers. It was clear that they were going to be difficult to maintain on Mahe, but Collier was not prepared to listen to their pleas to be transported away from the colony on his vessel. The situation was aggravated because the deportees insisted on being regarded as political detainees, and had no interest in working. Even worse, in the eyes of the white settlers, they preached the new code of liberty and common property. They were a direct threat to continuation of slavery and several of them began consorting with a freed negress, Vola-Maffa. One of the French detainees, Louis Francois Serpolet, who had arrived on "La Fleche", began preaching the principles of revolution to the enslaved Africans and proposed they should regain their freedom by taking-over the settlement. Alarmed at the prospect of insurrection, and, greatly outnumbered by slaves and detainees, De Quinssy took rapid evasive action, banishing the central figures in the plot to Frigate Island, and sending a petition to Ile de France, demanding that the detainees be removed. For most of the Jacobin prisoners it turned out to be a sad ending since thirty-three of them, including Serpolet, were transported on "Le Belier" which left Mahe on 18th March 1802 to carry them to Anjouan in Comoros. Almost all of them died there as a result of poisoning by the local chief, Sultan Louis Seyed Ouloni, who feared the consequences of allowing such a large group of "dangerous" people to settle in his territory. Those deportees remaining behind at Mahe were generally more fortunate. Over the next few years many of them began to adjust to life on the island, taking-up trades they had followed in France. In 1807, sixteen of them left Mahe for Ile de France, and, of those few who remained, only Joseph Quinon left any descendants in Seychelles. He took up his previous occupation, as a baker, and died on Mahe in August 1828. A resume of what happened to the French deportees is shown below.

Summary of French Deportees sent to Seychelles on La Chiffon and La Fleche

Total number originally embarked. 71
Died during the voyage (on La Fleche). 1
Died after landing at Mahe 1
Deported to Anjouan, Comoros 33
Died in Seychelles before 1806. 6
Escaped from Seychelles on visiting vessels 6
Authorised to sail to Ile de France in 1807. 6
Settled down and eventually died in Seychelles 8

Not everyone who made an enforced stay in Seychelles wanted to leave. One result of the demise of "La Fleche" and capture of "La Chiffon" was the temporary deposition on Mahe of a large number of French sailors and their officers. Although Captain Collier detached a captured brig to sail to Ile de France with French sailors from La Chiffon and La Fleche, several chose to remain.

The Treaty of Amiens, signed on 27th March 1802, brought a brief halt to hostilities between France and England, and it reinstated the right of French colonies east of the Cape of Good Hope to possess slaves. News of this did not reach Seychelles until August of 1802, when it was greeted with considerable rejoicing by the white settlers. Treatment of African slaves was controlled by the famous "Code Noir" which laid down conditions designed to protect slaves from greater abuse than was already inflicted on them by their status as human merchandise. The code prohibited owners to make their slaves work on Sundays; it required that they be instructed in the Christian faith; and it insisted that adequate food and clothing be provided, according to their needs. Nevertheless, one should not lose sight of the fact that the vital work-force consisted of slaves and their equally entrapped but euphemistically titled colleagues, "bonded labourers", whose suffering, degradation and misery remains unrecorded. Previous claims of "good treatment towards slaves" in Seychelles emanated from the slave owners themselves and are best regarded as a misguided contradiction in terms!

A letter written in 1803 by Malavois on behalf of De Quinssy to General De Caen at Ile de France provides a useful summary of the colony, as it emerged into the nineteenth century. He stated that the population stood at 1,820 comprising 220 whites, 100 liberated negroes and 1,500 slaves. While turtles and fish remained plentiful, efforts to conserve the Giant Land Tortoise had basically failed and the animal was now quite scarce. Commercial products included high quality cotton; coconut oil; hawksbill turtle-shell; together with small quantities of sugar, rum and the local drink, arrack. He noted that, during peacetime, the Colony was a useful provisioning station for slavers from the African coast, and for vessels enroute to India, together with general coasting vessels and even fishing-boats based at Ile de France. In addition to fresh food and water, there were skilled boat's carpenters who could effect repairs to visiting vessels.

In wartime the colony was regularly visited by privateers from Ile de France, some English warships, ships from neutral countries and those French cargo boats willing to run the risk of capture by the British. Malavois noted that French naval squadrons had often received unexpected support from the colony, but that further details on this point were best kept secret! It would, he warned, be unwise to store supplies for French warships in Seychelles, since these ran the risk of being captured. On the subject of communications between Ile de France and Seychelles, he commented that, whereas the sail to Mauritius may take only seven or eight days in the SE monsoon or ten to fifteen days during the north-westerlies, it often took twice as long for the return journey.

News of the renewed war between England and France reached Ile de France on 25th September, 1803, carried by captain of the corvette, Berceau. The status of Seychelles had been somewhat confused by the short lasting peace with England, and the colonists felt they were once more legitimately on the side of France. On September 21st 1804 the English man-of-war, HMS Concord sailed into harbour at Mahe and its captain, John Wood, demanded a new capitulation, the main wording of which was based upon the document signed in 1794. De Quinssy was later severely reprimanded by General de Caen for not having put up more resistance to the English. He was also instructed to lower the British flag and to fly only French colours. In defence of De Quinssy it must be said that, as man on the spot he was much more appraised of the position than General de Caen, and he was concerned to avoid unnecessary harm to the settlers. For the most part, visiting English war-ships presented no real problem to the colonists. Their main objective was to replenish with fresh-water and some supplies, and perhaps, for the sailors to spend a little time ashore. Once they sailed away, the colony continued to operate as a French outpost. Indeed, French naval vessels called and were officially received. Such visits included the arrival, in 1805, of the 40 gun frigates, Canonniere and Piemontaise, carrying orders from France, and that of the renowned Rear Admiral Linois who arrived on board the 74 gun Marengo, accompanied by the 40 gun Belle Poule. Linois was heading a renewed attempt to mount an effective opposition to British shipping in the Indian Ocean with a plan for well armed French men-of-war to patrol along routes followed by English vessels enroute to India. Upon discussion between de Quinssy and the French Admiral, it became clear that Linois held the view that, since it would be extremely costly to maintain an effective defence force in the colony, Seychelles should remain under capitulation until the present war ended. In this regard he differed sharply from General de Caen. In August, 1805, de Quinssy did give a token demonstration of resistance when HMS Terpsichore and HMS Pitt arrived. This amounted to raising the French flag and firing a single shot. It was sufficiently defiant however to have de Quinssy placed under temporary arrest by the British. Honour was thus maintained and General de Caen kept happy. Meanwhile, after the vessels departed, de Quinssy was left to carry on as governor, and Seychelles reverted to its normal peaceful atmosphere. A few months later however, HMS Duncan arrived (November 7th 1805) on a mission to seek-out and arrest French privateers. She was accompanied by a smaller brig, "Emilie", which had been previously captured by the British and subsequently fitted-out for a cat and dog match against her erstwhile sister-ships. Emilie's master discovered the slave and privateering boat, 'Courrier des Sechelles', off Therese Island and, when the British crew failed to locate the slaves which had been hidden on the island, they attacked settlements of the vessel's owners, Sieur Blin and Dupont. HMS Duncan's sailors also destroyed the goelette La Rosalie and brig Le Syrius, correctly assuming that both boats engaged in privateering.

HMS Duncan returned to the colony, accompanied by HMS Russell, on June 14th 1806 when Captain Lord George Stuart renewed the capitulation. The final surrender, prior to the fall of Ile de France, took place in 1806 when three ships, the 74 gun HMS Albion, HMS Drake and a smaller 20 gun corvette arrived at the anchorage. These were ships engaged in the blockade of Mauritius. The last few years of French rule at Ile de France, i.e. from 1806 to 1810, were a period of relative tranquility in Seychelles. The capitulation flag, raised at the sight of any English vessels, effectively gave Seychelles craft freedom of the seas. Privateering was on the wane, but slave trading continued to be profitable and a new activity, that of whaling, was beginning to capture the colonists attention. The first British whaling ships had rounded the Cape of Good Hope and entered the Indian Ocean in 1789; their target: Southern Right Whales off the Cape and Sperm whales found near Delgoa Bay. Whales around Seychelles had been commented on as early as 1608 when Jourdaine referred to "a quanti-tye of whayles". Whaling ships were among the vessels which called at Seychelles in this first decade of the nineteenth century. While communications between Seychelles and Ile de France became both strained and difficult, de Quinssy was in better touch with France. A series of corvettes called there having sailed direct from France; the "Amazone" in January 1807; the "Venus" in August and October 1808; and Manche and Caroline in the same year. The 40 gun Bellone also visited in May 1809.

Pressure by British colonists in the region had been mounting for some time (particularly at the burgeoning settlements in India itself) for the English navy to put an end to the deprivations on their commercial shipping wreaked by French corsairs. As early as 1801, the commander of Fort St. George had become so frustrated at the ineffectual protection the navy was providing, and so concerned at his fellow citizen's losses, that he issued a public letter, dated 18th March. It read as follows:

"*At our consultation of the 31st October last, the Merchants of this settlement submitted to us an address on the subject of the losses, which had been sustained from the success of the enemy's cruisers, in the Bay of Bengale, and stated their opinion of the practicality of affording security to the trade of India by the Blockade of the French Islands.*

We concurred in the opinion of the merchants, that the effectual blockade of the Isles of France and Bourbon would afford ample security to the trade of India and informed them that we had reason to believe that, if the normal force allotted for the service of the Indian seas, had been sufficiently numerous to admit a system of regular relief, the plan would have been carried into execution by His Excellency Vice Admiral Rainier. But it must be obvious that unless the blockade can be effectually maintained no vigilance or activity on the part of His Majesty's Naval Officers can be adequate with the ships now in India to protect the extensive limits of the India trade against the desultry attempts of the enemy's cruisers. Such a protection it might be difficult to establish under any circumstances, but under the general aspect of Public Affairs, His Majesty's Navy in India is destined to perform and has actually performed service of great political and national importance....".

The document then continues by blaming the merchants for not arranging to group their vessels together so that they could form convoys to which a naval vessel could be seconded for protection purposes.

In an urgent plea for greater cooperation, the merchants petitioned for a blockade of Ile de France:

"*...We have to regret that His Excellency's want of means to protect our general trade has exposed it in the years 1799 and 1800, in the Bay of Bengal only, to the losses of upwards of 15,700 tons of shipping besides many valuable cargoes...*".

Eventually the British took note, and their blockade was established, gradually squeezing the blood out of the French colonies, until they were no longer sustainable.

The British cordon around the French colony eventually took its toll on the islands' occupants and on 7th July 1810 Reunion, or Ile Bonaparte as it was then known, fell. On December 3rd of the same year, General de Caen was forced to capitulate and Ile de France was finally occupied by the British. News of this important event reached de Quinssy on 23rd December, 1810 by Captain Smith who sailed in on "Les Freres", followed not long after by the Seychelles based vessel, La Favorite which had been present in the harbour at Ile de France when the British invaded the island: the vessel had escaped destruction by flying the Seychelles Capitulation flag. The official notification was not delivered until the following April however, when HMS Nisus, commanded by Captain Beaver arrived at Mahe. Since Seychelles were themselves an official part of the administrative territory of Ile de France, Captain Beaver announced that they must abide by the terms of that colony's capitulation. De Quinssy, on the other hand, argued that Seychelles had already capitulated, long before the Ile de France, and that he had been governing the islands on the basis of that agreement. Surely, therefore there was no need for him to ratify the capitulation signed by General de Caen? In a compromise move, Captain Beaver agreed to the fact that Seychelles were being administered under terms set out in its own earlier capitulation, but he continued to demand that de Quinssy also recognise the application of the Ile de France capitulation to Seychelles. In order to formalise the arrangements whereby the islands were an official British colony, Captain Beaver landed a wounded officer, Lieutenant Bartholomew Sullivan, to act as a token British observer. Although he was given a grand title ("officier des troupes royales de Marine de Sa Majeste Britannique, agent civil et commandant pour le gouvernement anglais aux iles Seychelles") he was instructed to leave all administration of the colony to de Quinssy who was asked to do the best he could until the end of the

Old cemetery at L'Union, La Digue provides many poignant memories of Seychelles' early history. (Harrison).

Above
Coconut plantation worker's house at Silhouette. (Vine).

Below
Old houses of Leper Colony at Curieuse Island. (Vine).

war at which stage the status of the colony would be settled. Interestingly enough, this first English Governor was lodged under the care of the distinguished privateer, Captain Hodoul, at the house of Ma Constance.

Even after this however, de Quinssy was faced with the difficult task of dealing with a request for military help by his fellow countrymen, while continuing to adminster a British protectorate. The French frigate "Chlorinde", having sailed from Brest with supplies destined for Ile de France, had been damaged by English frigates, patrolling off the coast of Madagascar. She arrived at Mahe on 29th May and requested de Quinssy's assistance to refit and repair. Despite the presence of Lieutenant Sullivan, de Quinssy felt he had no choice but to assist the vessel. Fearing the return of an English naval ship, the "Chlorinde" mounted a battery of guns on shore and recruited the assistance of all willing inhabitants and their slaves to effect a very rapid repair and replenishment of supplies. After six days the "Chlorinde" sailed, once more in a sea-worthy condition, to the cheers of French settlers living under the British flag!

Seychelles remained in this political limbo until 1815, when England officially took it over as a dependancy of Mauritius (formerly Ile de France). De Quinssy (or de Quincy as he now spelt his name) remained in office with a fresh title, First Civil Agent, Commandant and Judge: for the colonists, the formal change of ownership had little effect. French laws and land titles remained in force, and the planters continued to grow their cotton, utilising slave labour. A visitor in 1819 noted that the effects of agriculture and the lumber trade had taken a severe toll on Mahe's original forests, and that there was extensive erosion on upland sites where land clearance had removed the natural factors protecting a thin soil covering. The main town, still simply referred to as "l'Etablissement", was comprised of a few wooden houses. Development of the colony under the British made slow progress, marked by a gradual growth of interest from the Colonial Office in London.

The anti-slave movement, led by William Wilberforce, gained momentum early in the nineteenth century and, while the possession of slaves continued to be allowed in Seychelles, the first steps towards their emancipation came in the form of a ban on slave-trading. In June 1812 Sullivan was responsible for confiscating 41 slaves brought to Seychelles from the East African coast. Other islands (including Praslin, Frigate and Daros in the Amirantes) continued to be used by slave-traders right up until the early 1830's.

In the early part of the nineteenth century Seychelles experienced a dramatic increase in population. As the British blockade of Mauritius took effect, many families of planters from those islands moved to Seychelles where they were initially attracted by the promise of free

Plantation owner's house at Silhouette. (Vine).

plots measuring 112 acres. Later, others followed with plans to set-up farms on outer islands. Seychelles cotton was gaining a world-wide reputation for its fine quality and it soon became the number one commodity of the group. Settlements, consisting of the 112 acre plots defined by Malavois, had been allotted around virtually the whole coast of Mahe and planters were also established on Praslin, La Digue and Silhouette. In 1810 there were around four thousand inhabitants and in less than a decade the population almost doubled (7,500 in 1818) and, for a short while, it seemed that nothing could go wrong. In 1816 De Quincy commented as follows: "*La population des Seychelles commence a etre consequente, les cultures de coton, de girofle, du cafe, les bois, les constructions de navires, le commerce, tous ces objets augmentent et sont susceptibles d'augmenter*". 'It is said', wrote a Mauritian who settled in Seychelles, marrying a Seychellois, 'that cotton is cultivated by poor people. In Seychelles, cotton cultivation has made the poor rich'.

Unfortunately,this lucrative form of agriculture did not continue. Less expensive cotton from America began arriving in Europe and the Seychelles cotton industry was immediately affected: during 1822 the price dropped from 80 dollars to 30 dollars per bale. Within a matter of months many planters and their slaves departed for Mauritius. By 1840, five years after abolition of slavery, the population had dwindled to 5,400 with over eighty percent of these living on Mahe.

While disillusionmemt with agricultural prospects in Seychelles seemed, for a while at least, to take a grip, other activities brought renewed optimism of an economic revival. The sea, once again, seemed to be the one natural resource which Seychelles possessed in such abundance that prospects for its exploitation appeared to be limitless. In earlier days privateering had brought wealth to the colony, now it was another form of bounty hunting, not from capture of ships, but through slaughter of large whales. A whaling expedition to Seychelles waters by a small whaler: the Swan, in 1823, resulted in such a good catch and enthusiastic report by its captain that its British owners instructed the vessel to return for a second trip. They also despatched the "Asp", a 345 ton vessel, which returned with a cargo worth eighty thousand dollars and the whale-rush began in earnest. By 1829, at least seven British whalers operated in Seychelles waters and the American whaling fleet began to take an interest. In 1828 four of the Nantucket whaling fleet hunted on the Seychelles bank, and buoyed by their results, in 1832 they opened a whaling station on St. Anne island. The crews of whaling vessels were apt to be quite a rough crowd of men leading very hard lives. An incident, occurring in May 1834, provides an insight into life among the whalers at this time. In May 1834, the American whaler, "Amanda", arrived in Seychelles but because she was taking water her commander, Captain Cross, arranged to have his cargo of whale-oil transferred to the British whaler "Thames", under command of Captain Dunn. Following a dinner ashore, a fight broke out between Dunn's first officer, Day, and a resident of La Digue by the name of Mellon. When the latter drew a knife, Dunn separated the two men. Incensed at Mellon's ungentlemanly behaviour however, several crew members hitched a rope noose around Mellon's neck and led him to the door, as if to lynch him, whereupon Captain Cross jumped to his rescue. When the "Thames" was departing, five days later, a naval pinnace carrying a Lieutenant Creagh with 15 soldiers boarded the whaler and delivered a summons from Judge Fressanges to appear before him. Following a very aggressive questioning session, they were taken to Praslin, where both men spent several days in prison before being released without formal charges being made against them.

Another incident documented in Seychelles Archives is that of the supposedly missing seaman, "Bill in the Bunk", so named by his compatriots because he was always sick. Family in Britain were anxious to hear news of him and the Governor of Seychelles eventually received an official request to investigate his whereabouts. A number of handwritten affidavits are preserved and tell the story of how he left England on board the whaler, Greenwich (belonging to Messrs Bennett and Son from Rotherhithe, Surrey), in September 1838. "...*on board was a seaman who called himself James Martin, who was in person, about 5 feet and a half high, with a red face and a red nose, his forehead bold, and hair dark in colour, with whiskers not of the same colour as his hair...*" During the voyage he stated his real name was William Whitehead, but to the crew he was known as "Old Bunk" and the captain referred to him as "Bill". The statement continues: "...*the Greenwich sailed from England towards the Cape of Good Hope and having rounded the Cape, cruised off the Eastern Coast of Africa, and the said William Whitehead or Martin, being ill from venereal disease, which he had when he left England, and being unable to work, he was put ashore to recover at Denis Island, one of the Seychelle Islands, about 8 or 9 months after the Greenwich left England....*" The writer goes on to claim that he had seen "Old Bunk" quite recently when he was in good health and seeking a passage home.

With the question of sovereignty settled, Seychelles experienced a relatively quiet period of slow development. Natural resources, such as timber, were exploited with far too little regard for preservation of the unique island habitats, but most of the damage had already been done in the last century. The disparity in numbers between voluntary settlers and slaves was quite dramatic. In 1827, for example, a total population of 685 "free-men" was complemented by 6,638 slaves! This pattern

Old jail building of Leper Colony on Round Island, Ste Anne Marine Park. (Vine).

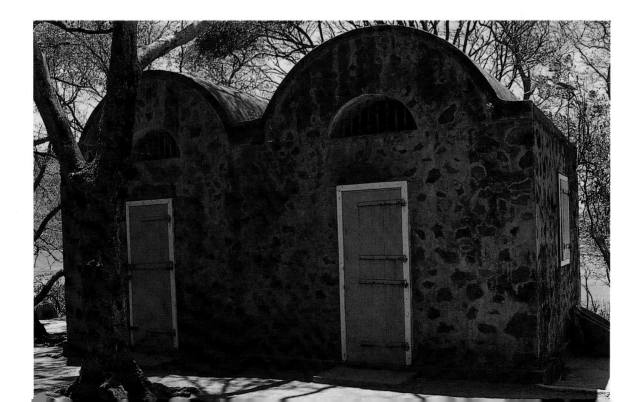

One of the first Catholic churches to be built in Seychelles. (Vine)

The memorial to a two year old girl's death is a sad reminder of the difficult conditions faced by settlers in Seychelles. (Vine.)

continued so that, by 1835, when slavery was abolished, the vast majority of Seychellois were of African descent. These people, together with an additional influx of slaves liberated by British naval vessels cruising the Indian ocean, provided a labour force for establishment of large coconut plantations and, in the final decade of the nineteenth century, for extraction of guano. By the end of the nineteenth century, the population had risen to almost twenty thousand people. The economy depended, almost completely, on coconuts.

While the affairs of Seychelles during the nineteenth century continued to be administered via Mauritius, this situation changed very early in the present century, with King Edward VII's declaration of 1903 that Seychelles would henceforth exist as a separate Crown Colony. This momentous step forward for Seychelles was commemorated by the erection of a clock-tower in the centre of Victoria. British administration of the Colony was, however, somewhat less than dynamic. The islands were left, more or less, to sink or swim by themselves. In the early part of the century guano was mined for all it was worth, causing irreparable damage to the natural vegetation on a number of islands. Green turtles were hunted under licence with at least three thousand a year being taken from Aldabra. Cinnamon, an introduced tree which had spread and rapidly colonised land cleared of natural vegetation, rose in economic importance early in the century. Vanilla production on the other hand crashed as a result of a fall in world prices. In 1899 it had been the prime crop in Seychelles with a value considerably in excess of that of coconuts:the discovery, in 1906, of an artificial substitute for natural vanilla brought about a dramatic decline in its production. The 1914–1918 war generated severe problems for Seychelles since shipping links were erratic and copra was not collected.

A visitor to Seychelles in 1933 was moved to comment as follows:

"The great majority of the people are engaged in agricultural and piscatorial pursuits. Such people can supplement small or sporadic earnings in cash by planting sweet potatoes or other cash crops even between coconut trees where necessary, and by drawing on the abundant fish supply available to anyone who chooses to fish in the sea by placing a basket trap with bait in shallow water and retrieving it and its contents a

Post Office, Victoria, Seychelles

Queen Victoria Clock and Post Office, Victoria photographed by Okashi c.1908. (courtesy S.Hopson, Indian Ocean Studies Circle).

few hours later. At present the Colony, from an investment point of view, has put all its eggs in one basket, that of the coconut industry. Not only that, but it has narrowed down its operations to one branch of that industry, the manufacture of copra. There are about 28,240 acres of coconut palms and a few thousand acres of cinnamon, while very small extents have been cultivated in other products. At present the essential oil industry, depending on cinnamon, patchouli, palmarosa, citronella, and lemongrass, is struggling for existence, and the exports of oil made from these plants threaten to reach vanishing point owing to the abysmal fall in commodity values in a period of unprecedented world-wide depression in industry. The London price of copra is now about £11 to £13 a ton, though in Seychelles a price of at least £15 a ton is required to give even a tolerable return to the grower of coconuts. The present Government of Seychelles is that of a Crown Colony in which the Governor, subject to the terms of the Letters patent establishing his Office, the Royal Instructions and the local laws carries on the administration on bureaucratic lines. The Government has an official majority in the Executive and Legislative Councils. French is the language of all classes..."

A chronology of events in the life of Seychelles, commencing at the beginning of the nineteenth century, is briefly listed below. And so we approach the present, a period of important development for Seychelles during which the country has made considerable strides, particularly since independence. In the final chapter we examine some modern aspects of this vibrant young nation.

Main Events of Nineteenth and Twentieth Centuries in Seychelles

1801   La Chiffon arrives with Jacobin deportees expelled from France by Napoleon. Naval battle between La Chiffon and HMS Sybille results in capture of the French vessel. La Fleche arrives with second consignment of deportees. Naval battle between La Fleche and HMS Victor results in British victory.

1802   Thirty-three of French deportees transported to Ajouan in Comoros where most of them died through suspected poisoning. Treaty of Amiens brings a brief peace between France and Britain.

1803   Population = 1,820 (220 whites; 100 liberated negroes and 1,500 slaves). War again breaks out between France and Britain.

1804   HMS Concord arrives and its captain demands a new capitulation by Governor De Quinssy.

1807   Abolition of slave trade in British Colonies.

1810   Reunion falls to Britain. Ile de France (Mauritius) falls to Britain.

1815   Seychelles officially declared a British Colony administered as a dependency of Mauritius.

1826   Sterling currency system introduced.

1827   Population: 471 whites...95 "men of colour", 119 free blacks; 6,638 slaves.

1832   Whaling Station opened at Ste Anne Island.

1833   The whaler "Sophie" burnt out at sea while enroute to Mahe. Whaler Greenwich wrecked at Bird island.

1835   Abolition of slavery. Death of Jean Francis Hodoul, 69 years old, former corsair and inhabitant of Seychelles.

A page from the "Register of Liberated Africans" listing and depicting slaves landed in Seychelles following British naval activities in the Indian Ocean between 1861 and 1872. Once landed in Seychelles they were "indented" to Seychellois planters and continued to provide low-cost labour for many years. (Courtesy of National Archive Centre). (Vine).

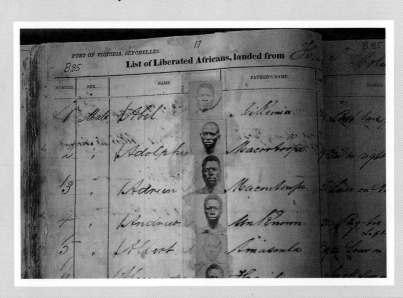

Queen Victoria shillings from National Archive Centre. (Harrison).

1836   Wreck of British Brig Aure on Providence.

1840   Coconut plantations...with capacity to produce "several hundred thousand litres of oil annually" established.

1841   Seychelles capital named Victoria.

1842   St Anne described as a "forest of coconuts".

1848   J.F.Lappussiere drowned and buried at Silhouette.

1850   Coconut plantations furnishing considerable quantity of oil.

1851   Letter from N. Savy to Governor of Seychelles requesting appointment of Roman Catholic priest, stating that for seventeen years he had not ceased applying for one!
Arrival on March 2nd of Catholic Rev Father Leon Des Avanchers. Alarmed at the challenge he posed to the Protestant church, the British administration succeeded in having him expelled. He was advised to seek permission from the Governor in Mauritius from where he had to travel to Rome and England.
First Protestant church erected....with boys' school attached...in Albert St.

1853   Arrival of first resident Catholic priests: Father Jeremiah and Father Theophile who began the work of the resident Catholic Mission in Seychelles.

1854   Wreck of S.V. "St Abbs" at Farquhar Is. Six survivors in grim battle to escape sharks and swim to shore. Seventeen days spent surviving on that waterless island before escaping by raft to Juan de Nuova where they found water. Five weeks later rescued by passing ship.

Middle to late nineteenth century: expansion of coconut plantations. **1860's:** Coconut oil, shipped to Mauritius...almost sole export. Cane, tobacco and coffee plantations kept on for local needs only.

1859   Victoria Anglican Church: "St Paul's Protestant Cathedral" completed....consecrated by Rt Rev. Dr Ryan...Bishop of Mauritius who travelled to Seychelles for the occasion....on board HMS Lynx.

1861   First Post Office opened in Victoria on December 11th. It was a sub-branch of GPO Port Louis, Mauritius. Seychelles still dependency of Mauritius, therefore Mauritian official seconded as "Resident Mail Agent in Seychelles".
"Voyageur" sank in Victoria harbour.
250 liberated slaves landed in Seychelles.

1862   Avalanche and hurricane caused considerable damage.

1863   Wreck of French Government Corvette: "La Perle" on Plate Island.

1866   Probable introduction of vanilla to Seychelles (see 1877).

1867   800 + slaves liberated by British vessels and landed in Seychelles.
Opening of St Louis College.

1861–1872 Almost 2,500 slaves liberated from Arab dhows...landed by British vessels and apprenticed to coconut planters, thus providing a dramatic increase to agricultural labour force (and a questionable form of liberty for the ex-slaves!).

1869   Suez canal opened and henceforth vessels from Mauritius were able to travel direct to Mediterranean, via Seychelles, thus improving communications with Europe.

1874   "Merry Monarch" wrecked on Cosmoledo Island. "DOT" wrecked at Alphonse Island.

Natural wood resources by now greatly reduced as noted by John Horne who commented that fine trees of exploitable size could only be found in the most inaccessible places in the mountains.

1875   Opening of hospital at Mont-Fleuri. Murder of first British Resident to Perak (Malay states)...Mr J.W. Birch...led to military expedition, occupation by British, and banishment to Seychelles of exSultan and various chiefs....becoming first political detainees to be held on islands.

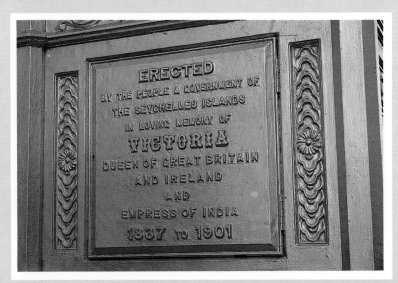

Presentation plaque from the "Queen Victoria Clock" which stands at the main cross-roads in Victoria. (Vine).

1876	The "Briton"...a British vessel of 166 tons...lost between Mauritius and Mahe.
	Rupee currency introduced, replacing sterling currency.
1877	Arrival in August of Ex-Sultan Abdullah of Perak plus entourage of 37 people in Seychelles. Commercial production of vanilla commenced (see 1891).
1879	Seychelles Government Gazette first published.
1880	General Gordon's visit to Seychelles (he was at time a Colonel) in order to report on cost of fortifying islands in view of trouble brewing between Britain and France over Madagascar....He concluded that they would be far too expensive to properly fortify....In something akin to a fit of passion he expressed the view that the granitic islands were part of a submerged continent...and that Valee de Mai on Praslin was the Garden of Eden with Coco de Mer the forbidden fruit!
	It was a theory which flew in the face of science and depended more on Gordon's legendary reputation than upon any sound evidence. Some would say that it provided an interesting insight into the mind of the man who, as a result of the same over-confidence in his own judgement finished up, four years later, being speared to death on the Palace steps at Khartoum.
1883	Volcanic eruption in Java...tidal wave in Seychelles. Visit by Marianne North..."coconut palms mounting higher up the mountains than any other place she had seen". Production of cloves reaches 21 tonnes.
1885	Population of Mahe...11,393....17 R.C. schools (1,084 pupils); 6 CofE schools (331 pupils).
1890	"Cupido", a British vessel of 140 tons, lost between Mahe and Mauritius. Seychelles issued its first stamps in April 1890 and parcel post begins.
1891	Guano digging begins...especially elevated deposits at Assumption and St Pierre (see 1907). First Government School established. Savy brothers drift to Muscat in maritime drama. Principle crop coconuts...next cloves(see 1893)...but vanilla increasingly important, with output this year at 41 tons (see 1901). Population....16,440....Victoria = 8,000. British vessel: "Sea Queen" lost. Coffee production begins (see 1899).
1893	Production of cloves reaches 49 tonnes but then collapses (see 1896). Account of the islands written by Mrs HE Edwards...New handbook for the Indian Ocean. Telegraphic communications with Mauritius and Europe...via Zanzibar completed in November, 1893. Eastern Telegraph Co. established on Mahe.
1894	Wreck of French bark "Federation" on Providence.
1896	Cloves production dropped to less than one tonne.

1897	Wreck of British ship, "Aymestry", at Farquhar Up to 1897 exports of guano from Seychelles reached 400,000 tons...leaving an estimated 50to100,000 tons of high grade guano available...rest lower grade (30–50% phosphates).
1899	Coffee production reaches 4.5 tonnes...peak...thereafter declines and ceased by 1908. In 1899 Vanilla was the prime value crop of Seychelles (worth 1.3 million rupees), overtaking coconuts in importance (value: 0.4 million rupees).
1900	Coconut had become almost sole support of a population of nearly 20,000 and still growing. First political detainees from Ashanti arrived...ie King Prempeh and entourage....while in Seychelles he was approached by both Catholic and Protestant missionaries who tried to "convert" him. After considerable deliberations he became a Protestant, embracing Christianity, and one of his sons later entered the priesthood. Having arrived in the colony in full tribal regalia....he left, almost twenty five years later, in full silk morning suit and top hat....tribal attire of another race. (see 1924).
1901	Wreck of British Schooner "Maggie Low" on sand-bank 20 miles south of Providence. New political detainees arrive...ie Mwanga, King of Buganda; John Kabarega...King of Bunyoro and his son: George Kabarega. Vanilla production increased to 72 tonnes...peak (see 1913). Population = 19,237. Unveiling of Queen Victoria Jubilee Fountain at junction of Albert Street and Long Pier.
1902	Wreck of SS "Hardwick Castle" on Farquhar Is.
1903	Seychelles made separate Crown Colony by declaration of King Edward VII (31st August, 1903). In a ceremony held on November 9th, in which HMS Pearl fired nineteen guns and all the towns bells were rung, the new colony of Seychelles inaugurated its first Governor and Commander in Chief—Sweet-Escott, who had campaigned on behalf of separation of Seychelles from the affairs of Mauritius. Clocktower erected in Victoria in commemoration of the

Early Seychelles stamps....1890 and 1892. (Courtesy of National Archive Centre and Indian Ocean Studies Circle). (Vine).

Ox power grinds coconut oil. c.1903. (courtesy S.Hopson, Indian Ocean Studies Circle).

event. It was funded by public subscription.
King Mwanga dies in exile, May 8th.
Wreck of British vessel "Tamatave" on Alphonse.

1905   Wreck of S.S. "Sir Celicourt Antelme"...at Marie Louise Is.

1906   Dramatic reduction in world price of vanilla created a severe shock to local economy. Coconuts once more became the prime crop; a change which resulted in grave social consequences since, while vanilla cultivation was carried out mostly by small land-holders (who now became poorer),coconuts for copra were raised by large plantation owners (whose profits rose).
Lugger "Alice Adeline" wrecked at Plate Island. Wreck of Bark "Norden" (Norwegian) at St Pierre Is. Wreck of Bark "Jorgen Bank"...Norwegian on Providence Organised exploitation of turtles by resident hunters begins at Aldabra (roughly 3,000 green turtles taken per year for next ten years)(see 1955). "Lord of the Isles" lost on north coast of Mahe without trace of wreckage.

Ex Kings Prempeh and Assibi, held political prisoners in Seychelles, received "western-style" education. 1912. (courtesy S. Hopson, Indian Ocean Studies Circle).

Court and Treasury building, Victoria in 1910. (courtesy S.Hopson, Indian Ocean Studies Circle).

1907   Output of guano...15,000 tons (see 1910).
Wreck of Norwegian bark: "Dagmar".

1908   Bark stripping of cinnamon at its peak. Cinnamon increasingly important. Andrew Carnegie donates £1,750 for construction of Public Library in Victoria.

1910   Output of guano 20,000 tons (see 1913)...peak production year (see 1960).

1911   Population = 22,691. An office of Commercial Bank of Mauritius opened (see 1916).

1912   Whaling carried out from whaling station at Ste. Anne.

1913   Output of guano 35,000 tons; Vanilla production dramatically reduced due to drought, disease, and a considerable fall-off in world price during first decade of century (resulting from an artificial substitute)...this year only 5 tonnes and still reducing (see 1934)
St Abbs whaling.
Wreck of Bark "Hamengia"...Norwegian at Cosmoledo island. Some "treasure trove" found at Astove..ie gold coins, silver spoons and forks salvaged from Portuguese vessel, Le Dom Royal (sunk 1760). Construction of Government House completed.

1914   German warship "Koenigsberg" is alleged to have hidden in Aldabra lagoon. Advent of First World War brings severe economic consequences for Seychelles since commercial links with Europe, its main market for guano and copra, are virtually severed.

Court and Treasury Building, Mahé, Seychelles

Post card of Albert street in 1910.
(courtesy S.Hopson, Indian Ocean
Studies Circle).

1915   Exploitation of cinnamon shifted to leaf oil distillation. Wreck of S.S. "Glen-Lyon" at Aldabra. Wreck of Lugger "Reve"...British ship..on Assumption Is. Whaling station closes at St Anne.

1916   Commercial Bank closes.
1,007 Seychellois were sent to join General Smut's army in East Africa. Many died of dysentery, malaria and beri-beri. A monument commemorates them in the cemetery at Mont-Fleuri.

1917   Severe economic depression. Only two copra cargoes to Europe.

1918   Worsening of economic depression. Only one copra cargo leaves. Petty crime rate rises dramatically as poverty striken islanders struggle to survive. Government response quite severe with 1,338 people imprisoned.

1919   Three members of the American Watch Tower Bible and Track Society were deported to Seychelles (via Mauritius) from Nyasaland where their teachings were causing disturbances.

1920   Political detainee, Mahmood Ali Shirreh, Sultan of Warsangli Tribe from Somaliland arrives in Seychelles where he is held until 1928.

1921   Population = 24,523 (11,974 males; 12,549 females).
More political detainees arrive, including Said Khalil Bin Bargash. Arabian claimant of throne in Zanzibar...arrested by British in Tanganyika... initially deported to St Helena...and from there to Seychelles. He came with two sons and nineteen others.

Ex King Kabarega of Uganda was held political prisoner in Seychelles. 1912 (courtesy S.Hopson, Indian Ocean Studies Circle).

Rickshaws await customers at the junction of Royal and Albert Streets, c. 1915. (courtesy S.Hopson, Indian Ocean Studies Circle).

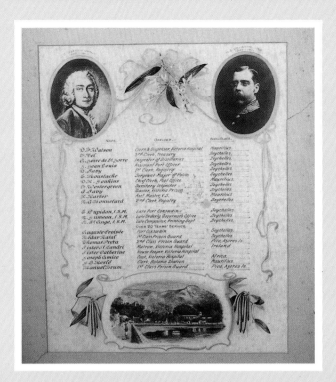

From the Address by Citizens of Seychelles on the occasion of the Coronation of King Gerge V. (National Archive Centre) (Vine).

King George V. Coronation presentation book with painting of old Government House. 1911. (National Archive Centre). (Vine).

| 1922 | Arrival of yet more political detainees...ie Egyptian premier, Saad Zaghloul Pasha and five cabinet ministers. Pasha was soon sent to Gibraltar for medical treatment. |

1922   Arrival of yet more political detainees...ie Egyptian premier, Saad Zaghloul Pasha and five cabinet ministers. Pasha was soon sent to Gibraltar for medical treatment.
Direct cable link to Aden and Colombo established by Eastern Telegraph Co.
Farquhar proclaimed a dependency of Seychelles (formerly of Mauritius).

1923   Production of Patchouli oil begins (see 1931).

1924   Prempeh, ex King of Ashanti, left Seychelles following almost 25 years exile, to return to Gold Coast where he was re-elected as Head Chief of Kumasi tribe.

1926   Electricity and telephone installations completed.

1927   Coconut is by far the most valuable plant in Seychelles (copra = 1.3 million rupees; essential oils = 0.4 million, guano = 0.3 million).
German cruiser, "Emden" (6,000 tons)—first German visit to Seychelles after 1914–1918 war.

1929–1930 Seabird egg landings on Mahe...average around 4.1 million eggs per year (see 1931).

1930   Peak year for export of sea-cucumbers...Trepang...10 tonnes.

1931   Population = 27,444; (13,289 males; 14,155 females...Europeans, their descendants and Africans...26,706; Indian community...503; Chinese community...235....Roman Catholics...24,054; CofE 2,611; 7th Day Adventists..25).
Peak year for sea-bird egg landings...possibly 10 million this year. (see 1944).
Patchouli oil production 3,900 L (see 1947).

Catholic Cathedral at Victoria. (Vine).

1933	"The great majority of the people are engaged in agricultural and piscatorial pursuits. Such people can supplement small or sporadic earnings in cash by planting sweet potatoes or other cash crops even between coconut trees where necessary, and by drawing on the abundant fish supply available to anyone who chooses to fish in the sea by placing a basket trap with bait in shallow water and retrieving it and its contents a few hours later." Arrival of six political detainees from Aden...all strict orthodox Muslims. "At present the Colony, from an investment point of view, has put all its eggs in one basket, that of the coconut industry. Not only that, but it has narrowed down its operations to one branch of that industry, the manufacture of copra. There are about 28,240 acres of coconut palms and a few thousand acres of cinnamon, while very small extents have been cultivated in other products. At present the essential oil industry, depending on cinnamon, patchouli, palmarosa, citronella, and lemongrass, is struggling for existence, and the exports of oil made from these plants threaten to reach vanishing point owing to the abysmal fall in commodity values in a period of unprecedented world-wide depression in industry." ..."The London price of copra is now about £11 to £13 a ton, though in Seychelles a price of at least £15 a ton is required to give even a tolerable return to the grower of coconuts." "The present Government of Seychelles is that of a Crown Colony in which the Governor, subject to the terms of the Letters patent establishing his Office, the Royal Instructions and the local laws carries on the administration on bureaucratic lines. The Government has an official majority in the Executive and legislative Councils". "French is the language of all classes..." First issue of Seychelles Clarion.
1934	Wreck of small Swedish yacht.."Nodeskalen" at Farquhar... Vanilla production down to less than one tonne.
1936	Sixty seven private cars in Seychelles; fifty-five distilleries and fifty copra producers.
1937	Deportation from Palestine...of five "freedom fighters": Ahmad Hilmi Pasha (60 yrs old, Arab Bank Managing Director); Rasheed Haj Ibrahim (50yrs old, Manager of Arab Bank at Haifa); Fuad Saleh Saba (35yrs old, Secretary of the Arab Higher Committee); and Dr Hussein Fakri Al Khalidi (42yrs old, former Mayor of Jerusalem (1934-37), medical practitioner, member of Arab Higher Committee) and Yacoub Ghussein...president of Arab Youth Congress. The group had been held morally responsible by the British for the disturbances leading to the murder of Mr L.W. Andrews, District Commissioner for Galilea. Wreck of British vessel SS "Endeavour on Providence. Exports: 5,611 tons copra; 9,594 tons guano; oils...72 tons; tortoiseshell 896 kgs; vanilla 466 kgs; calipee, 4.4 tons; birds egg yolk...liquid...27.9 tons. Agricultural Bank established.
1938	First pictorial stamps issued in Seychelles...depicting Giant tortoise; Coco-de-Mer and a fishing pirogue.
1939	Palestinian political prisoners repatriated.
1939-1945	Second World War...Seychelles becomes important refuelling base for flying-boats and British ships.
1939	Population 31,486 (15,462 males; 16,024 females).

1940   Population almost 32,000. No Bank in Colony (other than Government Savings Bank)...Local currency replaces coins and notes from Mauritius. British India Company steamships call once a month (on Bombay to E. Africa run)...and once every 2 months on return route...except June and July when fortnightly calls at Seychelles...by ships plying from Mombasa to Bombay. Also ships from Royal Dutch Mail Line and Scandinavian East Africa Line.

1941   900 Seychellois were sent to Africa to fight on British side. They saw action at El-Amein in October 1942; as well as at Tobruk and in Italy. Fishermen: Antoine Vidot, Vitalo Figaro and Robert Fred of Praslin rescued off Lamu, East Africa, following 36 days at sea in "Gypsy'.

1942   Governor Sir Arthur Grimble departs from Seychelles and is replaced by Charles Bernard Smith.

1943   Economy of Seychelles once more severely disrupted as a result of World War. Patchouli oil rises in price as a result of war in Malaya and Indonesia.

1944-1965 1.07 million sea bird eggs per year reach Mahe.(see 1955).

1947   Patchouli oil production 9,000 litres (see 1954). Population = 34,623.

1948   First elected representatives to government but franchise restricted to property

1949   Creation of first District Council.

1951   Population = 34,370.

1953   "Mary Jane" goes adrift on passage from Praslin to Victoria. Boat had eleven people on board on 31st January when saga began. After 72 days adrift in

A family of Seychellois Creoles photographed by G. de Comamond in about 1935. (courtesy of National Archive Centre). (courtesy S.Hopson, Indian Ocean Studies Circle).

Indian Ocean two survivors: Antoine Vidot (20yrs old) and Selby Corgat (15yrs old) are picked up (position:6.45South, 45.05 East) by Italian steamer Montallegro. They are taken to Kuwait. Six weeks later the "Mary Jane" herself drifts onto shore at El Balbile (30 miles north of Kismayu). Near the wreckage the dead body of a white person was found.

1954 Patchouli oil production collapses.

1955 Lease of Aldabra limits Green Turtle catch to 500 per year(see 1968) Seabird egg collection on Bird Island ceases.

1956 Issue of first commemorative stamp which was specific only to Seychelles.It depicted the Pierre de Possession—commemorating 200th anniversary of ceremony in which Captain Nicholas Morphey placed Stone of Possession on Mahe, declaring it as French territory. Visit of HRH Prince Philip to Seychelles.

1957 Peak year for export of Green Snail (29 tonnes).

1959 First commercial bank.

1960 17,000 acres coconut plantations listed...ie 36% of total land area; approx 700 acres of vanilla...usually grown under coconuts; 14,000 acres cinnamon. "Alone or together...coconuts and cinnamon occupy half the islands' surface area". Vallee de Mai one of last remaining primitive forest stands. Population census...41,425 people...80 percent on Mahe. 10,000 in Victoria.
Between 1895 and 1960 700,000 tons guano exported (half from Assumption and St Pierre)...see natural history and effects of guano mining on natural vegetation and wildlife.

1963 Americans commence construction of Satellite Tracking Station on Mahe.

1964 Stone of Possession removed from Government House grounds to Victoria Museum. Formation of Seychelles Democratic Party under James Mancham and Seychelles People's United Party under France Albert Rene who was strongly committed to achieving the independence of Seychelles.

1965 Creation of new British Colony: British Indian Ocean Territory comprising Aldabra, Farquhar and Desroche which were annexed with strategic defence considerations in mind. See 1976.

1966 Production of Tea commences (see 1970).

1967 Universal adult suffrage introduced.

1968 Taking of Green Turtles becomes illegal. Government adopts policy of acquiring large estates and dividing them into small-holdings. Two hundred year anniversary of arrival on Praslin of French colonists from Mauritius—on board "La Digue" and "Curieuse"—celebrated by stamp issue. Contract awarded to Costains for construction of Mahe International Airport.

1969 Rochon Dam completed.

A Pan American Grumman Albatross amphibian plane photographed by K.B.Fitton at Victoria Long Pier in 1968. (courtesy S.Hopson, Indian Ocean Studies Circle).

1970   First Constitutional Conference to discuss future of Seychelles. Creation of Legislative Assembly. 20 tonnes of tea produced. Royal Fleet Auxilliary, 47,000 ton tanker "Ennerdale" grounded in June and shortly after blown-up by Royal navy divers. 1971 Airport completed and first regular air service inaugurated. Population = 54,695; 5,120 tourists visited during 1971.

1973   New port in Victoria becomes operational.

1975   Seychelles becomes an autonomous colony.

1976   June 29th, 1976, Republic of Seychelles is declared. Coalition Government formed with President James Mancham, and Prime Minister France Albert Rene. Aldabra, Farquhar and Desroches redefined as Seychelles possessions.

When James Mancham declared his intention to award himself the title of President for Life he pushed the patience of opposition members beyond breaking point.

1977   On June 5th a coup took place while Mancham was attending a Commonwealth Conference in London. France Albert Rene was requested to form a new government. This date became recognised as Liberation Day and is celebrated annually. Official documents stated Governmental philosophy as follows:

     1. Government of the people and by the people.
     2. Government is Socialist and Seychellois.
     3. Government will promote and safeguard popular democracy.
     4. Government seeks a system free from all discrimination.
     5. Government wishes to create equal opportunities for all.

Population...61,786...Victoria...over 23,000; 54,490 tourists visited in 1977.
Oil exploration in Seychelles begins with 47 blocks awarded under three separate licences. Development Bank of Seychelles established.

1978   Seychelles becomes single party country in which people are represented by Seychelles People's Progressive Front.

Seychelles declares Exclusive Economic Zone.

Giant tortoises transported to Curieuse Island to establish a breeding colony there.

1979   General Elections held (55 candidates stood for twenty three seats) and new Constitution published.

Establishment of Seychelles Islands Foundation...for management and conservation of natural life of Aldabra and of any other land in Seychelles designated by Seychelles Government.Peak tourism year with 78,852 tourists.

Purse seining for Tuna commences in Indian Ocean. Seychelles grants fishing licences to Korean longliners to fish for Tuna in its waters.

1980   Population = 63,261. National Development Plan published in which education was "the priority of priorities". The plan also tackled housing development; public transport; agricultural development; fisheries development and tourism. Of the latter, the Government's strategy was summed up as follows: "The Government of Seychelles will not accept exploitation of its people by tourism, nor exploitation of tourists by its people, therefore tourism will be properly controlled and tourism development encouraged".

1981   November 25th mercenary aggression against Seychelles ends in failure for mercenaries and is followed by their arrest, trials and imprisonment in Seychelles and South Africa.

Headquarters of the S.P.U.P. Party in Victoria is in an attractive traditional building. (Vine).

1982	Aldabra becomes world's first coral atoll designated as a World Heritage Site by UNESCO. Relative lull in tourism with numbers cut back to 47,280.
1983	Agreements signed for EEC vessels to fish in Seychelles EEZ.
1984	Tourism in revival again with 63,417 in year.
1985	Population = 65,244; Number of tourists: 72,542.
1987	Major Tuna processing plant opened in Seychelles. Commercial port extension and major coastal reclamation underway. 10 year celebration of Liberation. Direct non-stop flights from Europe operated by Air Seychelles.
2000	Projected population = 82,443.

The National Library (formerly Carnegie Library), Victoria. (Vine).

NATURAL
HISTORY

GEOLOGY

As the once great mega-continent of Gondwanaland, comprising Africa, Madagascar, Seychelles, India, Antarctica and Australia began to crack around 130 million years ago, the major continents edged slowly apart, opening up deep rifts into which sea-water poured. At first India and Madagascar remained connected as they drifted north-eastwards at an estimated rate of 7.5 to 16 cms per year. In the late Jurassic or early Cretaceous period, India broke away from Madagascar, the latter remaining roughly where it lies today, separated from Africa by the Mozambique Channel. Seychelles and the Mascarene Plateau continued their drift, along with the landmass of India, towards the north-east. Approximately 75 million years ago, a second break occurred; the Seychelles-Mascarene bank became stranded on new ocean-floor but India continued to drift northwards. By 55 million years ago the major plate movements, creating the Earth's great oceans, had slowed down. Tectonic activity had far from ceased however since, about ten million years later, renewed activity broke-out along new ridges. In the vicinity of Seychelles, most movement was centred on the Carlsberg Ridge running NW-SE from the Horn of Africa.

The islands of Seychelles can be categorised, geologically, into three main types. Firstly, the high granitic islands including Mahe, Praslin, La Digue, Silhouette and their associated assemblage, comprising, in all, twenty-four islands; secondly, south-west of the Mahe group, many low sand-cays forming the Amirantes; finally, the slightly more elevated, limestone islands of the Aldabra-Astove group, situated even further to the west.

Mahe itself is covered, for the most part, by a grey, alkaline granite which, along its west coast and on the nearby island of Therese, tends to be porphyritic. The off-lying islands of Praslin, La Digue, Curieuse, Felicite, Marianne, Mamelles, Les Soeurs, Cousin and Cousine all have a fairly uniform, reddish-grey granite containing feldspars. The granitic rocks of the group have been dated to around 650 million years old, in the PreCambrian, long before Seychelles became separated from Gondwanaland. A series of NW-SE joints occur, penetrated in places by much younger (c. 50 million years old) basaltic dykes chemically similar to oceanic basalt and, therefore, not consistent with the original continental existence of Seychelles. They were exuded into the much older granite, when Seychelles had split from Madagascar and India, and achieved approximately its current position in mid-ocean.

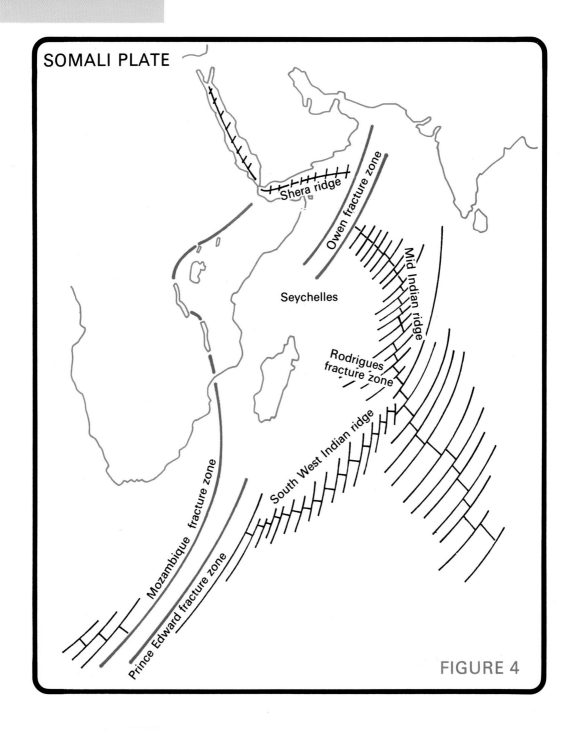

SOMALI PLATE

Shera ridge

Owen fracture zone

Seychelles

Mid Indian ridge

Rodrigues fracture zone

South West Indian ridge

Mozambique fracture zone

Prince Edward fracture zone

FIGURE 4

The red earth, often commented on by visitors to Seychelles, is formed primarily by weathered granite or laterite. Once surface vegetation is removed, for example by forestry, the remaining earth on the steeply sloping mountains of these granitic islands, is all too easily washed away, exposing the bare rock-face. At many sites around Mahe one can observe characteristically weathered granitic boulders whose surfaces bear a fluted pattern. Snorkel diving on offshore rocky outcrops, such as for example along the coast adjacent to Northolme

Hotel, reveals similarly weathered boulders patterned with deeply incut vertical grooves, beneath the sea. One such small outcrop was christened "The Cathedral" by the author, in recognition of its magnificent columnar grooves and the fact that it is frequented by hosts of Angelfish! This formation demonstrates clearly that the lengthy process of weathering took place when sea-level was considerably lower than it is today and such rocks were exposed to the atmosphere. It is difficult to state exactly what forces combined to create the dramatic modern rock-sculptures, but it seems likely that considerable weathering was caused by rain during the Pleistocene pluvial period. Coastal plains on these granitic islands are either formed by marine deposits cast ashore, or by phosphate (derived from guano) cementing sand grains to form sand-stone. The sand thus formed may be of marine, bioclastic, origin or lateritic. In river-estuaries a very fine silt, derived primarily from laterites, occurs and in those areas where they have not been removed, the fine sediment provides an ideal environment for mangroves. Before Man appeared on the scene a large area of the coast around Mahe was densely wooded with mangroves but they have today, with several notable exceptions, been largely extirpated. Examples of guano-related plateaux are evident on Cousin, Cousine, Aride and Frigate, each island still famous for its sea-birds.

The granitic slopes of Mahe have been worn smooth by rainfall, and over the course of millions of years, deep channels have been gouged in the rocks, often resulting in quite regular scalloping. North-west side of Mount Jasmin on Mahe. (Vine).

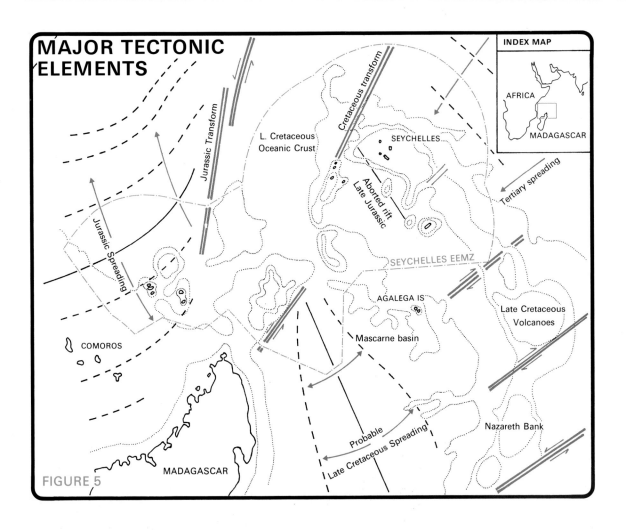

MAJOR TECTONIC ELEMENTS

FIGURE 5

INDEX MAP

AFRICA

MADAGASCAR

Jurassic Transform

Cretaceous transform

L. Cretaceous Oceanic Crust

SEYCHELLES

Tertiary spreading

Aborted rift Late Jurassic

Jurassic Spreading

SEYCHELLES EEMZ

AGALEGA IS

Late Cretaceous Volcanoes

Mascarne basin

COMOROS

Nazareth Bank

Probable Late Cretaceous Spreading

MADAGASCAR

The low coral islands of Bird and Denis situated on the northern rim of the Seychelles Bank are also renowned for their sea-birds: their guano deposits have been largely removed by mining. Platforms of, what is appropriately called, "beach-rock" are much in evidence along the shores of these islands. The process by which this forms deserves a brief explanation. Rain falling on the beach, being very slightly acidic, tends to dissolve calcium carbonate from the marine sediments; as the dilute solution drains down the shore, it comes in contact with alkaline sea-water, whereupon the calcium carbonate is precipitated once more, this time forming congealed "beach-rock" along the water's edge. Coetivy, the only other significant sand-cay on the Seychelles Bank, is characterised by high wind-blown dunes, partially related to guano deposition.

A rim, covered by coralline algae (*Archaeolithothamnion*) and other loose debris, surrounds most of the Seychelles Bank, rising to within about 20 metres of the surface. Bottom deposits within the "bowl" formed by this Seychelles bank rim (area: 43,000 sq.kms) are primarily derived from the skeletal remains of marine organisms such as planktonic foraminiferans (*Globigerina*), pteropods, algae, bryozoa, echinoderms, molluscs and non-reef-building corals (*Heteropsammia*). Snorkelling in the shallows around Denis Island, one may easily observe the process by which such organisms create the white sands

Rugged terrain on Aldabra can provide a daunting barrier for both man and beast to traverse. (Guy de Moussac).

associated with idyllic "coral-island" beaches. Growing in clumps attached to coralline rocks is the calcareous alga with fleshy disc-shaped leaves, *Halimeda*. Closer inspection of the lagoon floor reveals that the white "sand" is comprised, almost exclusively, of dead "leaf-discs" from this sea-weed. One can delve deep into the sediment and still grasp nothing but the bleached remains of *Halimeda*. Closer to the shore, the fragments are broken-up and less easily identified and the beach itself owes much to the prolific growth of this calcareous alga.

The three major "Banks" forming the Seychelles; i.e. the Seychelles Bank, Saya de Malha Bank (40,000 sq.kms.) and Nazareth Bank (26,000 sq.kms.) were all above sea-level during the Pleistocene glacial period, forming a combined land mass of 125,000 sq kms in sharp contrast with the presently shrunken land area of Seychelles, covering less than 500 sq.kms.!

The low coralline islands of Desnoefs, Marie Louise, Etoile, Poivre, Desroches, D'Arros, Remire and African Banks, none of which rise more than 2-3m above sea-level, comprise the Amirantes Group, roughly two hundred and fifty kilometres south-west of Mahe. While the islands themselves are formed of bioclastic sands, displaying no evidence of volcanic rock, there is little doubt that they are resting on a volcanic mound since magnetic profiles indicate that oceanic basalt lies less than one kilometer beneath the Bank.

Situated just over one thousand kilometers south-west of Mahe are a group of somewhat more elevated limestone islands known as the Aldabra group and comprising, in addition to Aldabra itself, Assumption, Astove, and Cosmoledo. The islands, although formed by limestone, are volcanic in origin and the coral-cappings are relatively recent. Evidence of their lengthy inhabitation by wildlife is provided by sediments in which skeletal fragments of giant tortoises, crocodiles, an iguana, other lizards, and birds feature prominently. The effects of the drop in sea-level during the Pleistocene glacial period (causing a total lowering of 120m.) are apparent on Aldabra as two terraces at +4m

Aldabra Sacred Ibis (*Threskiornis aethiopica abbotti*) is a subspecies of Sacred Ibis restricted to Aldabra in which the eye of adults is china blue. It is a rare bird with probably less than two hundred birds living on the atoll. (Guy de Moussac).

An old ship-wreck in shallow-water at Aldabra. (Jacques Fauquet).

and + 8m. The "atoll" shape of Aldabra is not due to growth of coral in the classical Darwinian model of atoll-formation, but by erosion of the central land-mass and the consequent creation of a shallow lagoon. The rock surface on Aldabra, and the adjacent islands, is, in places, extremely pitted, forming razor-sharp edges. This pitting is the result of solution of limestone by rain.

Coral-reefs surrounding the islands of Seychelles have mostly developed over a period of six to eight thousand years, i.e. very recently in geological terms. The great variety of marine habitats present in Seychelles waters support a huge range of coral communities, described further under the section covering marine-life.

CLIMATE

Separated, in some cases, by distances of more than a thousand kilometers; extending over a latitudinal range of almost seven degrees; and consisting of both mountainous islands and low-lying coral cays, it is not surprising that climatic variations exist within the country. Nevertheless, some generalisations can be made. Seychelles has a tropical, humid climate modified by monsoonal winds. Winter, i.e. May to October, is characterised by steady South East Trade winds in the southern hemisphere, deflecting to become south-westerly monsoons in the northern hemisphere. The south-easterly trades bring cooler, drier, remarkably stable weather to Seychelles. Around the higher granitic islands, this is modified by a frequent build-up of cloud in the afternoon, accompanied by short but intense rain-storms. Summer months, i.e. December to March, are affected by the NW monsoon winds bringing more moisture and much higher rainfall to Seychelles.

Studies indicate mean annual temperatures of 26.6 deg.C. at Port Victoria and 27 deg.C. at Aldabra, with little monthly variation. The coolest month is August, when the mean monthly temperature in Victoria is 25.7deg C. with an extreme minimum of 20.9deg.C., while the hottest month is April, with a mean temperature of 27.8 deg.C. The surrounding ocean plays a key role in moderating temperature extremes, as is evidenced by the fact that the lowest ever recorded temperature in Port Victoria is 19.3 deg.C. and the highest, only 32.8 deg.C. Temperatures higher up the mountains reduce with increasing altitude

at a rate of approximately half a degree per 100 metres.

Relative humidity at, or near, sea-level is fairly constant throughout the year, with lowest mean levels in April (75%), and highest in the middle of the January rainy season (80%). Steady winds tend to prevent relative humidity from rising to uncomfortable levels. High in the mist-shrouded mountains of Morne Seychellois however, humidity levels are extremely elevated, frequently exceeding 90% and characteristic "mist-forest" vegetation is associated with this moisture level.

Rainfall records for all the islands are still somewhat incomplete. North-westerly monsoon winds bring rain-bearing clouds over Seychelles, particularly during December-January and October-November. The southern islands, such as Aldabra, tend to lag behind, with peaks occurring in March-April. Mean annual rainfall in Victoria is 237.7cms. while that on the low level islands ranges from 173cms at Denis island in the north, to only 96 cms at Aldabra. There is a distinctly diurnal pattern to precipitation, with a concentration of rain falling in the afternoons (from 12pm to 6 pm). The granitic islands, including Mahe, are in a cyclone free-zone whereas the Aldabra group is occasionally affected by cyclones. During the past century there have been several major fluctuations in rainfall at Mahe and current levels are once more on the increase, in line with the climate of the equatorial Western Indian Ocean as a whole.

Windspeeds are generally moderate, stronger in the south than around the granitic islands. At the height of the SE trades, in August, average windspeed in Victoria is 9.2 knots while the NW monsoon is a weaker wind averaging around 3.5 to 4 knots. The period of lightest winds and calmest seas is during the April transition from NW Monsoon to South-Easterly Trades when average wind-strength at Victoria is only 3.2 knots.

An indication of the climatic stability of Seychelles is provided by its vegetation. Commenting on the wide range of habitats occupied by endemic palms, Procter (1984) commented as follows: "*This evidence suggests that past climates in the Seychelles have fluctuated between humid (as at present), and semi-arid, and that both the extremes and the intermediate stages have remained stable long enough either for the evolution or the arrival and adaptation of species to match them. It also suggests that past climates have never been either so arid as to eliminate*

Fossil-coral overhung cliff coastline of Aldabra with a small shark seen in the foreground. (Guy de Moussac).

Small islets such as this one in Aldabra's lagoon provide important nesting grounds for a number of sea-birds. (Jacques Fauquet).

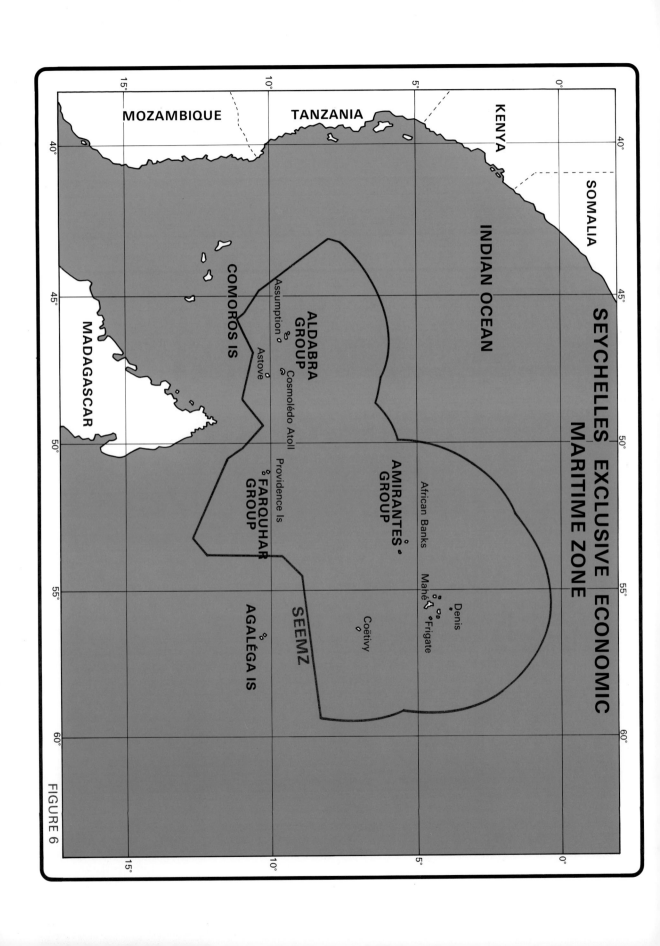

SEYCHELLES' EXCLUSIVE ECONOMIC MARITIME ZONE

FIGURE 6

rainforest species or so humid as to eliminate the more xerophytic species."

MARINE LIFE

A map of the Seychelles Exclusive Economic Zone illustrates the vast expanse of Indian Ocean falling under this young nation's jurisdiction. Whilst early settlers sought to exploit the limited land-mass of Seychelles, its' marine resources were, with the exception of turtles, left largely untouched. Coastal fishing yielded sufficient food for immediate needs and very little exploration of underwater resources took place. From a scientific viewpoint, there have been a number of intensive investigations of particular aspects of marine-life around Seychelles, especially at Aldabra, but these have barely skimmed the surface. To the visitor, intent on donning face-mask and snorkel, it is the coral-reefs of Seychelles which provide the big attraction. Sports fishermen come here for exciting game-fishing, while others are content to SCUBA dive among its underwater gardens and simply admire the rich assemblage of marine-life found here. For everyone there remains a true sense of excitement at the possibility of discovering the unknown.

J.L.B. Smith, the great South African icthyologist whose book Fishes of Seychelles remains the fish-watcher's bible for this part of the World, experienced his moment of adrenalin pumping excitement when he discovered a living "fossil", the Coelacanth: *Latimeria chalumnae*, a deep-water fish thought to have become extinct 70 million years ago. While Professor Smith eventually tracked down its habitat to the vicinity of Comores, there is no reason to suppose they do not also occur in the depths around Seychelles, for example off the edge of the Aldabra Bank. On a less dramatic note, today's marine biologists are continually recording either new species of fish or new records in Seychelles waters.

Shallow-water marine environments around Seychelles are generally dominated by sea-grasses, soft-corals, hard corals, sea-weeds or possibly loose sediment. Sea-grasses are of great importance, as a primary food-source for green-turtles as well as a key habitat for many invertebrates and fish. Two families are present; the Potamogetonaceae, in which the principle genera are *Thalassodendron*, *Syringodium*, *Halodule* and *Cymodocea*; and secondly the Hydocharitaceae, including *Halophila* and *Thalassia*. The major species found in Seychelles are *Cymodocea rotundata*, *Halodule uninervis*, *Syringodium isoetifolium*, *Thalassodendron ciliatum*, *Halophila minor* and *Thalassia hemprichii*. Sea-grass meadows are frequently very extensive and may have several species of sea-grasses within them. The different species do, however, tend to favour slightly different environments in terms of depth, exposure and sediment types. Some of the largest marine grass-beds are formed by *Thalassia hemprichii*, a widespread Indo-Pacific species growing on both sand and mud.

Apart from Green Turtles and juvenile Hawksbill Turtles, both of which graze sea-grasses, the sea-cow or Dugong is also dependent on undersea grass meadows for its food. While early visitors to the islands reported sightings of dugongs, it is not so certain now whether they were sea-cows or a since vanished seal or sea-lion. Suffice it to say here that there were, and still are, adequate sea-grasses around Seychelles islands such as Bird and Denis to support a sustainable population of sea-cows.

The large reef-grouper, *Epinephelus tauvina*, can grow to a considerable size. This relatively small individual is resting beneath a brain-coral head in Aldabra lagoon. (Jacques Fauquet).

Yellow-lipped Snapper swim in a tight bunch above Acropora coral on the reef at Aldabra. (Jacques Fauquet).

Seychelles coral-reefs are of three main kinds, i.e. fringing reefs, platform reefs and atolls. Even where they do not form distinct reefs many corals are to be found, attached to hard substrata in shallow-water, such as on the weathered granitic boulders around Mahe. Coral taxonomy is a highly specialised field and one in which it is easy to make mistakes. Coral species are defined, not by macro-characteristics such as colony shape, but by intricate details of their skeletal structure. Whilst the general shape of corals does usually follow a species pattern, this is not true in all cases and it is quite possible, and indeed not infrequent, for two quite different growth forms to be conspecific. Investigations of corals in Seychelles waters have recorded forty-five genera of reef-building corals around the granitic islands, and forty-four at Aldabra. Although Mahe is a granitic island, its shallows greatly affected by run-off and turbidity, there are several areas where quite well developed fringing reefs may be observed. The choice of snorkelling venue, however, may be partially influenced by the season. During the south-easterly trades (April–October) it is quite difficult, if not dangerous, to dive along the southerly oriented shores of Mahe and visits to these areas should be made during the period of the north-westerly monsoon (November–March), or in the generally calm change-over period between the SE trades and NW monsoon winds. The assemblage of corals, present at any particular location, depends upon a number of factors such as depth, local turbidity, degree of exposure to wave-surge, etc. A study carried out by Brian Rosen (1971) recognised three different assemblages of corals on reefs surrounding Mahe; *Pocillopora*, *Acropora* and *Porites* assemblages. The *Pocillopora* community, comprising primarily *Pocillopora danae-meandrina*, *Acropora humilis* and the yellow, stinging hydrocoral *Millepora platyphylla* occurs in areas of moderate to strong water movement. The *Porites* community, on the other hand, tends to be found in more turbid water, in harbours for example, where water movement is much less. *Pocillopora* communities may be seen along the reef crest of reefs in the south-eastern part of Mahe, at, for example, Anse aux Pins where a groove and spur sculpted reef face attests to the exposed character of this reef system. Surge channels along these reefs are likely to have branched colonies of *Stylophora mordax*. *Acropora* communities may still be seen in St Anne Marine Park and are dominated by banks of stagshorn coral (mainly *Acropora formosa*). More sheltered zones in the Marine Park have large rounded colonies of *Porites* together with numerous faviid corals. A reasonably well developed reef may be seen during the south-easterly trades along the protected north-west facing entrance of Baie Ternay at Mahe where Acropora communities dominate the reef-face, together with some large Porites knolls. Away from Mahe, extensive fringing reefs may be observed around Praslin and La Digue, where the reef width tends to be greatest to the west and south-east, being narrowest to the south-west.

Platform reefs may be observed at many locations including African Banks, Coetivy, D'Arros, Platte and Providence. In some cases the platform reefs have much of their area above water, forming islands, whilst in others only very small sections of the total reef area are raised above sea-level. The islands of Assumption and St Pierre are in fact raised platform reefs.

The third reef-type, atoll formation, is represented in Seychelles by several examples. A true atoll is one in which corals developing on an undersea mound, generally of volcanic origin, have grown up and outwards so that as the central mass of coral dies-back and erodes, a lagoon is formed, surrounded by a circle of coral reef, sections of which may emerge to form islands. Farquhar is the largest true atoll in Seychelles waters and other, smaller examples are those of St Joseph, St Francoise and Alphonse in the Amirantes.

Aldabra, Cosmoledo and Astove are raised atolls in which a complex history of submergence and emergence have led to a series of erosional features including, on Aldabra, distinct terraces at 4m and 8m above sea-level. Unlike the lagoons of the atolls mentioned above, that of Aldabra is very shallow, much of it above low-water spring-tide level, but it seldom dries since water exchange rates with the open ocean are greatly retarded. An interesting example of a drowned atoll is provided by Desroche, a sand-cay situated on the western edge of a submerged atoll, approximately twenty kilometres in diameter.

It is readily apparent to anyone who swims out from the shore of Mahe, or its adjacent islands, that there is a distinct zonation of marine-life as one moves from the extreme shallows out towards deeper-water; or, alternatively, in those areas where fringing reefs exist, through a shallow lagoon, across the back-reef zone, over the reef platform, and past the reef-crest to the shallow reef slope, beyond which is a more gently sloping terrace. In each of these "zones" the characteristic assemblage of corals, algae and other organisms differs. On a typical swim out from the beach along the east coast of Mahe, a swimmer wades out a short distance across a sandy zone and begins snorkelling over sea-grass beds, formed primarily by *Thalassia hemprichii*. Towards the sea-ward side of these grass beds, isolated colonies of corals provide a habitat for a variety of small fish. As one leaves the grass-beds, corals become more prolific and the brown algae *Sargassum* and *Turbinaria* cover large patches, broken here and there by sandy pockets. The sea-bed takes on the form of a series of ridges and troughs, and in the deeper water large colonies of *Porites*, *Pocillopora* and *Heliopora* occur. Then, as one swims closer towards the breakers, the water suddenly becomes shallower and it is possible to stand and walk again across the algal-ridge, formed by the pink calcareous cementing algae *Lithophyllum* and *Porolithon*, together with toughened stands of the brown sea-weeds, *Sargassum* and *Turbinaria*.

A *Promicrops* grouper dwarfs the other residents of Aldabra's reef-face. (Jacques Fauquet).

Here the waves create a strong surge and it is pleasant to force one's way forward, and out across a reef-crest formed by stands of yellow hydrocoral (*Millepora dichotoma*) and wave-resistant corals such as *Pocillopora danae*, out into deeper water where one can look down at the reef-face clothed by dense stands of stagshorn coral and large tabular Acroporas such as *A.pharaonis*. Here is the area of most active coral-growth and most prolific fish-life.

Black, sharply spined sea-urchins are amongst the first marine creatures encountered by swimmers, as they enter the sea around the granitic islands of Seychelles. These are of two main species, the longer spined *Diadema setosum* and the more stoutly spined *Echinothrix calamaris*. Both are nocturnal reef-grazers, feeding on algae, and avoiding direct daylight, aggregating on shaded rock-faces and in crevices, but, where shade is limited, they tend to gather in the open, forming hazardous patches of needle-sharp spines best avoided by novice swimmers. Not all sea-urchins have such painfully sharp spines however. An abundant small urchin, *Echinometra mathaei* is found lodged in crevices near the reef-edge while the broad spined "pencil-urchins", *Eucidaris metularia* and *Prionocidaris verticillata* are common on sea-grass-beds; the former species usually hiding under boulders while the latter may be seen out in the open. Another pencil urchin: *Phyllacanthus imperialis* occurs in somewhat deeper, sheltered habitats, frequently in association with the coral *Porites*. One can hardly fail to notice the large sea urchin, *Tripneustes gratilla* on the sea-grass beds, although it makes an attempt to partially camouflage itself with sea-grass blades. A somewhat similar, but more dorso-ventrally flattened sea-urchin, exhibiting a more effective camouflaging behaviour, is *Toxopneustes pileolus* whose unusually large pedicellariae are poisonous. Digging in the sand, especially among sea-grass roots, may lead to the discovery of beautiful sand-dollar sea-urchins, most probably *Clypeaster reticulatus*, or heart urchins such as *Metalia spatagus*.

Sea-cucumbers, also members of the phylum Echinodermata, fre-

quently cause interest among skin-divers. The common black sea-cu-
cumber, *Holothuria atra*, may be seen lying on the sea-bed with much
of its body camouflaged by mucus adhered sand grains. Several other
sea-urchins occur on sandy and hard substrata, but one worth men-
tioning here is the long sinuous species *Synapta maculata*, which can
move in an almost snake-like fashion and has been known to alarm
swimmers mistaking it for just such a creature. The surface of Synapta
sea-cucumbers seems sticky to the touch due to the presence of hook-
shaped spicules in the body-wall.

Other Echinoderms present in shallow water include brittle-stars
such as the surface-feeding, intertidal species, *Ophiocoma scolopen-
drina*, which anchors itself to the rock with one or two arms while the
others bend over and use a combination of tube-feet and mucus to
capture food particles at the surface. The most spectacular of all brittle-stars,the magnificent *Astroba clavata*, a basketstar, crawls to a suitable promontory at night, extending its arms into a large fan-shaped
net used to capture plankton. Sea-stars also come in a range of shapes
and sizes, with thirty-two species so far recorded. The large Cushionstar, *Culcita schmideliana*, is sometimes found on sea-grass beds, while
the tiny cushionstar, *Asterina burtoni* occurs on the underside of boulders, often in the algal-ridge zone. The coral-eating sea-star,
Acanthaster planci is also found in Seychelles but is not particularly
abundant. Finally, there are the feather-stars or Crinoids with nine
species recorded from Seychelles: of these, the most frequently observed shallow-water species is the multi-armed *Stephanometra indica*.

Whether scrambling across intertidal rocks or pacing along a sandy
beach, a group of animals one unfailingly meets with in Seychelles are
the crabs. Of special interest are the stalk-eyed, ghost-crabs whose
burrows are often marked by volcanic shaped sand mounds. Common
species are *Ocypode ceratophthalma* and *Ocypode cordimana*, the former occuring lower on the beach: the speed with which these crabs
escape from one's path is evidence of the predatory pressure upon

Ghost crab (*Ocypode* sp.) at water's
edge on Mahe. (Vine).

89

them. I recently watched a Whimbrel on the sea-shore at Denis island, as it caught and dismembered such a ghost-crab, before eating it. Also occuring on the beach, often ranging inland for quite a distance, are hermit-crabs such as *Coenobita rugosus*. These scavengers have been observed to eat just about everything, from the faeces of giant tortoises to moth caterpillars. Shallow mangrove areas provide a habitat for fiddler-crabs (*Uca spp.*) which have the peculiar habit of waving one claw in a come-hither gesture. Crabs scuttling over rocks near the water's edge are likely to belong to the genera *Grapsus* or *Metograpsus*, with *Grapsus tenuicrustatus* being particularly abundant. The large Coconut crab, *Birgus latro*, lives in burrows just above high-tide level and feeds on a variety of vegetation, including fallen coconuts. A large agile crab, capable of climbing Pandanus or coconut trees in order to attack their fruit, its numbers have been reduced on some islands through intensive hunting, but it remains present on Mahe, where I recently observed some specimens among a collection of opened coconuts, at the head of Anse Souliac.

Sea-shells or marine molluscs are abundant in local waters and are legally protected from collection for private or commercial purposes. In order to observe a wide range of species it is necessary to search in the various represented habitats, from among mangrove thickets, to beaches, shallow muddy areas, sea-grass beds, rocky shore-lines, shallow waters with sand, gravel, rock or coral substrata, and in the different zones already mentioned on the reefs themselves. Each habitat tends to have a characteristic assemblage of molluscan species. Thus, the mangroves generally contain *Littorina scabra* crawling over trunks, branches and leaves in the intertidal. The oysters *Crassostrea cucullata* and *Isognomon dentifer* occur lower down, frequently attached to prop roots or pneumatophores. On the silty or muddy bottom, among the mangroves, where water circulation is frequently limited, large num-

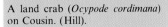

A land crab (*Ocypode cordimana*) on Cousin. (Hill).

Rock-hoppers (possibly *Damania anjouanae*) agilely cling to the rock surface in the splash zone at Bel Ombre, Mahe. They graze on the thin algal film coating rocks in the splash zone. A male is seen displaying with erect dorsal spines. (Vine).

bers of *Cerithium* and *Nassarius* gastropods are found, while *Terebralia palustris* is also present at some sites. Burrowing within the sediment are clams such as *Anadara antiquata*.

Sandy beaches, where wave-motion continually sorts the sediment, are not so densely populated by molluscs but two suspension feeding bivalves: *Atactodea glabrata* and *Donax faba* occur here. Sea grass beds on the other hand provide rich hunting grounds for shell-spotters. Here, one may find cowries, cone shells, strombs and a wide range of burrowing bivalves and errant gastropods. Deeply buried within the sediment are bivalve suspension feeders such as *Codakia*, *Anodontia* and *Ctena*. Buried less deeply are pinna shells such as *Atrina vexillum* and *Pinna muricata*: these have razor-sharp shell margins flush with the sea-bed, frequently the cause of cut feet among unwary swimmers. The burrowing shiny-shelled gastropod *Natica* is also present and feeds on the bivalves. Strombs such as *Strombus gibberulus* and *Strombus mutabilis* and spider-shells, including the large *Lambis lambis*, are found among sea-grasses while the main cowries are the Ring Cowrie, *Cypraea annulus*; the Money Cowrie, *Cypraea moneta*; and the Tiger Cowrie, *Cypraea tigris*. The Lettered Cone, *Conus litteratus*, and the Leopard Cone, *C.leopardus* are some of the large cone-shells found in this particular environment.

Molluscs on rocky shores include the intertidal littorinid: *L.glabrata*, a number of limpets such as *Cellana* sp. and the large chiton *Acanthopleura brevispinosa*; several *Nerita* species; *Monodonta* spp.; oysters such as *Crassostrea cucullata*; the mussel *Brachidontes variabilis*; and the cone-shells *C.ebraeus* and *C.sponsalis* both of which feed on polychaetes. Sheltered rocky shores are characterised by large numbers of *Planaxis sulcata* and *Cerithium morum*.

Boulders in the back-reef zone yield a rich assemblage of molluscs

Once caught, sharks are frequently left to hang from the ship's side in the belief that this discourages other sharks from attacking their hand-lines. Such sharks are sold for consumption but fetch a relatively low price compared with favoured species such as snappers. (Guy de Moussac).

including coneshells such as the Textile Cone (*Conus textile*) and many other cone-shells together with the cowries: *Cypraea histrio*, *C.lynx*, *C.isabella* and a number of others. On the coral-reefs one finds small muricids such as *Coralliophilia costularis* and *C. violacea* which actually feed on corals (especially *Porites*, *Pocillopora*, *Stylophora* and *Seriatopora*). Among the bivalves, the Giant Clams: *Tridacna maxima* and *T.squamosa* together with a number of other byssate bivalves such as *Barbatia helbingi*; *Pteria* and the Pearl Oyster, *Pinctada* are conspicuous. A distinctive clam, often observed while snorkelling, is *Trapezium oblongum*, the zig-zag clam, whose valve edges mesh together in a zig-zag pattern. Under coral slabs one may find a wide range of gastropod molluscs including *Cyprea* spp; *Conus* spp.; *Trochus maculatus*; and *Lambis crocata*. The giant Triton shell, *Charonia tritonis* is usually well hidden during the day but emerges at night to feed on sea-stars including the coral-predating *Acanthaster planci*.

A prime attraction of snorkelling or skin-diving among the shallow-waters of Seychelles is to admire its colourful and varied fish-life. On one memorable swim out from the rocky shoreline in front of the Northolme Hotel I was entranced by the richness of marine-life within a few yards of my hotel bedroom! After clambering over the rocks into the sea, I swam first over a bed of soft corals and algae, thinly coating granitic boulders. Small shoals of glimmering damsel-fish (*Pomacentrus pulcherrimus*) darted from rock crevices in search of planktonic prey while several yellow damsels (*Pomacentrus sulfureus*) paraded above the rocks. Parrotfish (*Scarus sordidus*; *Scarus niger* and *Scarus ghobban*) ranged over the sea-bed, browsing on algal coated rocks and even on the corals themselves. Here also were the cosmopolitan Butterflyfish: *Chaetodon auriga*, sporting large clear black spots on the rear portion of their dorsal-fins: a characteristic frequently absent from their Red Sea relatives. Other Butterflyfish sighted among the coral-encrusted rocks were the delicate, long-nosed *Forcipiger flavissimus* and *Chaetodon trifasciatus*. I was also pleased to renew my acquaintance with the graceful Lined Surgeonfish, *Acanthurus lineatus*, a close relative of *A.sohal* from the Red Sea, recognisable by the bright orange markings on its flanks. A dense cluster of Striped Catfish grubbed the sand in front of a large shaded cavern under a huge boulder while, not far away, a magnificent Lionfish (*Pterois volitans*) was "sunning itself", out in the open, with all its feathery fins extended. In less than five minutes I had met with all of the above plus several species of Snapper, including *Lethrinus harak*; a large school of Mullet; the Moon Wrasse (*Cheilinus lunulatus*); juvenile and adult African Coris (*Coris gaimard*); the Emperor Angelfish (*Pomacanthodes imperator*) and the Blue Angelfish (*Pomacanthops semicirculatus*); a shoal of Rabbitfish (*Siganus oramin*); the Barred Tang (*Acanthurus triostegus*); innumerable damselfish including *Abudefduf sexfasciatus*; *A.vaigiensis*; *Amblyglyphidodon leucogaster*, and the larger *Abudefduf sordidus* lurking among boulders; the Flutemouth (*Fistularia petimba*); Squirrelfish (*Holocentrus seychellensis*); a pair of Moorish Idols (*Zanclus cornutus*); a tame Eagle Ray which allowed me to swim alongside it for as long as I could hold my breath; and finally, to cap it all, a Barracuda and a tantalisingly elusive shoal of squid.

A useful small guide to coral-reef fish of Seychelles, prepared by Nicholas Polunin, has been published in the Seychelles Nature Booklet Series, now alas out of print but still obtainable at some shops on

Mahe. A much more comprehensive and erudite book is that by Smith and Smith: Fishes of Seychelles, listing and for the most part illustrating, 820 species. In addition to these Nicholas Polunin (1984) has recently listed a further seventy-nine marine fish since reported from Seychelles waters. He also provided a brief summary of distribution patterns for some of the shallow reef-fishes noting that the damselfish, *Pomacentrus pulcherrimus* and *P. sulfureus*; the Slingjaw-wrasse, *Epibulus insidiator*; and the Rabbitfish, *Siganus corallinus* are particularly abundant around the granitic islands whilst reefs in the Amirantes and at Aldabra are frequented by large numbers of *Chaetodon mitratus*; *Chromis pembae*; *Lepidozygus anthioides*; *Pseudocheilinus evanidus*; *P.margaretae*; *Acanthurus thompsoni*; *Naso vlamingii and Balistoides conspicillum*. Among the fishes he notes as either rare or absent from around the granitic islands is the Long-nosed Butterflyfish: *Forcipiger* sp., rendering my own observation of this fish swimming in front of the Northolme Hotel all the more remarkable! The record in no way invalidates Polunin's remarks; instead it highlights the particularly rich assemblage of marine-life within a stone's throw of the Northolme's bar! If one really wants to see a large number of coral-reef fish however it is worth travelling further afield, to coral islands such as Denis or even to the distant atolls of the Aldabra and Amirantes groups. In a single section of reef at Aldabra, having an area of 3,000 square metres, Nicholas Polunin observed 185 fish species!

As well as providing a colourful spectacle for the diver, fish are a vital food source for the people of Seychelles. A list of the main species caught by artisanal fishermen, together with their local names, is provided on page 180. Industrial fishing, carried out by vessels fishing deeper waters, produces a different assemblage of species. In recent years Tuna fishing has taken-on a major importance in Seychelles and this subject is treated separately in the final chapter of this book.

A monospecific catch of Red Snapper is recorded by artisanal fisheries officer, Guy de Moussac. (Guy de Moussac).

Lodoicea maldavica, the strange coco de mer tree, bears the largest seed in the plant kingdom, weighing up to 20 kgs. The seed takes two years to germinate while the tree is twenty five years old before it begins to bear fruit. It also takes seven years from fertilisation of the flower to maturation of the coco de mer nut, fruit of this ancient and unique tree. (Vine).

Bird's eye view of tree canopy on Mahe. (Vine).

PLANT-LIFE

The visitor to Seychelles is immediately struck by its lush green vegetation. The Government's determination to maintain buildings at less than coconut tree height (a maximum of three stories) has helped to preserve the appearance of the islands. Indeed, from the sea, they probably appear much as they did when John Jourdaine visited and made his first report in 1609. It will already be apparent however, upon reading the first section of this book, that there have been dramatic changes in the main composition of the islands' vegetation. Coastal mangroves, forming dense protective barriers around many of the granitic islands, have been largely removed and many of the native trees, previously forming thick jungle on mountain slopes, have been either cut down or burned. They have been replaced by Cinnamon and Coconut palms or by secondary growth of other native and introduced species. Despite this devastation by past generations, there has been, from the early days of its settlement, an awareness that efforts should be made to protect some examples of the group's native flora, particularly on Mahe and Praslin, where the effects of Man's disturbance were perhaps greatest, and where some of the most unique plants grow. Today Seychelles is at the forefront of nature conservation and is firmly committed to providing adequate protection to its endemic plant-life.

In considering Seychelles native plants it is pertinent to ask ourselves about their origins. There are three possibilities; they may be of ancient, primeval descent, having direct links with the vegetation of Gondwanaland before the landmass of Seychelles split away (first from the African landmass, then from Madagascar, and finally from India); or else they have evolved into new and distinctive species while Seychelles has been an isolated archipelago; or finally, their origins lie in natural transportation of seeds from plants living elsewhere. There are examples of all three explanations among Seychelles native flora, and we are indeed fortunate that, despite the effects of Man's settlement on the islands, specimens of most of Seychelles native flora have been preserved. Most of the vegetation comprises species which have, over the long period of the islands' existence, arrived from "neighbouring land-masses" (Procter 1984). Of the two major continents between which Seychelles are situated, Africa and India, Seychelles coastal flora shows a closer affinity with that of India. As one might expect, the further inland one moves, on the granitic islands at least, the more distinctly Seychellois the vegetation becomes; and the greater the level of endemism.

High on the granitic rock slabs of Mt. Bernica there lives what has been described as the rarest tree in the world. The Jellyfish Tree, *Medusagyne oppositifolia*, is an example of a primeval species. Interestingly enough, it does not occur in the damp, humid rain-forest for which Mahe is noted, but in quite dry conditions, among granitic boulders. Reaching about 8m. in height, it possesses extraordinary flowers and fruits whose appearance of upturned jellyfish have given the plant its common and Latin names. The endemic palms appear to have evolved in Seychelles: there are six species, each classified into a separate monotypic genus. Among these are species occupying each of the major habitats; *Roscheria* and *Verschaffeltia* living in the rainforest proper; *Lodoicea* (the famous Coco de Mer) grows on well drained valley soils of Praslin's Valee de Mai, sometimes in association with

Male inflorescence of Coco de Mer tree. (Vine)

Seed pods of *Medusagyne oppositifolia*, the "Jellyfish tree", possibly the world's rarest large tree. (Vine).

Nephrosperma but more frequently the latter species occurs in rocky areas at moderate altitudes. *Deckenia* is a hardy species, exposure resistant, favouring well drained soils sometimes inhabiting cliff-edges while *Phoenicophorium* prefers a relatively dry forest habitat such as occurs on Praslin. The Seychelles are of course famous for the Coco de Mer (*Lodoicea maldivica*), an extraordinary plant by any standards. Contrary to generally held belief, Coco de Mer are not confined to the Vallee de Mai, but occur at many sites on Praslin, and at Curieuse. Commenting on its unique biology, Procter (1984) states:

"*From the botanical point of view it is noteworthy because it bears the largest seed in the plant kingdom—weighing up to some 20 kg—perhaps the ultimate example of dispersal by gravity! Also its slow-moving biology—2 years for germination, 25 years for a tree to begin bearing fruit, 7 years from fertilisation of the female flower to maturity of the fruit—makes the species vulnerable to short-term changes in its environment.*"

Within the Vallee de Mai Nature Park one may wander along a marked trail leading through this unique forest. The pillar-straight upright trunks of some trees exceed a hundred feet; rigid broad fan-shaped leaves creating a jungle canopy through which little light penetrates. If there is a breeze blowing, the alarmingly loud creaking of massive leaves, accompanied by the occasional deep thud as heavy Coco de Mer nuts fall to ground, together with the strident calls of tantalisingly elusive birds, create the feeling of having been transported by some ingenious time-machine into a primeval forest, before Man arrived on this Earth. Wherever one ventures within the park area one is assailed by such powerful impressions, not only from the Coco de Mer trees, but also from other vegetation. Despite the encroachment of fires within the valley, some sections of the park remain as it appeared thousands of years ago and provide an indication as to the state of the islands' vegetation prior to the beginning of the eighteenth century.

The history of human settlement on Seychelles is so brief that we may turn to several written descriptions of the islands' vegetation as it appeared to the first explorers and settlers, before massive destruction of native forests took place. Nicholas Morphey, captain of the Cerf which visited in 1756 noted that mangroves fringed long sections of coastline: "*The coast, on the east side, is in many places bordered by thick mangrove growth where one can only penetrate at several openings*". The Coconut tree was already present in large quantities along the coastal-fringe: "*The shore is fringed by coconut palms which the sea without doubt has thrown up there in view of the fact that one does not find more than 20 toises [c.40m] depth of shore-land*". This appears to have been the result of natural dispersal rather than evidence of earlier activities of Man. The fact that many of the low-lying islands of the group were covered by sea-water during the last interglacial period would have devasted the region's coconut population and the elevated granitic islands of Seychelles must have provided local refuges for the coconut trees from which dispersal to the coral-islands could recommence after sea-level subsided. As Morphey noted, the coastal plains were populated by tall trees which immediately attracted attention as a source of wood for construction purposes: "*The space between the rocks and the mountains, just as in the plains, is covered with large trees, similar to those near the harbour, and one saw several which were of a circumference of 15 to 16 feet, and more than 75 to 80 feet high.*"

Palmiste, (*Deckenia nobilis*) is an endemic palm once common on the lower slopes of the granitic islands.(Vine)

Accounts by early administrators including Malavois and Rosnevet
mention other native trees such as Takamaka (*Calophyllum inophyllum*), a favourite timber for local boat construction and a tree whose
massive spreading arbours create welcome shade on many Seychelles
shorelines; Bois Chauve-Souris (*Ochrosia oppositifolia*), much sought
after due to the medicinal qualities of its bark, the stripping of which
kills the tree; the yellow flowered Bois de Rose (*Thespesia populnea*);
Bois de Table (*Heritiera littoralis*) a species dispersed by the sea and
usually found at coastal sites such as around the littoral marshland on
La Digue; Pin (*Casuarina equisetifolia*) whose ability to rapidly re-
colonise ground exposed by fires has already been mentioned); Faux
Gayac (*Intsia bijuga*) whose local name results from its similar qualities
to the Central American species: *Guaiacum officinale*; and extra large
specimens of Badamier (*Terminalia catappa*), the Indian Almond.

As we have seen already, settlers were not slow to exploit these
natural timber resources, and by 1874, John Horne was moved to

comment that the only remaining large trees of exploitable size on Mahe were high in the mountains, at relatively inaccessible locations! In his well known book, 'Island Life', A.R. Wallace (1880) wrote; *"Mr Geoffrey Neville tells us, that at Mahe, it was only in a few spots, near the summits of the hills, that he could perceive any remains of the ancient flora. Pine-apples, cinnamon, bamboos and other plants have obtained a firm footing, covering large tracts of country and killing the more delicate native flowers and ferns. The pineapple especially, grows almost to the tops of the mountains"*. Perhaps more than any other factor it was the widespread expansion of cinnamon leaf-oil distillation which led to destruction of upland forests, particularly in the first thirty years of the present century. Wild timber was consumed at a frightening pace as fuel for the distilleries, of which, by 1933, there were 82 on Mahe alone! Most of these have now closed however, since the market price of cinnamon leaf-oil has fallen. A more complete review of the effects of Man on the vegetation of Seychelles has been written by J.D. Sauer (1967).

Procter (1984) classified the major habitats for plant-life in Seychelles under three major headings: (1) The Moist Forest Habitat; (2) The Dry Forest Habitat; and (3) The Lowland or Coastal Habitat. This ecological classification, together with the major vegetational elements of each environment, is briefly discussed below. Readers seeking a more complete account are reccommended to consult the quoted references.

(A) THE MOIST FOREST HABITAT

Above
"Badamier" tree. (Harrison)

This is further sub-divided according to local environmental conditions.

1. Boulder/Peat

The soil in this upland habitat is usually a mossy peat. Plants occuring here but also widespread in other habitats include the Capucin, (*Northea hornei*) (named after Marianne North—whose painting of it is displayed in the Marianne North Gallery at the Royal Botanic Gardens, Kew, and John Horn a nineteenth century botanist and conservationist who contributed much to the knowledge and appreciation of Seychelles plant-life); Bois Rouge (*Dillenia ferruginea*); Cafe Marron Petite Feuille (*Erythroxylum sechellarum*) bearing oval red berries; and Bois de Pomme, (*Eugenia wrightii*). More or less confined to this habitat are Manglier de Grand Bois (*Glionettia sericea*), a short crooked trunked species clinging to the mountain ridges; the Pitcher Plant (*Nepenthes pervillei*), whose modified leaves form pitcher-like traps capable of catching and devouring insects, has a creeping growth-form spreading over trees in the forest or on granite slabs in exposed sites; the miniature palm, Latanier Hauban, (*Roscheria melanochaetes*), seldom more than two or three metres high; the rare, delicately flowered *Seychellaria thomassetti*; the epiphytic, compound leafed species: *Schefflera procumbens*; the endemic shrubs: *Canthium sechellense*, *Rapanea seychellarum* and *Psychotria sechellarum* and the Mangasave (*Dianella ensifolia*) a large herbaceous plant growing on the summit of Morne Seychellois and down to as low as 50m in some localities.

2. Glacis

Areas of bare rock, high-up in the mountains, may be due to natural topography or to soil erosion following forest clearance or fires. Isolated pockets of moist soil harbour a characteristic assemblage of plants including the Pitcher Plant (*Nepenthes pervillei*); the tenacious

On glacis slopes, north-west of Mt Jasmin, plants cling to the bare rock face. (Vine).

Opposite
Glacis vegetation.(Vine).

Jack fruit have the peculiar characteristic of arising directly from the main trunk. They are used in desserts. Mahe. (Vine).

Zat fruit has an aromatic flavour and is used in desserts. Frigate Island. (Vine).

knarled *Glionetta sericea*; and the rare endemic: *Garnotia sechellensis* only recorded from mountain tops on Mahe and Silhouette. To these we may add a number of plants occuring on slightly lower glacis; such as Colophante (*Soulamea terminalioides*) and Bois Jasmin (*Excoecaria benthamiana*): a shrub whose milky white sap, or latex, causes painful burns if brought in contact with skin. There are also other plants found here but which are not confined to the glacis habitat. These include the shrub: Vacoa de Riviere (*Pandanus multispicatus*) with, as its Latin name suggests, sharply spined leaves; and the endemic sedge: *Lophoschoenus hornei* together with the dramatically formed Vacoa Marron (*Pandanus sechellarum*) whose stilt-roots extend to a staggering height of upto ten-metres or so before they congeal into a short or almost non-existent trunk supporting a bushy crown of pandanus leaves.

3. Ravines

Protected from severe exposure to sun and wind, stream-banks of the moist forest provide shady, humid conditions where many ferns, including impressive species such as the Tree-Fern (*Cyathea sechellarum*) and the Giant Fern (*Angiopteris evecta*) flourish. Unfortunately however, the Tree-Fern or 'Fanjon' as it is known locally, has been heavily collected in the past for converting its fibrous trunk into plant-pots. In his recent book on plant-life of Seychelles, Francis Friedmann (1986) provides an excellent picture of a mature Tree-Fern growing in a sheltered location between two huge granite blocks at La Reserve, Mahe.

4. Slopes and Valleys

It is on the mountain slopes, where reasonable depths of soil could accumulate, that the formerly dense natural forests really flourished. This is also the forest area which was most thoroughly exploited by settlers, and where Cinnamon has been planted or colonised as a replacement crop. Despite the widescale destruction however, there are sites where most of the original elements of the natural forests have been preserved. Figure 7 (after Procter 1984) lists the presumed constituents of the primeval forest which not so long ago clothed the slopes of the tall granitic islands such as Mahe and Silhouette.

**Composition of Primeval Forest
on Mountain Slopes
(after Procter, J. 1984)**

CANOPY:
>   Campnosperma seychellarum
>   Dillenia ferruginea
>   Mimusops sechellarum
>   Northia hornei
>   Vateria seychellarum

UNDERSTORY:

Drypetes riseleyi	Planchonella obovata
Gastonia sechellarum	Tarenna sechellensis
Grisollea thomassetti	Verschaffeltia splendida
Pandanus hornei	Wielandia elegans
Pandanus sechellarum	

Cashew trees have probably been spread by Fruit Eating Bats since they are found throughout the main islands, often in remote situations.(Vine).

LARGE SHRUBS/ SMALL TREES:

Aphloia seychellensis	Indokingia crassa
Brexia madagascariensis	Ixora pudica
Canthium bibracteatum	Ludia sessiliflora
Colea seychellarum	Pittosporum wrightii
Craterispermum microdon	Psychotria sechellarum
Eugenia wrightii	Roscheria melanochaetes
Ficus bojeri	Timonius sechellensis

SHRUBS AND LIANES:

Canthium carinatum	Gynura seychellensis
Dracaena angustifolia	Psychotria pervillei
Flagellaria indica	Tournefortia sarmentosa

HERBS, EPIPHYTES AND PARASITES:

Begonia (3 species)	Procris latifolia
Bryophytes	Protarum sechellarum
Curculigo (3 species)	Scleria angusta
Ferns etc	Thoracostachyum (2 species)
Orchidaceae	Viscum triflorum

Figure 7

Coco-Plum (Chrysobalanus icaco) with fruits on Mahe. (Vine).

(B) DRY FOREST HABITAT

Procter (1984) includes under this heading: north and south Mahe, peripheral areas of Silhouette, together with the majority of Praslin, La Digue, Curieuse, Marianne and Felicite. He also notes that fire has caused major destruction among the dryer forest areas, leading to severe soil erosion in some places. The Vallee de Mai also falls into this category however and represents one of the best preserved examples of primeval forest to be seen anywhere.

1. Glacis

Arising from wedges of soil among massive slabs of granite, the Jellyfish Tree, *Medusagyne oppositifolia*, occurs at a few locations within this habitat. The spiny leaved *Pandanus multispicatus* and Cafe Marron (*Randia lancifolia*) are also found here, together with several species characteristic of glacis habitats in the moist forest. Lower down, nearer to the coast, *Pandanus balfouri* and *Euphorbia pyrifolia* replace some of the more upland species.

2. Ravines

These somewhat more accessible ravines than those of the moist-forest have been more affected by Man than their upland counterparts. Vegetation is fairly similar but some endemic species, such as the tree fern, do not occur.

3. Slopes and valleys

This is the habitat under which the Vallee de Mai is categorised. The natural vegetation consists of a range of palms but many areas have been cleared for cultivation. Although the Vallee de Mai represents a unique preserved environment, it is also a sad fact that numerous ornamental plants have been introduced or invaded from surrounding countryside, and have thus altered the vegetational composition of the valley. There is little doubt however that the Coco de Mer on Praslin formed dense stands and occupied a much larger area than it does today. In such forests, there may have been relatively few other species growing among the Coco de Mer since its large, heavy, broad leaves would have regularly fallen, damaging any young saplings and forming a thick carpet covering the ground.

(C) LOWLAND OR COASTAL HABITAT

The original lowland forests have been almost completely denuded. Procter (1984) however points out that vestiges of this community are preserved on Felicite, Silhouette and parts of south Mahe.

(1) Mangrove Swamps

Known locally as "Mangliers", mangrove trees have in the past been cut down, either for timber or as part of coastal clearance programmes. We are extremely fortunate however that the extensive mangrove area at Port Glaud on the west coast of Mahe, has not been destroyed. There, one may see large 'red mangroves' or Manglier Hauban (*Rhizophora mucronata*), easily identified by its arched roots and terminally pointed leaves. Other mangroves include Manglier Jaune (*Ceriops tagal*); Manglier Gros Poumon (*Brugiera gymnorhiza*); Manglier Fleur (*Sonneratia caseolaris*); Manglier Blanc (*Avicennia marina*) and Petit manglier (*Lumnitzera racemosa*).

(2) Swamps and Lagoons

Shallow swamps formed by fresh or brackish water occur in several coastal plains, such as at La Digue. These environments are often dominated by reeds, sedges and grasses (eg *Typha javanica*; *Cyperus articulatus* and *Eleocharis dulcis*) and by a range of water-plants (eg. *Ipomoea aquatica*).

(3) The Plateaux

An area of intense cultivation and/or removal of timber for fuel or boat-building, the coastal plateaux have little remaining of their original plant communities. Extensive coconut plantations were established in this habitat and, in places where these have become neglected, some elements of the aboriginal flora have begun to re-establish themselves. The Takamaka tree, *Calophyllum inophyllum*, can still be seen along various shore-lines, despite intense cutting for boat-building.

Mangrove channel formed by 'Manglier Blanc' (*Avicennia marina*). (Vine).

Aerial roots of a large mangrove tree on the shore at Anse La Mouche, Mahe. (Vine)

(4) The Sea Coast, or Littoral

A dominant tree on low-coastal land, near the sea-shore, is *Scaevola sericea*, known locally as Veloutier. It flourishes in exposed situations where few other trees occur. Another common shore-line tree is 'Porcher' (*Cordia subcordata*) whose attractive orange flowers are frequently commented upon. The yellow-flowered Hibiscus (*H.tiliaceus*) is often found growing close to mangroves or along open-shorelines.

FLOWERING PLANTS

Procter (1984) states that there are approximately 766 flowering plants and 85 ferns (or fern allies) in Seychelles. The recent account by Francis Friedman (1986) claims that between six and seven hundred exotic species have been introduced, and that despite the enormous changes which have occurred, most,if not all, of the indigenous flowering plants have survived. One interesting observation regarding supposedly 'native' plants is that the presence of four species (*Casuarina equisetifolia*; *Tacca leontopetaloides*, *Terminalia catappa* and *Adenanthera pavonina*) has been invoked as circumstantial evidence for earlier visits to Seychelles by boat-people who either planted or inadvertently transported these species. As Procter (1984) states, "*These four species may antedate the modern colonisation of the Seychelles and I suggest that they did not arrive by 'natural' means. I also suggest that the supposed arrival of coco de mer (Lodoicea) nuts in the Maldives on ocean currents is a myth. The routes and means of transport of the successive non-African colonists of Madagascar are not known. I suggest that these people may have used the Seychelles as at least a temporary staging post, and brought with them seeds or tubers of Adenathera, Casuarina, Tacca, Terminalia and perhaps others (bananas?) not now found wild in the Seychelles or faut de mieux, classes as 'of uncertain status'.*"

Many of the above comments refer, primarily, to vegetation on the granitic islands. Detailed investigations of plant communities on the coral-islands of the Western Indian Ocean, including Seychelles, have been summarised by Dr David Stoddart and Dr F.R. Fosberg (1984). In addition to numerous published papers on the subject, "The Flora of Aldabra and neighbouring islands" (F.R. Fosberg and S.A. Renvoize, 1980), provides a detailed review of flora on the elevated limestone islands of Aldabra, Assumption, Cosmoledo and Astove. This latter work lists 272 angiosperms of which 185 are indigenous, and 43 endemic to the group. In classifying the major habitats on the low-lying coral islands of the western Indian Ocean, Stoddart and Fosberg listed the following: (1) Coconut Forest; (2) Casuarina Forest; (3) Broadleaf Forest; (4) Mangrove Forest; (5)Mixed Scrub and Scrub Woodland; (6) *Scaevola* Coastal Scrub; (7) *Tournefortia* Scrub and Scrub Woodland; (8) *Suriana* Scrub; (9) *Pemphis* Scrub; (10) *Lumnitzera-Thespesia populneoides* Scrub; (11) *Typha-Acrostichum* Marsh; (12) *Sporobulus* Grassland; (13) *Sclerodactylon* tussock grassland; (14) Tortoise turf; (15) *Bacopa-Molluga* Meadow; (16) *Sesuvium* Mat; (17) *Boerhavia-Portulaca* Mat; and finally vegetation of disturbed areas such as airstrips. While it is beyond the scope of this book to discuss all such habitats, or to mention all the plants represented, the lay-reader will be immediately familiar with some of the above communities. The beach crest at most coral islands within the region are fringed by a uniform barrier of *Scaevola* scrub. Open grassland on Bird Island has numerous

Tournefortia argentea trees, about 5m in height. We have already mentioned Mangroves, Coconuts, *Casuarina* and the broad-leafed Takamaka (*Calophyllum*).

Mahe's Botanical Gardens.

The fifteen acre Botanical Gardens on the southern side of Victoria were created, in 1901, by Rivaltz Dupont, and are now a fascinating public park, where visitors may examine, in comfort and delight, the six endemic palms of Seychelles, together with a host of other spectacular local or introduced trees, shrubs and flowers. On entering the park by the main drive, one first encounters Mauritian Bottle-Palms, complimented by a magnificent Madagascan Flame-tree, situated towards the rear of the lawn on the left of the drive. Also within sight, at this stage, are the Albizia tree, much sought after for house construction, and the strange Silk Cotton tree, or Kapok, from South America: its pods contain a white, cotton-like, material used locally for stuffing pillows. The towering Malaysian Breadfruit tree grows here, as it does throughout the Seychelles, producing large, nutritious fruit. For many visitors it may be their first encounter with the Nutmeg Tree bearing apricot-shaped fruit which split, when ripe, to expose the nut. The famous Seychelles Coco de Mer, occuring naturally in the Vallee de Mai on Praslin, throws its leafy shade over the main path through the gardens, offering a unique opportunity for photographers whose efforts at capturing this singular tree on film may have been daunted by the tangled vegetation and dark, shady conditions within the valley itself.

I was particularly struck by the Asian Elephant Apple tree, resplendent with pretty, white, magnolia-like flowers; the Vacoa Parasol Screwpine; the tall, straight trunked Queensland Kauri Pine; the Norfolk Island Pine and the Traveller's Palm, a Madagascan species whose clusters of long, fan-shaped leaves bring to mind ancient tropical scenes, when such leaves were actually used as fans. Other intriguing exotic species found here include the Torch Ginger plant of Madagascar, the Lobster Claw of South America, the Rose of Venezuela and, among the most striking of all, the Cannon Ball tree, so named after the cannon-ball sized, brown fruits protruding directly from the trunk.

Passion-flower on La Digue (Vine).

A walk towards the rear of the gardens, among the tall trees situated alongside the stream, will invariably be accompanied by the high pitched squeaks of Fruit Bats flitting through the vegetation. For, orchid lovers a visit to the gardens is a must, since they have recently incorporated a special orchid display garden, comprised of orchids from all over the world, especially Malaysia.

The endemic palms found here are:

Deckenia nobilis	*Palmiste*
Lodoicea maldivica	*Coco de Mer*
Nephrosperma vanhoutteana	*Latanier Millepate*
Phoenicophorium borsignianum	*Latanier feuille*
Vershaffeltia splendida	*Latanier latte*
Rocheria melanochaetes	*Latanier hauban*

REPTILES

Among the reptilian fauna of Seychelles, the Giant Tortoise is one of the most visually impressive creatures. The most primitive reptiles surviving on Earth, they are also a real link with the ancient past of Seychelles. Evolving in the Triassic period, about 180 million years ago, at a time when the great continents of Africa, India and Australia were still part of Gondwanaland, they are living reminders of this prehistoric period. In times past they inhabited many of the Indian Ocean islands but, today, wild populations occur only at Aldabra. While several species may have existed, the surviving Giant Tortoises of Aldabra are, remarkably, the same genus (i.e.: *Geochelone*) as the World's only other surviving population of wild Giant Tortoises at Galapagos. We are indeed fortunate that the population at Aldabra does still exist since, in relatively recent geological time, the island has been repeatedly submerged by sea-level rises. On each occasion when this occurred all the island's terrestrial life was wiped-out. Recolonisation took place from population resevoirs on more elevated islands. In the case of tortoises it is believed that animals which had accidentally fallen into the sea, or perhaps been trapped by rising tides when feeding at the shore-line, drifted on ocean currents. Those landing on reasonably predator-free islands where suitable vegetation occurred formed the nucleus for new colonies.

Studies carried out on Giant Tortoises at Aldabra reveal how remarkably adapted they are to survival in this harsh environment. As cold-blooded vertebrates, they must rely on a combination of their unique structure and behavioural patterns in order to modify body temperature. The prime risk is that of over-heating and a range of responses combat searing midday temperatures. Tortoises emerge from sleeping sites about an hour before dawn, when they range out in more or less random directions until they reach suitable grazing. As the sun-rises, they orientate the rear of the carapace to face the sun so that the extended neck is shaded by the front of the carapace. By concentrating feeding towards dawn, the quantity of fresh-water consumed as condensation on plants is maximised. Before midday the tortoises have retreated to the shade of local trees, or in the case of young individuals, to shaded crevices. Often a whole group rest under the same tree,

Giant tortoises are herbivores, feeding mainly in the early morning or evening, and retreating from the intense midday heat by seeking shade under bushes or rock-ledges. (Hill).

FIGURE 8

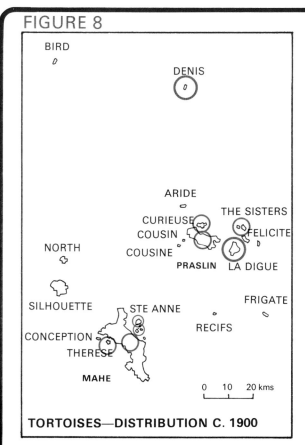

TORTOISES—DISTRIBUTION C. 1900

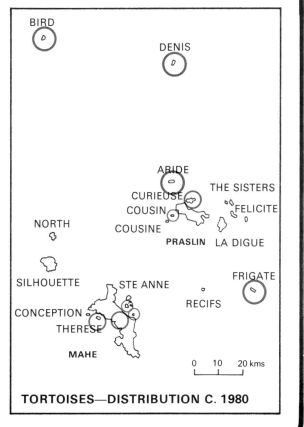

TORTOISES—DISTRIBUTION C. 1980

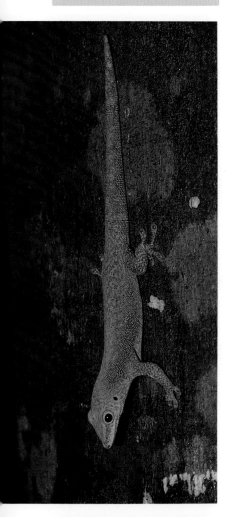

The Green Gecko, *Phelsuma* sp. is a common sight on many of the islands. This one was photographed at Praslin. (Hill).

sometimes partially on top of each other. While thus protected from the fierce rays of midday sun, they may also extend their necks, exposing unprotected skin and permitting a degree of heat exchange. The presence of shade trees is a controlling factor for tortoise populations. Individuals unable to locate protection at midday often die. In addition to resting in the shade, the tortoises also dig shallow pits so that their plastron lies in close contact with the relatively cool ground. In so doing they tend to uproot trees and when their numbers result in high densities, many trees are killed. This, in turn, leads to a reduction in shade, the death of more tortoises and a drop in population. As the numbers fall, grazing pressure eases and young saplings, which had little chance to develop when heavily predated, can now grow taller, creating more shade where tortoises can shelter.

Giant Tortoises at Aldabra mate from December to June with maximum copulation occuring in April. It is a process frought with difficulties since the massive, heavy and cumbersome male has to climb on top of the female and, some how or other, coordinate his position to permit insertion into the female cloaca. The process is accompanied by what has been aptly described as a noisy "groan and thrust" phase, and the difficult manoeuvres involved ensure that the success rate is low, with less than two percent of the tiring mountings by males resulting in fertilisation. Giant Tortoise nest building commences in May or June with the females excavating nests at night time using their hind legs. Once the hole is dug, but before eggs are laid, the female urinates copiously into the hole and on the surrounding ground so that the whole region around the nest is saturated. Then from four to fifteen eggs are laid, depending on population density (with more eggs deposited when populations are lower). Once the eggs are laid they are carefully covered over by the female tortoise; the entire process taking eleven or twelve hours. Less than two days after egg-laying, the soil around the nest has hardened, as a result of drenching with urine and mucus, into a concrete like encasing, providing protection for the eggs from their major predator, the Robber Crab (*Birgus*). Incubation lasts 73 to 160 days and young tortoises emerge from the nest about two weeks after hatching. At this stage they are threatened by a number of potential predators, including Robber Crabs; Land Crabs (*Cardisoma carnifex*); rats; the Flightless Rail and Ibis.

Their greatest enemy, however, is Man himself and, as we have already seen in the historical section, literally thousands of giant-tortoises were removed from the granitic islands by early settlers. As a result, they have only survived on Aldabra where activities by Man are now carefully controlled. In 1978 a population survey there estimated the entire number of tortoises then present at 150,406. At that time it appeared that the population was on an upward curve.

LIZARDS OF SEYCHELLES.

The bustling noise of scurrying skinks in crunchy leaf litter; exquisite green, diurnal geckos gazing dolefully from tree trunks; and the comforting presence of their graceful, wide-eyed nocturnal counterparts, patiently waiting to trap insect prey, provide the visitor with a constant reminder as to the abundance and diversity of the lizard fauna in the Seychelles. In fact, besides birds, reptiles have been the most successful vertebrate colonisers of islands in general. Reptiles possess a hard,

LIZARDS OF SEYCHELLES*

	Aldabra Group	Amirantes	Central Seychelles
Phyllodactylus inexpectatus			x
Phelsuma astriata astriata			x
P.a.semicarinata		x	x
P.astriata (intermediate form)			(x)
P.astriata astovei	(x)		
P.abbotti abbotti	(x)		
P. a.sumptio	(x)		
P. laticauda	(*)		x
P. longinsulae longinsulae			(x)
P. l. pulchra			x
P. l. menaiensis	(x)		
P. sundbergi		x	x
Ailuronyx sechellensis			x
Hemidactylus frenatus		x	#
H. mercatorius	x		
H. brookii		(x)	
Gehyra mutilata	x		x
Mabuya sechellensis		x	x
M. wrightii			(x)
Cryptoblepharus boutoniii	x		
Scelotes braueri			x
S. gardineri			x
Zonosaurus madagascariensis	(x)		
Chamaeleo tigris			x

Brown skink at Cousin Island. (Vine).

Key: x = occurs on some islands within group
   (x) = reported from only one island in the group.
   (*) = present in the Farquhar group
   # = refers to sole record from C.Seychelles, on Bird Island.

* adapted from Cheke, 1984.

FIGURE 9

cornified, desiccation-resistant skin and a very low metabolic rate, enabling them to endure long sea journeys, probably on vegetation 'rafts', in extremely harsh conditions and without nourishment. Both of these factors, along with the evolutionary acquisition of the amniotic egg, greatly reducing dependency on freshwater, also facilitate their establishment on newly colonised islands. It is probably no coincidence that geckos, possessors of the most dehydration-resistant eggs, are also the most successful vertebrate island colonisers.

The lizard fauna of Seychelles is varied in origin; Malagasy influence predominates, but there is also a small African and Indo-Pacific input along with some forms of uncertain derivation.

As we have already mentioned, the flora of the Seychelles possesses many ancient elements however, the absence of an equally venerable land fauna—no flightless birds, giant lizards or unique snakes—has perplexed interested observers. The *Scelotes* skinks (*Pamaelaescincus* & *Jantaescincus*), *Chamaelo tigris*, *Phyllodactus inexpectatus* and *Ailuronyx sechellensis*, although somewhat overshadowed by the pre-Quaternary Amphibians, caecilians and frogs, have some claim to fame as constituents of such an ancient fauna, though probably not quite as archaic as the aforementioned plant-life. The remaining lizards are purported to be of more recent origin. Endemic species, such as the *Mabuya* skinks, probably journeyed from the Comores via Aldabra and the *Phelsuma* geckos may be an even more recent arrival (Cheke 1984).

Attempts to map the complex radiation of Phelsumas in the Seychelles has met with considerable difficulties. Cheke has isolated three species-groups of the genus.

1. *P. laticauda*
   Madagascan/Comoran species....   Farquahar/Providence group.

2. *P. astriata*
   allied to Madagascan species....   granitic islands, two of the
                                       Amirantes, and Astove

3. This complex is related to *P. madagascariensis* and consists of
   P. abbotti........   Aldabra, Assumption and N.W.
                                       Madagascar

   P. longinsulae. (Cosmoledo)
   P. sundbergi   granitic islands, Amirantes.

The distribution of lizards (other than *Phelsuma*) within the granitic islands is relatively predictable, although the detailed pattern of distribution is still rather poorly documented. The table on page 109 attempts to give a reasonably clear picture of the information as it now stands. *Phyllodactylus inexpectatus*, *Chamaelo tigris* and *Scelotes gardineri*, representing the more ancient stream, are found throughout the archipelago; certain discrepancies in the distribution pattern can usually be attributed to ineffective collecting, although chamaeleons are definitely absent from Frigate and La Digue (Cheke 1984).

The impact of topographical parameters, other than the above-mentioned ocean currents and island age, on lizard ecology is difficult to separate entirely from vegetation and climatic factors. It may be possible to conclude that the height of the island does not have a major effect ecologically: as Cheke points out all the endemic lizards of the granitic islands can be found within 50m of sea level, and only the two semi-fossorial *Scelotes* appear to be frequent above 500m (Boulenger 1909). The plundering of the primary lowland forest and its replacement on the central islands by secondary forest and coconut plantations doesn't appear to have been catastrophic, as far as the lizard population is concerned, although it has been suggested that a few species such as *Chamaelo tigris*, *Scelotes gardineri*, and possibly *S. braueri* and *Ailuronyx sechellensis* may have been adversely affected. However the confinement of some species to forest may be more due to rats than any unsuitability of coconut plantations (Cheke 1984:349). In fact, the presence of large numbers of seabirds and the absence of marauding rats may be two of the most significant factors influencing both the dispersity and density of lizards on any particular island. *Mabuya wrightii*, for instance, flourishes on rat-free Frigate but is extinct on Marianne. Introduced Tenrecs and Barn owls as well as cats, dogs and pigs have also made their predatory impact to a greater or lesser extent on lizard populations. As a result of work done on Cousin island, one can now really understand something of the interaction between the lizard fauna and the sea-bird colonies [Houston (1978) & Brooke & Houston, and Hunter (1978 MS)].

Cousin has a breeding population of some 200,000 pairs of seabirds of which two-thirds are lesser noddies, and boasts a lizard population estimated at 50,000 *Mabuya sechellensis* and 20,000 for *M.wrightii*. These skinks, are the major exploiters of the sea-bird biomass comprising of dropped food, chicks, eggs and faeces, varying in availability depending on nesting activity, the peak occurring from July to Septem-

Mabuya wrightii, seen here on Cousin island, is a predatory skink, feeding on birds eggs and young fledglings. (Hill).

ber. Interestingly, but perhaps not surprisingly, the lizard faunas' weight cycle reaches its' zenith during this peak period.

The change in social organisation correlated with density highlighted by these studies is reported also in other lizard species. The skinks on Cousin are not territorial (Houston 1978), although they do have home ranges (Brooke & Houston 1983). In contrast, according to work done by Evan and Evans (1980) on Praslin, *Mabuya sechellensis*, found in all forest habitats and coconut plantations there but in much lower densities than on Cousin, exhibits territorial behaviour, each male enjoying a harem of females.

Scelotes gardineri also behaves differently on Praslin and Cousin: on the former island this skink is relatively scarce, occurring only in residual lowland and intermediate (palm) forest, generally active in the morning but apparently not at night and living in and under the leaf litter. Its rarity and diurnal activity can possibly be attributed to the presence of predatory rats and Barn Owls on Praslin. On Cousin, the same species is larger and heavier and strictly nocturnal, its activity pattern probably influenced by the high densities of *Mabuya skinks*. (Cheke 1984).

It has been observed that the two diurnal *Phelsuma* geckos (*Phelsuma astriata* and *P. sundbergi*) common on Praslin, display distinct preferences for particular species of tree within each habitat. In the palm forest, for instance, both species gravitate towards the coco-demer and are rarely found other than on palms or pandans. Within the same habitat, the two Phelsumas will often favour trees of different size. In coconut plantations, *P. astriata* and juvenile lizards of both species occupy young palms, whereas *P. sundbergi* is dominant on large palms. As well as eating insects *Phelsuma* species sip the nectar from flowers. In fact Evans observed *P. sundbergi* chasing nectar-feeding sunbirds from coconut flowers. In contrast to the sunloving skink *Mabuya sechellensis*, these geckos court the shade and possess much lower mean diurnal body temperatures (29–30 degrees centigrade compared to 34.7 degrees centigrade). Thorpe and Crawford (1979) postulate that the two Phelsumas still exhibit the behaviour typical of nocturnal geckos rather than of diurnal arboreal lizards (e.g. *Anolis* sp.)

Honegger observed a very interesting association between *Phelsuma abbotti* and the giant tortoises *Geochelone gigantea*—lizards were seen hitching a ride on the back of the tortoise and feeding on the insects exposed by the heavy, ambling gait of their benefactor. He reported that one gecko remained on the same tortoise for at least 36 hours, and hid at night and when alarmed under the carapace near the tail.

Another interesting interaction occurs between the lizards on Frigate and the very rare Magpie Robin endemic to that island: the robust robin feeds on both Mabuyas (only the young of the larger *M. wrightii*), *Scelotes brauerii*, young *Ailuronyx* and *Phelsuma* species garnered from coconut crowns. But the predation isn't all one-sided, *M. wrightii* apparently raids robin nests, and is possibly the main cause of nest failure. The *Mabuya* skinks are indeed quite fearless on this rat-free island. Having become quite used to hand-feeding, from the dinner table, the teeming bird life on Frigate, I was quite astounded to see a large, sleek *Mabuya* patiently waiting to be fed some of my papaya and obviously relishing it once I had complied with its wishes.

SNAKES OF THE SEYCHELLES

Visitors can rest assured that the snake fauna of the Seychelles is comprised of three entirely harmless species; two endemic colubrids, *Boaedon geometricus* and *Lycognathopsis seychellensis* and one member of the Typhlopidae, the small secretive burrowing *Ramphotyphlops braminus*. These three species can be found on the four largest granitic islands (Mahe, Praslin, Silhouette, La Digue) and on Frigate. In addition, they are probably present, but unreported, on some of the other central granitic islands. This low level of speciation and dispersion is in complete contrast to that of lizards: we have seen that the Seychelles Archipelago supports fifteen species of lizard and a population can be found on almost every island whether older granitic or younger coralline. Dietary considerations have probably had a major influence in the widely different colonising ability existing within the herpetofauna. Lizards, as we have seen, are primarily insectivorous but some species are herbivorous and some omnivorous. Insect and plant food are always readily available on even the youngest of islands. Snakes, in contrast, basically feed on higher order prey such as lizards, mammals, and birds. Since amphibians and mammals are rare on oceanic islands, a majority of the world's snakes are effectively barred from becoming established on distant islands. Those that prey on lizards and birds, as well as the rarer insectivorous snakes, will obviously be the most successful island colonisers. However, because most snakes are in fact higher order predators, they require broader feeding ranges and are usually less abundant than lizards. Snakes are rarely found on far islands. Other than the islands of the Seychelles, Round Island near Mauritius is the only distant island of the Indian Ocean inhabited by snakes.

As far as origins are concerned, the similarity between the African and Seychellean house snake probably points to a relatively recent origin of the latter from an African ancestor. It is possible that housesnakes were introduced to the Seychelles by Man. *L. seychellensis*, on the other hand, is probably native whereas Honneger claims that *R. braminus*, a tropicopolitan species, was introduced between 1936 and 1939.

The following brief descriptive notes, based on Nussbaum's work, should facilitate the identification of any snake encountered in Seychelles.

Boaedon geometricus. (Seychelles house snake)

A thick bodied, smooth scaled snake, the brown iridescent dorsum has 3 narrow longitudinal stripes. A certain amount of variation occurs in the colouration of the ventral surface, but it is usually grey, and appears to be banded with white. The snout is also white and two short white stripes extend from behind the eye to the neck area. This species is readily distinguished from *Lycognathopsis seychellensis* by its' plumper, smooth-scaled body, white stripes behind the relatively small eyes and broad muzzle. *B. geometricus* couldn't possibly be mistaken for the small, drab thread-like *Ramphophylops braminus*. The life history of the Seychelles house-snake remains obscure but one can speculate to a certain extent on the basis of its very common African relatives. Nocturnal and oviparous, all house snakes kill their prey, rats and mice, bats, birds, lizards and frogs, by constriction. It is primarily

Seychelles Wolf Snake (*Lycognathopsis seychellensis*) feeds on lizards and is active during daytime. This specimen was photographed on the settlement plateau at Frigate Island. (Harrison).

113

a terrestrial creature but, like most snakes, it can climb trees and houses. *B. geometricus* is found in dense moist forest, coconut forests, in villages and on open rocky slopes from sea level to 430 metres: likely nocturnal predtors are Barn Owls and Tenrecs as well as feral cats.

Lycognathopsis seychellensis

This species is commonly known as the 'Seychelles Tree Snake', however Nussbaum (1984) points out that, since it is more often encountered on the ground and doesn't have the classical morphological adaptations associated with arboreal snakes, the common name amounts to a misnomer and suggests that it be corrected to 'Seychelles Wolf Snake', in deference to its Latin title.

L. seychellensis occurs in two different colour phases, slight variation occurring within each phase. 'Yellow phase' snakes are usually brown with faint, dark spots on the back and and a bright yellow ventral surface in contrast to the 'dark phase' snake which is normally dark grey dorsally, with distinct black spots and a basically white ventral surface, flecked by a multitude of small dark dots. It is a svelte, elegant creature up to 1.2m in length possessing a small head, a relatively narrow muzzle and keeled dorsal scales.

An active, diurnal species, probably oviparous, this species is found in nearly all habitats, and at all elevations on Mahe and Silhouette. On Frigate, it has been encountered mainly on the low-lying settlement plateau but this may be coincidental since this is the only area of concentrated human activity. Lizards seem to be the principal component of this snakes' diet but it has been known to feed on small birds. The Seychelles kestrel is probably its major predator.

Ramphotyphlops braminus Black Burrowing Snake

Although it is frequently stated as resembling a black earthworm, the body colour of this small, blind elusive snake is, in fact, a uniform

dark grey; it has no distinct neck, vestigial eyes, and the ventral scales do not vary in size and shape from the dorsal, like the other two species. It would be impossible to confuse this snake with the other two, but it has been frequently mistaken for a juvenile caecilian, differentiated by the series of continuous rings encircling the body. *R. braminus* usually burrows in damp soil, decaying logs and rotting humus, but is also found living in sand on beaches near sea level.

Because of its retiring nature, there is very little known about the life-history of this snake, but we can extrapolate, from its tunnelling propensity, small mouth and the peculiar jaw mechanism of typhlopoids, that all species of this family feed on small, soft-bodied invertebrates such as ants and termites. Most typhlopids are oviparous and Nussbaum (1984) suspects that this is an all-female species.

TURTLES

We know from the historical section of this book that marine turtles were abundant in the eighteenth century when Seychelles was formally discovered and settled by Europeans. But first-hand accounts of this and later periods have also underlined the high level of exploitation suffered by these creatures, leading to rapidly diminished populations. In fact, numbers have declined so dramatically that there is now considerable concern for their future. Four out of seven species of marine turtle are recorded from Seychelles. Two of these four; the Leathery Turtle (*Dermochelys coriacea*(L)) and the Loggerhead (*Caretta caretta*(L)), although common in the western Indian Ocean, do not occur in significant numbers in the Seychelles. But the Hawksbill (*Eretmochelys imbricata* (L.)) and Green Turtle (*Chelonia mydas* (L)), both widely distributed throughout the western Indian Ocean can be found on almost every island, the Green turtle apparently more numerous than the Hawksbill. Hawksbills feed during daylight and seem to be most abundant in areas of rich coral growth: the narrow bird-like beak of the Hawksbill is ideally adapted for cropping soft-bodied invertebrates like sponges, so plentiful on tropical coral reefs. The Green Turtle on the other hand, is the only marine turtle that feeds mainly on plants, once the early planktonic phase in their life-cycle has ended. Here again the beak is admirably adapted, this time for grazing marine pastures. The feeding grounds for both Green Turtles and Hawksbills are restricted to areas shallower than 15 fathoms where light can penetrate to facilitate the growth of favoured plant and animal food. The feeding areas of Green Turtles are often separated by large distances from the nesting beaches. Adult Hawksbills too may migrate between distant feeding grounds and shallower island nesting sites. Green turtles breed throughout the Seychelles, nests having been recorded from more than 20 islands representing all island groups. Aldabra has earned a reputation as the main breeding area for Green Turtles in the western Indian Ocean, but, although it is still a major nesting site, other large rookeries outside of Seychelles now compete for the primary position. In contrast to the situation in Aldabra (estimated nesting population 1,980–2,420), probably fewer than 10 green turtles nest each year in the Granitic Islands. Hawksbill nests have also been reported from more than 20 islands, involving all island groups in the Seychelles. Cousin Island with an estimated 30–40 animals nesting annually is reported by Frazier as having the largest known concentration of nesting Hawksbills in the western Indian Ocean. Mortimer (1984) has also recorded surprisingly heavy nesting of Hawksbills on the granitic islands in the vicinity of the Ste. Anne Marine National Park (55–70 females annually). Although Hawksbill and Green Turtles often nest on the same islands, there seems to be some attempt at partitioning valuable nesting resources. The Green Turtle, nesting at night and favouring beaches with direct access to the open sea, excavates its nest just above the beach crest in firm but friable sand, lacking vegetation and shade whereas Hawksbill nests are made on reasonably protected beaches, higher above the beach crest, in dense ground vegetation, usually shaded by bushes. Nesting is also concentrated in different seasons: Green Turtles nest from June to September, and the Hawksbill, from October to January. The Seychelles Hawksbill, known for its propensity to nest during the day doesn't show the same tendency to nest in groups as Green turtles. Frazier comments that the latter apparently adopts a strategy of overwhelming the enemy by sheer force of numbers whilst the former adopts a sneak attack approach. This is best illustrated as hatchlings of both species emerge to commence the planktonic stage of their existence. Green turtle hatchlings, emerging at night in large numbers exhibit a very strong sea-going response, orientated towards light, running the gauntlet of predatory ghost crabs and birds, (Frigate birds, pied crows, turnstones etc.) and eventually fish as they swim out to sea. There is some evidence to indicate that Hawksbill hatchlings may not emerge in such large numbers, possibly leaving themselves open to more intensive predation. The Hawksbill hatchlings certainly seem to lack a strong sea-going response. Both species of turtle supported extensive commercial fisheries in the Seychelles which still linger on to some extent. The Hawksbill fishery centres on the production of tortoise-shell from the epidermal scutes of the turtle, the meat, considered poisonous, is rarely consumed. Captured by harpooning or upending females on nesting beaches, the Hawksbill is fished throughout the year. Tortoise-shell is worked by local craftsmen but large quantities were also exported. The Green Turtle is highly valued as a traditional food source, the main constituents of the fishery being live animals, meat, dried salted meat (mainly quitouze), dried salted flippers, 'tortue marinade' (meat in oil), oil, blood, bone meal, 'cawan' (yellow belly scales) and 'calipee' (cartilage). Originally, live animals were the most important product but during this century calipee, destined for the European market, assumed primary significance.

There are various legal restrictions on turtle hunting in Seychelles. The Turtle Act of 1925 is the basic legislation applicable and, although there have been many changes in the law since that date including absolute protection extended to turtles in the nature reserves, it is inadequate to meet the present challenge. In 1981, in an attempt to discourage the capture of Hawksbill Turtles, the government made it illegal for anyone but the state-owned company, Seycom, to export raw hawksbill shell. Despite the fact that the price offered was lower in 1982–83 than during the previous seasons, the number of Hawksbills declared at the police stations (as dictated by the legislation) was actually higher in 1982–3 (647) than in either 1980 (560) or in 1981–82 (537). In 1983, Seycom stopped buying shell completely. Mortimer comments *"despite the progress made, problems remain. Seychelles does not yet fully honor her obligations to CITES, for raw shell is still exported. Much poaching occurs in all but the Cousin Island and the Aldabra reserves. The only restriction on the capture of hawksbills outside the reserves is that they must have a carapace length greater than 24 inches. There are no seasonal restrictions. Both males and females can be captured, and females may even be captured while up on the nesting beach."* In 1968 a total ban on the capture of green turtles was imposed. The ban was both unenforcable and unpopular. Hence, in 1976 it was replaced by a measure that allows the taking of male turtles during the the months from March through October. No green turtle products may be exported or sold in restaurants, and butchers may not sell more than 2kg. of meat to any customer. Recommendations by Mortimer to safeguard turtles include the complete protection of adult female turtles everywhere in Seychelles; the prohibition on the export of raw hawksbill shell (export of stuffed hawksbill is prohibited and enforced); and steps to be taken to prevent the destruction of breeding and feeding habitat from construction development and pollution.

AMPHIBIANS

Unlike reptiles, amphibians do not have physical characteristics, such as dessication-resistant, salt-tolerant skin and a low metabolic rate, enabling them to endure long ocean odysseys on rafts of driftwood or vegetation in order to colonise new islands. In fact, the delicate amphibian integument has a respiratory function and is in constant need of moisture. This, coupled with the fact that amphibians never solved the problem of reproducing themselves away from moisture, always scarce on young islands, ensured their poor dispersion. However the Seychelles are particularly remarkable amongst distant islands in that they support an enormously diverse and highly endemic amphibian fauna, but only on the larger more elevated islands blessed with a high rainfall and moist forests. It seems logical that those genera that have relinquished the completely aquatic stage in their reproductive requirements for direct terrestrial development have a head start in the colonisation process. Three of the five species of frogs, and, at least, one of the seven species of caecilians, found in the Seychelles, lack aquatic larvae—whether this facility evolved after the ancient Seychelles land mass was colonised is uncertain.

Of the three extant orders of Amphibia, two are represented in the Seychelles—*Gymnophiona* and *Anura*—clearly underlining the archaic origins of its amphibian fauna. Caecilians (*Gymnophiona*), seven species of which occur in the Seychelles, are burrowing legless, tropicopolitan amphibians whose poor fossil record, morphology and distribution indicate that they are a Gondwanan group. Whilst some families of frogs (*Anura*) share this ancestry with the caecilians, others are clearly a Laurasian element.

There seems to be some evidence to support the theory that the caecilians of the Seychelles could have adaptively radiated on the Seychelles archipelago (or microcontinent) from a single ancestor—however, there is no published evidence which indicates the source of the ancestor. Nussbaum (1984) also feels that no definite conclusions are presently possible concerning the origin and affinities of the unique Seychellean sooglossids, but states that it now seems almost certain that they are not ranids with African affinities, as is widely believed. The caecilian and sooglossid species may have evolved from ancestors which were present on the Seychelles Microcontinent 75 million years ago, when it was still part of India: the ancestors of these two groups could also have dispersed to the microcontinent when it was isolated but still very close to India.

Ancestral *Megalixalus* almost certainly immigrated to Seychelles from Africa or Madagascar previous to the Pleistocene period, but there is no basis for speculation beyond this. The genus *Megalixalus* once included African, Madagascan and Seychellean tree frogs but is now reduced to a monotypic genus restricted to the Seychelles. *Rana mascariensis*, a relatively recent arrival, probably came to the Seychelles from Africa, as individuals from the Seychelles are nearly identical to those from that continent. The dispersal route, if not orchestrated by man, could have included island-hopping from Madagascar and/or the Mascarenes. (Nussbaum 1984).

As already emphasised, amphibians are found only on the larger granitic islands of the Seychelles. It is not difficult to deduce that dispersion problems, recency of emergence, and lack of suitable amphibian habitat are undoubtedly the factors responsible for the absence of amphibians on the coralline islands. One to eleven species of amphibian are found on eight granitic islands. (See Table pg. 121). Nussbaum (1984) points out that a few additional, undiscovered or unreported species may possibly be present on some other islands. He feels that the caecilian, *Grandisonia alternans*, and the frog, *Rana mascarensis*, may inhabit Cerf, Ste. Anne, and Curieuse islands: islands for which there are no amphibian records but may support a few species of amphibian, since they are small and water is scarce are Aride, Cousin, Cousine, Grand Soeur, Petite Soeur, Marianne, Felicite and North, the last two being the most likely candidates.

Generally speaking, there are more species of amphibians on the larger islands, however, although Silhouette has only 40% as much area as Praslin, it possesses one more species, probably because of its greater elevation. All three species of the secretive sooglossid frogs thrive in Silhouette's (and Mahe's) high elevation moss forest, a habitat completely absent on Praslin. In general, all three species of Sooglossid frogs can be found in suitable habitat above the 200m contour on Mahe and Silhouette, but have not been recorded from the north and south peninsulas of Mahe. *Sooglossus gardineri* is by far the most common and widespread species on Mahe, occurring at lower elevation and in drier and more disturbed sites compared to the other two species.

On the whole, the pattern of amphibian distribution, low island endemism, and the fact that islands in close proximity to each other are not any more similar in species composition than those that are widely separated, "*reflect recent partitioning of a once wide-ranging fauna into island refugia through submergence of the Seychelles micro-continent*", as is demonstrated by geological data (Nussbaum 1984).

Caecilians

Caecilians, elusive, burrowing, leg-less amphibians, spend much of their life secreted in moist leaf litter, soil, or rotten logs. Carnivorous, they feed on a wide variety of soil and litter invertebrates. Very little is known about caecilians throughout the tropics and even less about the life histories of the Seychellean species. Internal fertilisation is presumed to be the norm in all species: eggs are always deposited in moist, hidden, land-based sites, and, in the few cases known, females remain wrapped around the eggs until they hatch. (This appears to be the case also with Seychellean species, *Hypogeophis rostratus* and *Grandisonia alternans*.) Some species have larval stages whilst others undergo direct development, omitting the larval stage altogether. It appears that caecilians are not limited by elevation but rather by the availability of suitable moist habitat.

Sooglossid frogs

The female *Sooglossus sechellensis*, having deposited eggs in a concealed, terrestrial nest, apparently leaves the tending of the eggs to the male. On hatching, the tadpoles scramble onto the male's back, remaining there without feeding until they metamorphose into tiny froglets. Therefore, although development does include a larval stage, the ever-scarce water is not required.

Nussbaum (1984) has also thrown some light on the life history of *S. gardineri*. The female, having deposited eggs in concealed terrestrial sites, under or between rocks, in hollow stems, and between moist leaves, spends most of the time sitting on them. Unlike *S. sechellensis* however, no tadpole-carrying occurs, since full metamorphosed froglets emerge from the egg capsules.

The life-history of *Nesomantis thomasetti* remains obscure. Sooglossid frogs are found in moist creek bottoms, on deep-littered, shaded slopes, and on moist moss forest ridge tops. Dry, open coconut groves and glacis are not suitable habitats for Sooglosids. *Nesomantis thomasetti* is restricted to higher elevations compared to the other *Sooglossus* species, and is most often associated with rock outcrops or boulder fields. *S. sechellensis* is a forest litter species, usually found in deep accumulations of Cinnamon, Northea, or Bois Rouge leaves. *S. gardineri* is also a forest litter species, but it occurs in a greater variety of habitats than the two larger sooglossid species. *S. gardineri* frequently occur in piles of wood chips, in litter under cultivated plants, and in road cuts. This species has the greatest elevational range, from about 200 meters to the top of Morne Seychellois (914m) (Nussbaum 1984).

Megalixalus seychellensis are thought to breed throughout the year, peaking in December, at suitable sites ranging from sea level on Praslin and La Digue to 750 metres on Mahe. Eggs are usually deposited in vegetation above a stream; development through hatching normally takes place out of water, the young dorso-ventrally flattened tadpoles either falling directly into or travelling short distances to a stream. The tadpoles, equipped also with an elongated tail, are suitably adapted to exploit the available fast-flowing water, since there is very little standing water on the granitic islands. A nocturnal frog, this species inhabits trees: the reddish-brown male is smaller than the darkgreen female but both sexes can change colour—a lightish lemon-green is normal during the day.

Rana mascarensis

This is a wide-ranging, extremely versatile species, frequenting swamps, wet meadows, and marshes in Africa, apparently feeding on a wide selection of invertebrates. Breeding in lakeside marshes and temporary rainwater pools, takes place over an extended period. The eggs having been deposited directly in water, the tadpoles that emerge are of the usual pond-type. In the Seychelles, Nussbaum has collected this particular frog from sea level to about 450 meters elevation, in habitats ranging from brackish seaside marshes to mountain forest. The breeding season apparently coincides largely with the rainy season. The food habits of the Seychelles species are likely to be the same as those reported from Africa. Potential predators in Seychelles are snakes, caecilians, owls, kestrel, sea birds and tenrecs.

INSECTS

The Percy Sladen Trust Indian Ocean Expedition, visiting the islands in 1905 and 1908, completed and published a considerable body of work on insect taxonomy—"*an estimated figure of 3,500 species for the region is based on some 2,800 species recorded in the Percy Sladen works and approximately 700 additional species from Aldabra*" (Cogan 1984).

A well camouflaged introduced frog (*Rana mascareniensis*) seen at Frigate Island. (Harrison).

120

THE STATUS OF AMPHIBIAN SPECIES IN THE SEYCHELLES

RARE:
  Grandisonia brevis,
  Grandisonia diminutiva,
  Praslinia cooperi.

UNCOMMON:
  Grandisonia larvata,
  Grandisonia sechellensis,
  Nesomantis thomasetti.

COMMON:
  Sooglossus gardineri,
  Sooglossus sechellensis,
  Megalixalus seychellensis.

UBIQUITOUS:
  Grandisonia alternans,
  Hypogeophis rostratus,
  Rana mascarensis.

AMPHIBIA OF SEYCHELLES
(after Nussbaum, 1984)

GYMNOPHIONA
  Caecliidae. (Caecilians)
    Grandisonia alternans
    Grandisonia brevis.
    Grandisonia diminutiva.
    Grandisonia larvata.
    Grandisonia sechellensis.
    Hypogeophis rostratus.
    Praslinia cooperi.

ANURA (Frogs)
  Hyperoliidae
    Megalixalus seychellensis.
  Ranidae.
    Rana mascariensis.
  Sooglossidae.
    Nesomantis thomasseti.
    Sooglossus gardineri.
    Sooglossus sechellensis.

ISLAND	CAECILIANS	FROGS	TOTAL
Mahe	6	5	11
Praslin	6	2	8
Silhouette	4	5	9
La Digue	3	2	5
Curieuse	1	0	1
Ste. Anne	1	0	1
Frigate	2	1	3
Cerf	1	0	1

FIGURE 10

But, in the last twenty years, the subject has suffered through neglect so that, it is really only possible to discuss insect taxonomy, and therefore, phylogenetic relationships and zoogeographical considerations on a relatively superficial level.

The faunal composition of the Aldabra group and central Seychelles are quite different. Cogan et al (1971) estimated the Aldabran insect fauna to be in the region of 1,000 species on the basis of collections made during the Royal Society Expeditions: the same researchers gave a preliminary average figure of only 4.1% for the fauna shared by the two distinct regions. Legrand (1965) also came to the conclusion that, of the 363 species of Lepidoptera recognised by him from the Seychelles, only 32 species or just under 10.6% were common to both areas—and this percentage is very much above the average. Most of the non-endemic species of the Aldabran area have close affinities with the Afrotropical region, with a considerable input from the Malagasy sub-region. The insect fauna of the granitic Seychelles is characterised by a considerable degree of distinctive endemicity, often highly derived. It is possible that this most highly derived section has ancient Gondwanan origins—the rest of the endemic species probably colonised the islands at various stages of isolation. The majority of the non-endemic fauna must have crossed the Indian Ocean, some actively as part of migratory swarms, others passively and windborne. As Cogan (1984) succinctly remarks—*"invasion by rafting does not appear to be a very successful method for insect dispersal, as seawater acts as a very efficient insecticide"*!

Insect species introduced by man have made an impact on the island, far exceeding the relatively few species involved. This is understandable as these introduced species are nearly all cosmopolitan pests. For example, the Crazy-ant *Anopolepsis longipes* (Jerden) arrived in Mahe from S. E. Asia only about 1962, but is now a major nuisance.

Some individual members of the insect fauna and its more ancient allied class, the arachnids, are of particular interest to the visitor. Dedicated enthusiasts, in search of a more detailed account are referred to the appropriate scientific works listed in the bibliography. The family Tenebrionidae, in which 7 genera are apparently without related genera in other regions, is a good example of endemic elements which appear to be isolated taxonomically (Cogan 1984). The giant tenebrionid beetle, *Pulposipes herculaeanus*, has been recorded from only two places in the world, Round Island off Mauritius, and Frigate. It is now found only on Frigate and can be easily identified by the observant visitor because of its unusually large size.

The insect fauna of the Seychelles, however, is characterised by a low level of endemicity in the order Lepidoptera; in fact the number of all butterfly species recorded is relatively small. Visitors to the central Seychelles are often left with the distinct impression that there is a complete absence of butterflies on the islands, since even the diurnal species are not of the obvious colourful variety. Legrand (1965) observes that even the caterpillars of the majority of the 46 species he studied on the central islands lead, what he calls, a hidden life, being either nocturnal or concealed in rolled-up leaves. To offset this apparent paucity, numerous vividly coloured butterfly species can be spotted on the less frequented, elevated islands of the Aldabra group.

ARACHNIDS

The large spider *Nephla madagascariensis* is often observed motionless in its dramatic, glistening orb-web woven amongst the trees. Frigate, home of the tenebrionid beetle already mentioned, also plays host to a distinctive arachnid, a large (up to 12 inches) *Amblypige* spider with very long first legs characteristic of its order, and, reputedly, a painful bite. However these flattened arachnids live in constant

The introduced spider, *Nephla* sp., seen here on Mahe, is quite harmless, (Vine).

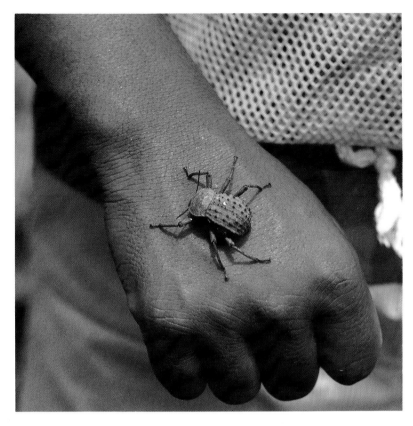

Giant Tenebrionid Beetle, *Pulposides herculaeanus*, is a unique and ancient species only found on Frigate Island.(Harrison).

concealment and are seldom encountered.

The rather large scorpion, *Chiromachus ochropus*, also occurs on Frigate under rocks, or in those large piles of coconut husks found frequently around the island. Its bite, although reported as painful, is not dangerous.

BIRDS

This book does not attempt to fulfil the role of an identification guide—Malcolm Penny's and Tony Beamish's useful reference works should satisfy the needs of any inquiring ornithologist—however, I would like to highlight some of the more interesting aspects of the fascinating birdlife flourishing in Seychelles, a knowledge of which will undoubtedly enrich any visit to these islands.

Although the exact timing is uncertain, the Seychelles Microcontinent was probably separated from the mainland too early in evolutionary history to support a relict population of birds. If this is the case, ancestors of the present avifauna will have arrived by invasion, except for those species artificially introduced by Man. The vast majority of species directly originated in Madagascar. This *"strong Malagasy element can be explained by the short distances to be covered and the prevailing winds from the south, although an apparent case of colonisation in the opposite direction is the Seychelles Bulbul, (Ixos crassirostris) from the Seychelles to the Comores"*. (Benson 1984). The direct African element is very low in comparison to the Asiatic input, one species, the Seychelles Scops Owl, (*Otus insularis*), is even of Australasian origin. Benson however, calculates that study of the putative indirect, earlier, origins, via Madagascar indicate a greater African input.

Unlike some of the other groups we have considered in our glimpse of Seychelles' natural history, birds are uniquely successful invaders for a number of obvious reasons; not least of which is their ability to travel long sea-distances—even the smallest of birds can cover over a 1,000 miles on a favourable wind (e.g. swifts and pigeons). But, successful colonisation of oceanic islands requires more than the ability to cross sea barriers: as far as birds are concerned, a male and female must arrive either together or at a reasonable interval—flocking (parrots and white-eyes), and long-lived birds (owls and kestrels), have a distinct advantage in this regard. The adaptability inherent in certain avian species such as finches (weavers), sunbirds, thrushes (Magpie Robin) is also a prerequisite as far as successful colonisation is concerned: birds whose feeding or nesting requirements are too specialised are unlikely to survive. There must also be enough invaders to give rise to a viable population; the lack of such vital necessiities as fresh-water, available food sources and space for breeding, may severely limit the successful invasion below the numbers necessary for continued survival.

Seychelles, a group of relatively small islands far removed from their source of colonisation, supports a predictably low number of bird species, with the resultant emphasis on intraspecific rather than interspecific competition. Many visitors, although delighted to become acquainted with such a selection of very rare birds, are rather disappointed with their drabness compared with the bird fauna of the tropical mainland. As Penny comments, this lack of dramatic colouration can be directly associated with an insular life; there is less need for interspecific recognition signals on the island because of the paucity of species. "*Where there are a lot of closely related species one would expect to find the greatest and brightest variety of colour*". Dull breeding plumage may also lead to reduced territorial aggression between breeding males, "*dull or drab breeding dress also permits the establishment of places where the birds can congregate on limited resources.*" Both of these factors may, of course, be interconnected, neither explanation providing the answer in itself.

Besides dull plumage, other characteristics such as large size, small clutch size, and broad ecological preference are common to bird populations confined to distant islands. Such isolation, without any genetic input from mainland stock, leads eventually to the separation of the species, sometimes through the creation of a subspecies, but often through the formation of a completely new species, and possibly even a genus.

Ecology, isolation and area are the main factors influencing landbird distribution on oceanic islands; ecology and area, of course, interlinking with habitat diversity. Diamond (1984) made an extensive study of the biogeography of Seychelles' land birds. He used the broad geological island categories as a qualitative measure of ecology, the high granitic islands providing a greater level of ecological diversity compared to the low coralline or elevated limestone islands. He concluded that the distribution patterns shown by the original land bird faunas were different on the granite and coralline islands: species number was related chiefly to isolation in the granite islands, and to area in the corallines. Inter-island immigration rates rose as the islands were located closer together. This helps to explain some apparent discrepan-

Sooty terns gather in the evening sky over Bird Island, preparing to roost for the night. Before the breeding season, at the beginning of May, there are no Sooty terns on the ground during daytime since the huge flock has moved off out to sea in search of food. By five o'clock they start coming in over the island—accompanied by the deafening chorus of almost a million screeching birds, wheeling closer and closer to their designated landing strip, adjacent to the settlement. During my observation I was forced in the end to cover my ears to protect them from the noise. Sun set at ten past six and the first terns began to land ten minutes later. During the next twenty minutes I watched over half a million birds touch down on the ground and continue to squawk at each other, presumably arguing over who should stand where. The noise continued for most of the night and the entire flock departed before sun-rise, once more out to sea in search of food. (Vine).

cies in bird distribution in the Seychelles, in particular the small number of species on large islands such as Mahe and Silhouette, both relatively isolated by Seychelles standards, and the unexpectedly high numbers on much smaller islands such as Praslin and Marianne, situated in closer proximity to other islands. Diamond also found that there was remarkably little difference in total species number between granite and coralline islands. The reduced habitat diversity of the coralline islands was probably compensated by their greater accessibility from Madagascar and also because inter-island distances were greater in coralline than in granite islands. However, species distribution patterns in the granite islands changed significantly after human settlement. Species number is now determined primarily by area, not by isolation. The reduction in the pool of potential recolonisers of small islands brought about by the extirpation of at least 41% of island populations, altered dramatically the influence of isolation. In the coralline islands area still determines species number, but to a lesser degree than before human settlement (Prys-Jones and Diamond 1984).

A taxonomic, rather than species number, comparison "*of the indigenous land-bird fauna of the coral and granite groups reveals almost complete divergence at the specific level; out of thirty species, only one, the Malagasy Turtle Dove is common to both. However, 30% of the genera are held in common which is indicative that many species in one group have close ecological counterparts in the other.*" (Prys-Jones and Diamond 1984). The following brief account of Seychelles avifauna centers largely on the central granitic islands and the associated coralline cays of Bird and Denis.

Modifications to the original avifauna brought about by the impact of Man on the Environment

Taking into account the extent of the destruction wreaked on the endemic woodlands, characterising the early history of Seychelles, it is remarkable that only three of the original land birds are known to have become extinct: the Green Parakeet, *Psittacula eupatria wardi*, and the Chestnut-flanked White-eye, *Zosterops mayottensis semiflava*, both probably in the first decade of this century, and, more recently through interbreeding, the Seychelles own subspecies of turtle dove *Streptopelia picturata rostrata*. However, other species may have disappeared before the first detailed accounts of the land birds by Newton (1867) and Oustalet (1878). Over and above habitat destruction, the introduction of mammalian predators (cats and rats) has had a very marked effect on abundance and distributional patterns. A number of exotic bird species have also been introduced by man for his own particular ends— as pest control, food source, and for purely decorative or entertainment purposes. Man himself played a direct role in decimating bird populations, by shooting large numbers of those they considered pests and by intensively cropping birds, eggs, and chicks as an easily exploited food source. Land birds, like the Blue Pigeon and the Turtle dove suffered at the hands of early settlers because of their tame disposition, but some seabird populations are still vulnerable to large-scale egg and chick collection, even though this is now regulated to some extent. Unfortunately these protective mechanisms came too late for a few species : the Great Frigate is now very probably extinct as a breeding species on the central group of islands, and the Red-footed Booby is locally extinct.

Although habitat destruction and predation have taken their toll on Seychelles avifauna and concerted efforts at conservation only commenced about 40 years ago, most of the endemic species have managed to survive, despite severe reduction in population sizes and drastic restriction of the numbers of islands occupied by many indigenous species. Four taxa, however, are considered greatly endangered, five vulnerable and the remaining three secure (Watson 1984).

LAND BIRDS

Introduced Species

The Mynah, the Cardinal and the Barred Ground Dove, all introduced species, are the most common land birds in Seychelles. The ubiquitous and unmistakable Mynah, *Acridotheres tristis*, renowned for it's mimicry, is said to have been introduced to the granite islands in the eighteenth century to control locusts although there is no evidence that these insects have ever been a problem in Seychelles. The Mynah, owing much of it's success to a well-developed scavenging ability, unfortunately, also preys on the chicks of smaller birds such as the Fairy Tern.

The finch-like Cardinal, *Foudia madagascariensis*, particularly common to the lowlands of all the granitic islands, is rumoured to have been introduced from Mauritius about 1860, by a vexed landowner attempting to seek revenge on his rice-growing rival. The male, resplendent in scarlet breeding plumage adds a much-needed dash of colour to the bird population, whilst females and juveniles have a nondescript, streaky-brown hue. Although primarily a seed-eater, the Cardinal feeds it's young on insects. As with the the endemic species of fody, *Foudia sechellarum*, nectar is also an important source of nourishment. Both species benefit from close contact with human habitation. Although the Seychelles Fody is very restricted in its distribution, there is no evidence that it is suffering from competition with the Cardinal.

The endemic subspecies of Turtle Dove, *Streptopelia picturata rostrata*, has not been able to achieve such peaceful coexistence with the introduced Malagasy form, the grey-headed *Streptopelia picturata*. Interbreeding has taken place to such an extent that the former is now considered to be extinct: the previously distinguishable species on Cousin and Cousine are thought to be hybrids. This kind of infiltration sometimes happens when an introduced species cannot displace the endemic form. Like the other highly successful introduced species, the small ground dove, *Geopelia striata*, barred with black above and on the neck and breast, has adapted its basically seed—eating habits to take advantage of a special relationship with Man. This ground-feeding bird, so tame that it barely moves out of the way as one approaches, is often found in close association with the Turtle Dove ; the Ground Dove taking small seed and the larger Turtle Dove feeding on larger seed and fallen fruit.

Ecologically speaking, one of the greatest disasters in recent years has been the colonial government's introduction of the East African Barn Owl, *Tyto alba*, in the 1950's as a possible method of controlling the rodent population. Unfortunately, for many reasons, it proved to be singularly ineffective at this designated task and, turning it's marauding intentions towards other birds, has practically decimated the Fairy Tern population on Mahe and Praslin. The Seychelles Kestrel has also suffered as a result of strong competition from the Barn Owl for nesting sites high up in buildings such as church towers.

Seychelles, for reasons we have already outlined, is blessed with a small but unique collection of endemic birds. Unfortunately, some of these birds are now amongst the rarest in the world although much has been done in recent decades to halt the decline in numbers experienced by these singular species. The following brief notes review some points of interest regarding a range of endemic birds and their habitats.

Endemic Species

The following four endangered species are largely confined to a single island, each in turn having a world population of about 100 birds, except for the Black Parrot about which there is some dispute over population size.

Indian Mynahs scavenging on shore at Mahe. (Hill).

Male Black Paradise Flycatcher (*Terpsiphone corvina*) seen in La Digue Verve Reserve. This endemic bird is now confined to La Digue (and possibly also a small population on the east side of Praslin) (Hill).

Female Black Paradise Flycatcher in the reserve created especially for its survival on La Digue. The pair build a tidy nest held together with material from spiders' webs. Breeding continues throughout the year, each clutch consisting of a single egg, and both sexes share the task of incubation. (Hill).

Paradise Flycatcher

A Special Reserve has been established jointly by the Seychelles National Environment Commission and the Royal Society for Nature Conservation to protect the endangered Seychelles Veuve or Black Paradise Flycatcher, (*Tersiphone corvina*) and its essential lowland forest habitat on La Digue. Once found on Marianne and Aride, this rare species, except for a few individuals on Praslin, is now confined to La Digue. The Reserve not only contains Badamier and Takamaka trees, favoured by the Veuve as resting places for its delightfully moulded nest, delicately held together by a spiders web, but also has a permanent water source and marshland to support the insects constituting the main diet of the Flycatcher. The long tail streamers sported by the beautiful black male has earned it the Creole name of Veuve (Widow). The La Digue Reserve, smallest in the Seychelles is entirely crucial to the survival of this rare and beautiful bird.

Black Parrot

The extremely rare endemic subspecies *Coracopsis nigra barklyi*, known as the Black Parrot, also owes its continued survival to a nature reserve, this time the rustling, primeval palm-forest of the Vallee de Mai on Praslin. It is unlikely that this species ever lived on islands other than Praslin and possibly Curieuse which has similar archaic vegetation, although some reports indicate that it was formerly on Marianne and Aride. A dusty grey-brown bird, not at all the colouration one associates with the parrot family, it, nonetheless, behaves in a typical parrot-like, acrobatic manner. Feeding on the fruit trees in and around the reserve, the elusive bird can be detected by its high-pitched whistle or, alternatively, the pitter-patter of discarded seeds dropping through the leaf canopy to the forest floor. However, one should be aware that many of the Mynahs on Praslin can imitate the parrot's distinctive call very accurately.

The Black Parrot nests in holes burrowed in decaying tree trunks, notably the decaying stems of the coco de mer and the screwpine (*Pandanus sp.*). It is possible that, as some commentators have suggested, the paucity of available nest cavities may be a limiting factor and the provision of suitable nesting boxes could well be the answer. (Penny 1965) (Watson 1984).

Stories are recounted of the slaughter of large Black Parrot flocks, because of their devastating effect on Praslin's fruit-trees, however populations may just as well have declined as a result of ecological changes. There has been some dispute about the population size but the total number of birds probably does not exceed 200(Watson 1984).

Magpie Robin

The Magpie Robin, (*Copsychus sechellarum*), is aptly named, since it does indeed resemble a robin masquerading as a magpie: although it possesses the colouration of the latter, blue-black plumage and white wing-bars, it displays many endearing characteristics, such as tail-cocking, of the familiar robin. Just to confuse matters even further, it is in fact a thrush. The present Magpie Robin population may be as low as 19 birds, all of which are confined to Frigate; with the exception of one solitary male still hanging on at Aride, the result of an unsuccessful attempt to re-establish this once widespread species. A ground-feeder, the opportunistic Magpie Robin can be observed in the shade, picking at the soil disturbed by the clumsy movements of the giant tortoise or foraging for worms or insects in the vicinity of farming activity.

Frigate is devoid of cats and rats, a factor which ensured the survival of the Magpie Robin. Its disappearance from at least six islands has been largely attributed to the predation of the domestic cat, particularly on recently fledged young which leave the nest before they can fly. In 1984 Watson reported that the population appeared stable at around 30 to 40 birds and "*was found to be limited by available feeding habitat with the bird's social behaviour playing an intermediate regulation role; removal experiments demonstrated that potential breeders were being excluded by the territorial behaviour of existing adult pairs*".

Seychelles Grey White-Eye

The Grey White-Eye *Zosterops modesta*, restricted to three sites in high and intermediate forest on Mahe, was presumed extinct until rediscovered by Philip Lalanne in 1962. The total number of birds is estimated to be in the region of 50 to 100 but very little is actually know about the Grey-White Eye. Confined to upland areas where there is very little human habitation, almost the entire range of the bird lies within the Morne Seychellois National Park.

The following five species are categorised as vulnerable, world population numbers are between 100 and 1000 birds and several are well established on more than one island.

Seychelles Kestrel

This tiny endemic bird of prey, *Falco araea* sporting chestnut wings mottled with black, buff underparts, and a dark crown, seems to be largely confined to Mahe and Silhouette, having once inhabited Praslin and La Digue as well. We have already alluded to competition from the introduced Barn Owl as a factor in reduction of kestrel numbers; predation by rats and cats also played a significant role in decimating populations. Unfortunately for the kestrel, it also suffers death and destruction from Man, because its appearance in the eaves of buildings where it likes to nest, is considered an ill omen. Breeding success is fortunately much higher in remote hill areas than in the more

Magpie Robin and skinks at Frigate Island. (Harrison).

Male Madagascar Fody at Praslin. (Hill).

Cattle egrets at Bird Island. (Hill).

Female Madagascar Fody at Praslin. (Hill).

Turnstone on rock at Cousin. (Hill).

The Seychelles Sunbird (*Nectarinia dussumieri*) is the most widely distributed of Seychelles endemic birds, apparently being one of the few species to have actually benefitted from Man's intervention on the islands, through the introduction of numerous exotic plants upon which the sunbirds feed. (Hill).

populated coastal regions. As a result the population on Mahe is considered to be in the region of 300 to 350 pairs with about 50 pairs on Silhouette.

The Cave Swiftlet

The endemic Cave Swiftlet, (*Collocalia francica elaphra*), can be easily spotted on Mahe, especially in Victoria, as dusk falls, and flocks of the elegant little birds, silhouetted against the darkening sky, swiftly swoop through by the telephone wires in search of insects, but the highest concentrations on Mahe are actually to be found over the boulder fields above Glacis. The bird isn't as common as first impressions might indicate and is considered vulnerable because of a restricted range and the 'vulnerability' of its breeding colonies to disturbance and destruction (Watson 1984). This species also inhabits some of the other larger granitic islands, particularly Praslin and La Digue, and it was in a granite cave on the latter that a cave swiftlets nest, "a typical upside-down nest agglomeration", was first discovered as recently as 1970.

Seychelles Bare-legged Scops Owl

The Bare-Legged Scops Owl (*Otus insularis*), like the Grey White-Eye, was considered extinct for fifty years only to be rediscovered by Seychellois ornithologist, Philip Lalanne in 1959. The nesting-site of this small, light brown owl, has not been found so far and little is really known about its ecology. Apparently restricted to the remote hill forests of Mahe, numbers are thought to be in the region of 75 pairs but "could be nearer twice this" (Watson 1984). Fortunately for the future of this species, about 80% of its range falls within Morne Seychellois National park.

Seychelles Brush Warbler

The lively, green Seychelles Brush Warbler, (*Acrocephalus sechellensis*), once occurred on Marianne but is now restricted in its distribution to the small granitic island of Cousin, (a small population had been artificially introduced to Cousine). This protected island, bought for the ICBP (British Section) in 1968 has witnessed a rapid increase in the numbers of this unique insectivorous warbler, apparently in response to an increase in suitable habitat, resulting from the deliberate replanting by reserve management of natural woodland to replace coconut plantation. Penny recorded 50 birds on Cousin in 1965, whereas by 1974 the island held between 250 and 300 birds (Diamond 1980).

Seychelles Fody

We have already mentioned that an endemic species of fody *Foudia sechellarum* coexists with the introduced Madagascar Fody on three islands, Cousin, Cousine and Frigate. It was once found on Marianne, and possibly Praslin and La Digue, but never on Mahe or Silhouette. Speculation that the introduced fody might be out-competing the endemic species, accounting for its restricted distribution, has been largely discounted. Recent data shows the species to be largely segregated by food—the Seychelles Fody feeding much more on insects and less on seeds than the Malagasy Fody. The Seychelles Fody is also reported to scavenge on eggs and dropped fish in the dense colonies of nesting seabirds on Cousin (Prys-Jones and Diamond 1984).

Fledgling White-tailed Tropic Bird at Cousin. (Vine).

Opposite

Red-Footed Booby (*Sula sula rubripes*) is a member of the Gannet family which breeds on Aldabra, Cosmoledo and Farquhar, nesting among mangroves. Following a day's fishing they may be seen approaching the islands towards evening when they are often attacked by Frigate Birds whose repeated harrassment causes the Boobies to regurgitate their catch of flying fish and squid. (Guy de Moussac).

As already indicated, nectar feeding is an important part of the diet of both species although they harvest this sweet substance in a completely different manner to the delicate, Sunbird. The fodies remove the flower with the beak, and secure it with one foot whilst probing the nectary from behind. The Sunbird on the other hand preserves the flower in pristine condition, probing the open end with its long slender curved beak. Both forms also feed happily and noisily from scraps laid out in front of the plantation house on Frigate, the Seychelles species distinguishable by its larger size and and rich dark brown colour, except for the yellow patch above and below the bill in breeding males. There hasn't been any recent reliable census of Seychelles Fody populations since the early 1960's but, from casual observation, it would be safe to assume that the numbers have increased since then and might even be better categorised under 'secure', rather than 'vulnerable'.

The remaining species have never really been considered threatened, although there has been some concern about the healthy state of Blue Pigeon (*Alectroenas pulcherrima*) populations. However this striking blue and silver bird, crowned with a blood-red wattle, seems to occur in reasonable numbers on Mahe, Silhouette, Praslin, La Digue and Frigate, with small populations also on Felicite and Marianne.

The Seychelles Bulbul, *Ixos crassirostris*, is also common on the four large islands, its disappearance from Felicite and Marianne is probably due to the clearance of forest on these islands. But the little Sunbird *Nectarinia dussumieri*, although it has disappeared from Aride, is the most common and widely distributed of all the endemic birds on the granitic islands. The introduction of numerous tropical flowering plants may have benefited the Sunbird, primarily a nectar-feeder, enormously.

SHOREBIRDS

The demarcation line between land and shorebirds is not so perfectly clear on a small island. Scavengers, like the Mynah, can often be seen foraging on the shore, even Ground Doves are common on the beach down to the tide line, and Feare (1977) records that, in December 1972, turnstones were observed feeding in rain forest at La Misere (500m). The granitic Seychelles, in fact has only three resident shore birds: the rare marsh-dwelling Yellow Bittern *Ixobrychus sinensis*, the Cattle Egret, *Bulbulcus ibis* commonly seen on rubbish tips, and the Green-Backed Heron. But, many migrant waders visit these islands, affording the dedicated birdwatcher ample opportunity to update existing records. Most migrant shorebirds arrive in the period August to November and are presumed to have travelled directly south from the northern coasts of the western Indian Ocean. Whether they deliberately head for Seychelles or are strays, which fortuitously find the islands while wandering south; is not entirely clear, but, Feare comments that the numbers involved of some species suggest that many of the birds were, in fact, heading for wintering grounds in the Malagasy region. But migrant shorebirds aren't the only visitors to the Seychelles, migrant land birds also arrive in November and December but in much smaller numbers and are very unpredictable in their occurrence. Their time of arrival, suggests that they too make a direct crossing of the Indian Ocean rather than arriving from Africa. The

Seychelles provides a variety of coastal habitats for visiting shorebirds: from intertidal flats, sandy beaches, muddy lagoons, mangroves and freshwater pools on the granitic islands, to sand bars, reef flats, and littoral fringes of coral cays. Victoria's intertidal mud flats provide the dedicated ornithologist with a fruitful hunting-ground for visiting shorebirds.

SEABIRDS

Except for the Sooty Tern, which we will discuss later, almost all of the extensive seabird population of the Seychelles is resident. Species diversity and colony sizes have decreased dramatically during the past century through heavy cropping of seabird eggs and chicks by Man to supplement both diet and pocket with habitat changes also taking their toll. As a result of these pressures, certain seabird populations have disappeared from some islands where they were abundant up until the beginning of this century. On the other hand, other islands retain populations which are significant on a world scale. Seychelles seabirds have been the subject of protective legislation since 1906, however, apart from the laws in force regulating egg collecting, the present emphasis is on the creation and policing of completely protected reserves. Stoddart (1984) emphasises that "*there is no relationship whatever between island size and number of breeding seabird species: the highest diversities reflect environmental diversity and habitat availability.*" The great seabird islands of, Bird, Aride and Cousin are particularly interesting to the visitor, Aldabra and Desnoeufs, of course, also fall into this category, although they are not so accessible. Aride, most northerly of the granite islands, is lushly verdant, belying an unpromising name. No doubt, its fertility owes something to the large quantities of guano deposited by the extensive seabird colony it supports. Although these species occur on other islands, nowhere else in the world will you see such large breeding colonies of the Lesser Noddy (c.115,000 pairs); Audubon's Shearwater (c. 50,000 pairs); Roseate Tern (25,000–50,000 pairs); White-tailed Tropicbird (c.10,000 pairs); and Fairy Tern (15–20,000 pairs). The Common Brown Noddy also breeds on Aride (c. 20,000 pairs), but can be found in even greater numbers on Frigate (c. 24,000 pairs) and in somewhat smaller colonies on Cousin. Both Cousin, and Aride support very small breeding populations of the Red-tailed Tropicbird and the Bridled Tern.

Cousin, 27 hectares of nature reserve just a few miles from Praslin, also plays host to breeding colonies of the Lesser Noddy (c. 100,000 pairs); the Wedge-tailed Shearwater (c. 35,000 pairs)—Aride's population of Wedge-tails is smaller at 20,000 pairs; the Fairy Tern (c. 10,000 pairs) and the White-tailed Tropicbird (c. 1000 pairs), as well as receiving frequent visits from the Little Tern (*Sterna albifrons*) in the Northwest Monsoon. The Crested Tern (*Thalasseus bergii*), more commonly associated with the limestone and low coralline islands, has also been recorded from Cousin. Both the Great Frigatebird (*Fregata minor*), and the Lesser Frigate (*Fregata ariel*) breed on Aldabra, however a few hundred of the former roost, but probably do not breed, on Aride and can be glimpsed, distinctive angular wings catching the wind, as it hangs over Cousin and other granitic islands. The large and powerfully built Red-footed Booby (*Sula sula*) is also restricted in its breeding activity to Aldabra, but is found ranging widely throughout the Sey-

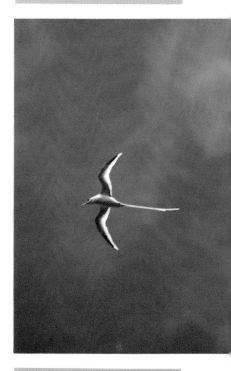

White-tailed Tropic Bird in flight at Cousin Island. (Vine).

Fairy Tern chick on Cousin Island. (Hill).

Photographer Dr. Mike Hill has captured a wonderful moment as this Fairy Tern settles down on its egg at Bird Island. (Hill).

Crested Terns on beach at Bird Island. (Hill).

Sooty tern adult feeds a chick at Bird Island. (Hill).

Young Noddy Tern at Cousin. (Vine).

Sooty tern in flight. Bird Island. (Hill).

Sooty tern at Bird Island. (Hill).

Breeding colony of Sooty terns at Bird Island. (Hill).

Noddy Tern adult and chick in nest at Cousin. (Vine).

Mating of Fairy Terns usually occurs in the early morning. This pair was observed for more than an hour while the author sat on an adjacent branch of the tree, apparently not disturbing the pair in their mating ritual. The female bird lands first, establishes a suitable position on the tree, and crouches rhythmically, pattering her feet. Next the male lands and commences his own posturing display, including wing stretches,, a little stamping of feet, and some half-hearted crouches. Finally he jumps on the female's back and they perform a balancing act while mating occurs. (Vine).

The Red-Tailed Tropic bird, (*Phaethon rubricauda rubricauda*) is rare among the central Seychelles islands, but relatively common around Aldabra where it nests on islets within the lagoon. (Guy de Moussac).

chelles, especially at Cousin and other granitic islands.

Bird Island is famous for its vast, raucous Sooty Tern colony, (c. 395,000 pairs) although Desnoeufs boasts an even greater abundance, estimated at 1.75 million in 1966. The Bird Island Sooty Tern population is discussed in more detail below. This island also supports an estimated 10,000 pairs of Common Noddy breeding in Coconut palms and Casuarina, accompanied by a few White-tailed Tropicbirds and approximately 720 pairs of Fairy Tern. Audobon's Shearwater is also recorded from Bird Island.

The nesting habits and preferences of the the various seabirds mentioned above vary considerably. The liquid-eyed, milk-white Fairy Tern (*Gygis alba*), nesting primarily in the December–January period, doesn't attempt to construct a nest but balances a single egg in a precarious position, on the branch of a tree, or other equally bizarre situation such as the one remarked on by many visitors to Cousin: on a conservation signpost! The Roseate Tern (*Sterna dougalli*—*S.d. arideensis* being the local race whose type locality is Aride) is also quite nonchalant about nest-building and lays its eggs on soil, sometimes with traces of nest material. The Lesser Noddy, breeding from May to August, diligently builds impressive nests, composed of Pisonia leaves cemented with brown algae, high up in trees. The two species of shearwater—Wedge Tailed (*Puffinus pacificus*) and Audubon's (*Puffinus lherminieri*) nest in large numbers in burrows dug out of the ground. The former species, breeding throughout the year, forms colonial nesting burrows of up to six feet long whilst the latter is not as gregarious, often making its narrow burrow around the edge of the Wedge-tailed colony. Both species spend most of the day fishing out at sea, leaving before dawn and returning late in the evening.

We have talked about the impact habitat destruction and replacement can have on colony sizes but it is also true that such large number of seabirds leave their imprint on island ecosystems, especially on vegetation. Seabirds too, play a pivotal role in the transfer of nutrients from sea to land, especially in the accumulation of guano and the formation of phosphate rock.

Sooty Tern

Sooty Tern range the vast expanses of the Indian Ocean, except in the breeding season when they congregate in noisy tumultuous colonies on specified breeding islands. Bird Island, a northerly situated sand cay, sixty miles from Mahe supporting approximately half a million pairs, is now the world's second largest breeding colony of this species. At the beginning of this century the Sooty Tern colony occupied the centre of Bird island. Fryer (1910) gives some indication of the raucous impact such an accumulation of birds can make—"*it is quite impossible to give any idea of the countless thousands which breed upon the island.... the confusion, noise and smell of such a 'fair' can only be realised by a visit, as any attempt at description would seem an unpardonable exaggeration.*" However, once the island was extensively planted with coconut palms, the birds became restricted to the northwest corner. Feare (1976) concludes that most of the decline in the Sooty tern population, experienced after this afforestation, can be attributed to the extension of the plantation, and not to over exploitation of the eggs for food as was commonly perceived, even though Bird Island was one of the most important egg producing islands up to 1955. Tree clearance carried out after 1967 and ongoing vegetation management provided much more valuable space for the terns, space they quickly occupied resulting in a 19% per annum increase in the population. Feare's intensive studies in the field support this point of view. He found that the terns ability to lay a replacement egg after loss of the first, whether by natural causes or cropping by Man, is much greater than previous estimates had suggested, and some individuals could be induced to lay a third egg, but both the ability to re-lay and the size and success of replacement eggs declined seasonally. Since early laying, as indeed synchrony, significantly increase breeding success, the productivity of late laid eggs is probably very low. Feare states that "*it is precisely these eggs that the present close-season regulations protect, and on biological grounds these regulations could be withdrawn without detriment to the birds. However, exploitation of eggs laid during the peak-laying period should be carefully controlled.*"

Feare also reported an interesting phenomenon which occurred in 1973 amongst the Sooty tern breeding population on Bird Island: in part of the colony, observers were startled to witness the mass desertion of well-incubated, hatching and newly hatched eggs which could only be attributed to a heavy infestation of *O. capensis* ticks in the area in question. The subsequent mortalities in orphan chicks were probably due to starvation but may have been aided significantly by the Soldado virus hosted by the tick.

Besides the impact of Man and ticks, the Sooty Tern population also has to contend with the usual natural predators. The large size of the breeding colony and advantages conferred by synchronous breeding provide a certain amount of protection for the eggs; hatching success at the centre of the colony is 75% whereas it declines dramatically to 10% at the extreme edge. Feare calculates that 40% of egg predation is carried out by turnstones and assumes that the remainder are consumed by rats. Rats also prey on chicks whilst the scavenging activity of land crabs has an important impact. Chick mortality can arise as a result of pecking injuries and, to a lesser extent, starvation. Rain increases mortality, especially of pecked chicks. However Feare calculated overall chick mortality to be only in the region of 26%.

Sooty Terns breed in June during the period when the south-east trade winds blow and the seas around the Seychelles are at their most productive. The extreme synchrony exhibited may not be entirely due to seasonal food influences, but can also have a social significance, since both egg and chick survival were higher where eggs had been laid at approximately the same time as the surrounding eggs. Laying takes place in a "scrape", hence the importance of clear ground and suitable vegetation. Initially the terns will fly away at the least disturbance, however, as incubation progresses, aggressiveness increases so that, immediately prior to hatching, some adults repeatedly attack any approaching human. Incubation lasts for 28 days—a task shared by both parents, the incumbent often flying to sea to wet bill, belly or feet in order to keep the egg moist and cool. The hatchling experiences rapid growth in the first 30–35 days but this can be impeded by food shortages. Chicks are fed on fish and squid and are regularly given drinks, often by adults other than their own parents. This dependency on parental care lasts for a period of two months and, although juveniles have been observed flying to sea with their parents, adults were not seen feeding juveniles at sea. Incidentally many Sooty terns from the

Sooty tern chick. Bird Island. (Hill).

SEYCHELLES BIRDS: ABBREVIATED CHECK-LIST

LAND BIRDS OF THE CENTRAL SEYCHELLES

Endemic Species
Bare-legged Scops Owl	*Otus magicus insularis*
Seychelles White-Eye	*Zosterops modesta*
Blue Pigeon	*Alectroenas pulcherrima*
Seychelles Sunbird	*Nectarinia dussumieri*
Paradise Flycatcher	*Terpsiphone corvina*
Magpie Robin	*Copsychus sechellarum*
Seychelles Kestrel	*Falco araea*
Seychelles Brush Warbler	*Acrocephalus sechellensis*
Seychelles Fody	*Foudia sechellarum*
Seychelles Bulbul	*Ixos crassirostris*
Cave Swiftlet	*Collocalia francica elaphra*

Endemic subspecies
Seychelles Black Parrot	*Coracopsis nigra barklyi*
Seychelles Turtle Dove	*Streptopelia picturata rostrata*
Seychelles Moorhen	*Gallinula chloropus sechellarum*
Cattle Egret	*Bubulcus ibis sechellarum*
Green-Backed Heron	*Butroides striatus degens*

Introduced species
Madagascar Turtle Dove	*Streptopelia picturata picturata*
Barred Ground Dove	*Geopelia striata*
Indian Mynah	*Acridotheres tristis*
Madagascar Fody	*Foudia madagascariensis*
Common Waxbill	*Estrilda astrild*
Barn Owl	*Tyto alba affinis*
Chinese Bittern	*Ixobrychus sinensis*

SEABIRDS OF THE CENTRAL SEYCHELLES

Common Brown Noddy	*Anous stolidus*
Black (Lesser) Noddy	*Anous tenuirostris*
White-tailed Tropicbird	*Phaeton lepturus*
Red-tailed Tropicbird	*Phaeton rubricauda*
Red-footed Booby	*Sula sula*
Great Frigatebird	*Fregata minor*
Lesser Frigate	*Fregata ariel*
Sooty Tern	*Sterna fuscata*
Roseate Tern	*Sterna dougalli (arideensis)*
Fairy Tern	*Gygis alba*
Little Tern	*Sterna albifrons*
Bridled Tern	*Sterna anaethetus*
Crested Tern	*Thalasseus bergii*
Black-naped Tern	*Sterna sumatrana*
Lesser Crested Tern	*Thalasseus benghalensis*
Wedge-tailed Shearwater	*Puffinus pacificus*
Audubon's Shearwater	*Puffinus lherminieri*

FIGURE 11

MIGRANT SHOREBIRDS.

Shorebirds that have been recorded on the central Seychelles (after Feare and Watson 1984).

Charadrius hiaticula	Ringed Plover
Charadrius dubius	Little Ringed Plover
Charadrius alexandrinus	Kentish Plover
Charadrius mongolus	Lesser Sand-plover
Charadrius leschenaultii	Greater Sand-plover
Charadrius asiaticus	Caspian Sand-plover
Pluvialis dominica	Lesser Golden-plover
Pluvialis squatarola	Grey Plover
Arenaria interpres	Turnstone
Calidris minuta	Little Stint
Calidris ruficollis	
Calidris subminuta	
Calidris temminckii	Temnick's Stint
Calidris melanotos	Pectoral Sandpiper
Calidris ferruginea	Curlew Sandpiper
Calidris canutus	Knot
Calidris alba	Sanderling
Philomachus pugnax	Ruff
Tringa erythropus	Spotted Redshank
Tringa stagnatilis	Marsh Sandpiper
Tringa nebularia	Greenshank
Tringa ochropus	Green Sandpiper
Tringa glareola	Wood Sandpiper
Tringa hypoleucos	Common Sandpiper
Tringa brevipes	
Xenius cinereus	
Limmosa lapponica	Bar-tailed Godwit
Numenius arquata	Curlew
Numenius phaeopus	Whimbrel
Numenius minutus	
Gallinago media	Great Snipe
Gallinago gallinago	Snipe
Limnocryptes minimus	
Himantopus himantopus	Black-winged Stilt
Phaloropus lobatus	Red-necked Phalarope
Dromas ardeola	Crab Plover
Glareola maldivarum	Maldivian Pratincole
Plegadis falcinellus	Glossy Ibis
Aythya fuligula	Tufted Duck
Limosa limosa	Black-tailed Godwit
Burhinus oedicemus	Stone Curlew
Larus ridibundus	Black-headed Gull
Sterna hirundo	Common Tern
Clamator jacobinus	Cuckoo
Clandrella cinerea	
Phoenicurus phoenicurus	Redstart
Corvus albus	Pale Crow
Ciconia ciconia	White Stork

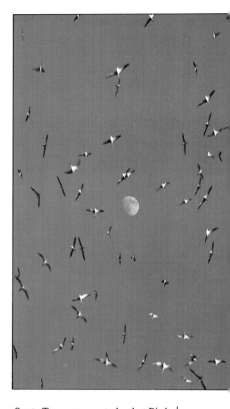

Sooty Terns prepare to land at Bird Island while a three-quarter moon has already risen. (Vine).

Bird Island colony feed between Silhouette and Mahe 80–100 Km to the south and can be easily observed from the deck of the inter-island launch, as they skim over the waves, frequently diving into the sea in pursuit of small squid or fish. Whilst fledgling birds are fed by their parents at their "nests", once young birds are capable of flying, the parents may feed them on the wing. This has been described by Feare who admired the Sooty terns antics at Bird Island; "*the adult bird flew above the juvenile while the latter gave the begging call. The adult then regurgitated food and passed it directly to the juvenile's bill beneath. In this way young birds could be fed at sea by their parents. This would be essential during the supposed period of juvenile dependence on the parents for food after leaving the colony.*"

MAMMALS.

The Seychelles Islands appear to be singularly devoid of mammals except for two endemic species of bat. This, in itself, is not remarkable since the break-up of Gondwanaland probably occurred early in the evolutionary history of land mammals. From our previous discussions on the difficulties associated with the colonisation of distant islands, we can also deduce that mammals are not particularly well-equipped for long sea-journeys. Man has been responsible for introducing a number of mammalian species, however, some of these 'aliens' are the source of very severe ecological problems.

Endemic mammals

Bats

Bats are found on most of the central Seychelles, with the exception of some of the outlying coralline cays such as Bird, Denis, Platte and Coetivy: they also occur on the atolls of the Aldabra group.

Seychelles Fruit Bat (*Pteropus seychellensis seychellensis*).

The Seychelles fruit bat, common throughout the central granitic Seychelles, belongs to a genus which extends from the South Pacific through Australasia and South East Asia to the islands of the Indian Ocean, but has never been located on the African mainland. Having a decided preference for tall trees such as Casuarina and Albizzia as roosting sites, the bats usually occupy two different sets of roosts: one from May to October in the south-east trade winds and the other from November to April in the Morth-West Monsoon (Racey and Nicoll 1984).

For most of the day, the fruit bat hangs upside down from one foot, wings tightly wrapped around the curled body. But these can be noisy creatures, and in addition to several variants of screech-like calls, they produce loud clapping sounds by the rapid beating of outstretched wings over the head in an attempt to frighten off intruders in territorial disputes. Scent plays an important role in the social life of the fruit bat. Recognition between individuals is apparently achieved through olfactory signals and the wing rubbing that takes place in grooming sessions may distribute scent over the wings. Racey and Nicoll (1984) point out that males scent-mark their usual hanging places by rubbing necks, equipped with special odour producing glands, against the chosen spot and sometines also against their females and sites on the territory boundary.

The female Seychelles fruit bat usually gives birth in late November and December. In the ensuing period most adults are organised into family groups of one adult female and male with a dependent juvenile. By April, the bats have moved to the roosts they favour during the south-east trades, the young forming large aggregations in the centre of the roost and the remaining bats in adult groups established and policed by the males. Some individuals occasionally hang on the edge of the roost by themselves.

The diet of the Seychelles fruit bat is composed mainly of soft, sweet fruits, such as jackfruit, fig, breadfruit, chinese guava, mango and cashew fruit. Nectar is also a significant source of nutrition. Racey and Nicoll in 1977 estimated the number of fruit bats on Praslin as somewhere in the region of 2,000 to 2,500 and on Mahe, 2,500 in 1979. They admit however, that this is probably a substantial underestimate and there may be as many as 10,000 bats on this island. The conclusion is reached that the cropping of fruit bats in order to supply restaurants with the essential ingredient for bat curry; the felling of roosting trees; and the possibility that control measures may be taken if bats become an increased threat to fruit growers; may combine to endanger "the viability of these vulnerable island populations of fruit bats".

Seychelles Fruit Bat in flight. Botanic Gardens, Mahe. (Vine).

Sheath-tailed Bat (*Coleura seychellensis*)

This less conspicuous species of the endemic Mammalia is a small insectivorous, cave-roosting form belonging to a genus found only in Africa. Originally very common on Mahe (Wright 1868), and also found on Praslin and Silhouette, the latter harbouring a smaller subspecies *C. seychellensis silhouettae*, this bat is now extremely rare. Racey and Nicoll report that, having spent 300 hours searching caves on Mahe, Praslin and La Digue, this intensive effort produced only two boulder caves occupied by *C. seychellensis*, "*one on Praslin in which the numbers of bats rose gradually over the years of study to* 12, *and one on La Digue in which a maximum of four bats were seen.*" They surmise that the reasons for the population decline, although unclear, may be loss of indigenous forest, increased human disturbance of caves and their occupancy by barn owls.

Indigenous Aquatic Mammals

Sightings of large marine mammals, considered by Stoddart (1972) to refer to seals, have been recorded from Denis and Bird, on the northern edge of the Seychelles Bank. Dugongs have been observed more recently off Aldabra. Whales, mostly sperm whales, were regularly caught near Bird and Denis and processed at a whaling station on Ste Anne. Sperm whales have beached in Beau Vallon Bay, and beaked whales on Bird and Denis in recent years. In fact, whales are still frequently sighted south or west of the Seychelles Bank.

Racey and Nicoll (1984) report that "*an aerial survey was conducted by a radial-line transect within a 200 mile radius of Mahe between mid-April and mid-July 1980 by R.W. Keller, N. Von Swelm and J. Mc Devitt. Over 50 sperm whales were observed, including several calves, indicating that this area may be a breeding and calving ground for this species. Several goose-beaked whales and False killer whales were also recorded. Over 400 Bottle-nosed dolphins and over 100 Rizzo's dolphin were observed, together with several rough-toothed dolphins which is often associated with Rizzo's. Several spotted dolphins were also seen.*"

Introduced Mammals.

The Tenrec (*Tenrec ecaudatus*)

"*Ancestral tenrecs arrived in Madagascar by rafting, or across a land bridge, and have radiated to fill a variety of terrestrial, semi-aquatic and semi-arboreal niches.*" (Eisenberg & Gould 1970). Tenrec, however, is the only genus to have been introduced in any significant manner to other Indian Ocean islands and is found on the Comores, Mauritius and Reunion, and on Mahe and Praslin in the Seychelles. *Tenrec ecaudatus*, brown in colour and equipped with soft hairs interspersed with spines, is the largest member of the Tenrecidae and was probably introduced to the Seychelles, about 1880, from Reunion as a source of food. Quickly establishing itself, this nocturnal creature is now found up to cloud forest elevation, although uncommon on sandy lowland plateaux. Rarely consumed in present day Seychelles, they are now of nuisance value only as they seriously damage seedlings whilst digging for food. In the section on Reptiles and Amphibia we mentioned that Tenrecs prey on lizards, snakes and caecilians, however their diet is mainly composed of discarded fruit, and invertebrates found in leaf litter. Young Tenrecs are themselves eaten by Barn Owls, but adults, equipped with long canine teeth and powerful jaws, are killed predominantly by dogs and Man. In the Seychelles, the Tenrec aestivates in burrows for part of the year, (approx. Feb. to August) and insemination takes place on arousal, most births occurring from October to December. Large litters are common, foraging family groups often comprising 19 young and two adults.

Rats and Mice. (*Rattus rattus L.* and *Mus musculus L.*)

Rats were most likely introduced into the Seychelles in the late eighteenth century and are now common in a variety of habitats, including intermediate forest and eroded hillsides as well as coastal plateaux, on all the central islands except Cousin, Cousine, Frigate and Aride.

We have already mentioned the effect of rat predation on birds, eggs and chicks, both land and sea; on turtle hatchlings, geckos and snakes; but rats also eat fruit, especially tomatoes, pineapples and coconuts, causing a considerable amount of damage in the process. Barn Owls were introduced into the Seychelles in 1949 in a well-meaning attempt to control rats, however the operation backfired since Barn Owls, for various reasons, were generally ineffective, and eventually ended up with a bounty on their heads because they had begun to prey with devastating effects on more vulnerable species, such as Fairy Terns.

Mice are common on Frigate and Aride, but also occur on Mahe Praslin, Bird and Farquhar.

Hares and Rabbits

Cousin island plays host to only one mammal, *Lepus nigrocollis*, a shy noctunal hare native of Southern India and Ceylon, probably introduced in the 1920's or 1930's Rabbits probably *Oryctolagus cuniculus* are found on a number of islands including Praslin of the granitic group, but they are also bred in captivity as a food source on Mahe and Praslin.

Cats and Dogs

Feral cats are frequently seen feeding at night by the roadside on

Praslin and Mahe. Tenrecs, rats, mice, lizards and birds form a major part of their diet. The introduction of cats can have serious consequences for the bird population—they have been associated with the decline and extinction of the Seychelles Magpie Robin on a number of islands. Despite the large number of dogs present on Mahe (about 40,000) very few could be said to be feral, although they have a significant impact on Tenrec populations.

Ungulates

Pigs play a major role in the native households of the central Seychelles. Dairy cows, fed on sugar cane, are becoming more important also, but domestic goats are less common and horses and donkeys are only seen occasionally. The only remaining evidence of Rusa deer, once introduced to Silhouette, Frigate and probably Cerf, are the antlers used as decorative features in some houses.

Seychelles Fruit Bats (*Pteropus seychellensis seychellensis*) roost in a tree at the Botanic Gardens on Mahe. (Vine).

TRADITIONS

Despite its relatively short history, Seychelles has inherited a unique combination of ethnic affinities, moulding them into a characteristic culture clearly recognisable today. as Seychellois. What of the ingredients in this fascinating pot pourri of traditions? By sheer force of numbers the influence of Africa dominates. Among the haunting beat of heated goatskin drums, so enthusiastically played at the "Moutia", one can hardly fail to appreciate the African tribal heritage of this music. The singing however is in Creole, a language derived from an oral interpretation of French as it sounded to Africans deprived of their own cultures and frequently seeking to bridge the gap between different tribal tongues. French based, with African and Malagasy elements, and partly Bantu in structure, Creole was regarded, during Seychelles colonial period, as an inferior language, banned in school classrooms. Today however Creole is a highly respected speech form and the lingua franca of Seychelles. It has proved itself to be a most versatile language and one which has recently been stimulated by production of literature, education texts, plays and many songs. To the visitor, Creole is a fascinating language and one which, as result of its similarities with French, is not too difficult to learn.

The Afro-French flavour of Seychelles has been maintained in other areas, as we shall discuss below. Early voluntary settlers in Seychelles, were primarily French and they brought with them customs and traditions of their native-land. Aspects of eighteenth century France are preserved in the 'serenade' sometimes performed at wedding ceremonies and up to recently the 'Levee de Chambre' in which parents of the newly-weds visit the couple on the day after the wedding, ostensibly to confirm the bride's purity, but in practice, to extend the celebrations by consuming a special cake and generally wishing the couple well. The widely popular 'contredanse' also has French origins and is reported to have been a regular feature of Louis XIV's court. Apart from language and musical heritage, the French brought Catholicism to Seychelles and it has remained the country's dominant religion to this day. Perhaps the most significant French contribution to the creation of the nation however has been genetic since, from earliest times, they intermarried with Africans and Asians living on the islands, thus contributing to the appealing racial blend we describe today as Seychellois.

A third influence in the Seychelles pot-pourri is Asian, in the form of Indian and Chinese culture and traditions. The Indians were among the first to come to Seychelles, and there is some evidence that their knowledge of the islands pre-dates that of Europeans (a concept many find hard to stomach, but which sheer logic dictates is most likely correct). Maldivians certainly recognised the Coco de Mer nut long

Opposite above
A Katyolo being paddled through shallow-water along the shore-line of La Digue. (Vine).

Opposite below
A beach seine net stowed aboard a pirogue on Beauvallon beach, Mahe. (Vine).

145

A collection of aberrant Coco de Mer nuts from the National Museum, Victoria. (Vine).

Seychellois lady in singing mood. (Vine).

before westerners came to Seychelles: it was a highly prized commodity believed to possess special healing powers. This was one of the enticing aspects of the islands, encouraging some of the first Asians to settle here, while for others it was a natural staging post between Africa and India and thus an ideal location for establishing trading companies. Whatever their individual reasons for settling in Seychelles, the Asian community, comprising Hindus from Tranquebar and Mayavaram (the Chetty's and Pillay's); Muslims from Kerala; Parsee merchants (Temooljee) and Chinese (Ahoy from Saakive in Canton) tended to preserve their separate identities and genetic integrity whilst dispersing other riches, in particular culinary skills and knowledge of exotic spices, greatly enhancing Seychellois cuisine.

Thus, the traditions of Seychelles, whose roots lie on the continents of Europe, Africa and Asia, have blossomed and borne fruit only among these islands where conditions differed, even from other western Indian Ocean territories, such as Mauritius, similarly occupied by French emigrants and African slaves. It is perhaps worth commenting that whilst the British maintained the longest period of colonial rule in Seychelles, her impact on the country's cultural heritage is so small as to almost defy measurement! That is not to say that the impact of Britain's presence was not felt, but once her administrative machinery was dismantled and Seychelles gained its independence, from a cultural viewpoint it seemed as if the hundred and sixty or so years of Crown Colony status had been nothing but an ephemeral dream whose plot, upon awakening, eludes recollection.

The slaves landed in Seychelles in the second half of the eighteenth century were brought to work the land. It was through their sweat, tears and unknown suffering that the dense, ancient jungles were cleared and planted with coconuts, cinnamon, sugar, tobacco, cotton, and other crops. Despite an enforced submission, and the erosion of tribal identities, they continued to treasure one of the only things left in their possession; something which not even their captors could eradicate: their cultural heritage, expressed through music and dance. When the day's forced labour was completed, and the slaves were left in peace to rest, they often gathered around an open fire, in a jungle clearing, as far from their 'masters' as they were able to go, and the rhythmic drum beat joined the night chorus, enjoining the secret revellers to abandon their worries and dance. A pliable framework made from the local hibiscus shrub, formed the framework of that most soulful of instruments, the Var. A long strip, about two inches wide was nailed into a circular rim over which they stretched a piece of cow hide. Drum sticks were made from a hard wood, carved into a sphere at one end, and sometimes covered in hide. Before creating haunting rhythms, they warmed the drums over the fire, and, when all was ready, began the beat.

To the uninitiated observer, it would have seemed at first as if the participants were not particularly interested in dancing, gaining sufficient release from the romantic timbre of the drums. As the beat gained confidence two men, stimulated by sugar-cane "bacca" or coconut palm derived "calou", would rise from the floor and enter the ring. While one of them cupped his hands and starts the music with a high pitched cry of "Ehhhhh, eh, eh," the other began to recite the words of a song. Frequently these would be composed by the singer, and might relate happenings within their group, or be derived directly from older

Traditionally clad women dance at an impromptu Moutia-style celebration on beach of S. Mahe. (Vine).

Gris gris, or witchcraft, has more or less died out in Seychelles but beneath a veneer of modernity, there remains a deep-seated tradition of superstitions. Seychellois witchcraft was brought from Africa by slaves of early French settlers and by Africans released from slave-boats. The tools of this mysterious voodoo consisted of various charms, amulets, and supposedly magical powders. Seychellois "witch-doctors" or "Bonhomme-du-Bois" were widely credited with miraculous powers of healing as well as, on some occasions, the power of creating trouble or even death. (Vine).

tunes, brought from the African homelands. As time passed however, more and more of the songs had their roots in Seychelles, inspired by the everyday lives of the enslaved workers. The male duet continued their performance with one repeating in song what the other recited. Often, songs were composed right there, in the midst of the circle, illuminated by the rising flames of a wood fire, among the dancing shadows of surrounding coconut trees. Finally, when the music was ready, the two men, totally engrossed in their chant, swayed towards their seated womenfolk, arms extended in a universal sign, beckoning them to join the dance. Their invitations, vocalised in a guttural tongue, clicking and chanting derived from their native languages, were met by an immediate response from all the seated men who

The "Evil Eye" will be cast on any trespassers on this privately owned plantation on South Mahe. (Vine).

Opposite
Christianity has been a powerful and guiding influence in Seychelles whose inhabitants are predominantly Roman Catholic. (Vine).

jumped to their feet, enjoining the women to dance. When the women eventually rose, the dance approached its climax and partners displayed their fine sense of rhythm in swinging provocative movements calculated to arouse while avoiding any physical contact. By now, the song seemed to have gained a momentum all of its own, driven on the still night air by the beat of the drums and the abandoned revelry of the dancers. The earlier pattern of repetition had been replaced by all the men chanting a phrase, followed by the higher pitched response of the women. As the song progressed, chants rose in tone and dancing became increasingly expressive, despite the fact that from the waist-up the men hardly moved their bodies, concentrating nearly all the action on rolling hips and in shuffling feet. Women often lifted up full skirts so as to display their legs, and to have greater freedom of movement. Suddenly the drum beat ceased, the dance was over, and everyone returned to their seats, while the fire was rekindled and preparations commenced for a new song.

The "Moutia", as this dance was called, has survived to this day in Seychelles, particularly on the outer islands: a strongly guarded Seychellois tradition. It remains a very personal, participatory celebration, rarely observed by total strangers. A looser version of the "Moutia" can however be seen throughout Seychelles, particularly on public holidays, when Seychellois families visit the beach to picnic and swim. Among shaded Takamaka or Coconut groves the local people enjoy an opportunity to relax and recall their valued traditions by music and dance in the "moutia" style, if not in its pure form.

I am indebted to Guy Lionnet, a longtime student of all things Seychellois, who has recently published the words of a Moutia song with French translation. This particular song, describing the indignation of a jealous husband, is reproduced below in both Creole and French.

Among the traditions of Seychelles, the role of superstitions in people's lives deserves comment. Tribal customs in Africa during the eighteenth and nineteenth centuries were at their height, frequently focussing on a fear of and respect for supernatural forces. Slaves brought to Seychelles carried these fears and superstitions with them and, however hard the missionaries tried, they were unable to stamp out what they regarded as "black-magic", but what might better have been regarded as an integral part of the cultural heritage of these displaced Africans. Many of their beliefs resulted in harmless practices designed to ward off 'evil spirits' and to protect suppliants from the 'evil eye'. Whatever one may think of such practices, the reality of people's fears cannot be doubted, and if possession of a talisman left the wearer with a feeling of protection from hidden forces, otherwise beyond his or her control, then what harm was done? Of course, the charms or 'grisgris' were not always aimed at guarding the individual himself from the unknown, but could also be directed against enemies. Witch doctors, locally known as 'Bonhommes' or 'Bonnefemmes du bois' played a pivotal role in the 'black-magic' scenario. The most famous of these was probably Charles Zialor ('Dialor') who lived to the grand old age of ninety two years old, dying in 1962, and leaving behind him a legendary reputation as a herbalist cum psycho-therapist par excellence. To the insensitive observer however, Dialor was simply

LAPLI PA TI A PE TONBE

Ou a la la ou a la la
Mon madanm ou dir mwan
Ou al lave larivyer
Ler mon vin larivyer mon vin bengnen
Mon war ou bake lo ros larivyer (2 fwa)
Be sa zour lapli pa ti tonbe ni nanryen
Be si lapli sa zour ti tonbe
Mon ti a mazinen ou n al kasyet lapli
Mon fanm si ou pa kite piten
Mwan mon a fer ou dimal
Ou lae lay lae ole lae lay lae-e-
Mon manman pa ti fer mwan mizer
Ae ee lala la la la la
Pa bat mwan ou a fer mwan dimal
Aa mon fanm
Si ou pa kite piten mon a bat ou
    mon a touy ou
Ae ee alae le le le le
Aa a oo mon vin bengnen larivyer
Mon war ou bake lo ros
Ole lele ley le la aa aa...

IL NE PLEUVAIT PAS

Ou a la la ou a la la
Ma femme vous me dites
Que vous allez fair la lessive a la riviere
Lorsque je me suis rendu a la riviere pour me baigner
Je n'ai vu que votre baquet sur la roche a laver (bis)
Mais ce jour il n'y avait ni pluie ni rien
Si la pluie etait tombee ce jour-la
J'aurais compris que vous vous etiez garee
Ma femme si vous ne cessez de faire la putain
Je vous ferai du mal
Ou lae lay lae ole lae lay lae-e
Ma maman ne m'a jamais fait de mal
Ae ee lala la la la la
Ne me battez pas vous me ferez mal
Ah ah ma femme
Si vous ne cessez de faire la putain, je vous nattrai,
    je vous tuerai
Ae ee alae le le le le
Aa a oo je viens me baigner a la riviere
Je vois votre baquet sur la roche
Ole lele ley le la aa aa....

Procession for Feast of the Assumption during August 1987 at the Catholic Cathedral in Victoria. (Vine).

a witch doctor and, as such, his activities were banned by an Ordinance of 1958. Strangely enough, just as Man has almost succeeded in eradicating all indigenous knowledge or memory of such unconventional practices, He is also recognising that tropical plants synthesise a host of valuable medicinal drugs, and that ancient herbal remedies were often based upon biochemically proven properties of the plants utilised by "witch doctors". This remains a topic worthy of investigation in Seychelles.

Cultural activity in Seychelles is not of the artificially created variety predominant in western societies, where the individual travels to a gallery, theatre or concert hall to experience the arts. In Seychelles there is a strong, people-centred, oral tradition from which different facets are plucked by interested observers as examples of Seychellois heritage. Even this process tends to break down the reality into discordant components, no longer meshed into an entire experience and lacking the same impact it holds in its natural setting. Thus, the real atmosphere of Seychelles evades description or recognition unless one actually visits the islands, escapes from the tourist facilities, and absorbs Seychelles life, learning at first hand the fascinating language and unique traditions. It is a most rewarding experience and one which has captivated many who have made the effort.

Surrounded by ocean, it is not surprising that the sea has played a central role in the lives of Seychellois and holds a key place in its traditional heritage. The maritime instincts of local people arise from a combination of ancestral background, upbringing, and sheer necessity. While many of the early European settlers were accomplished seamen and boat-builders, Africans, landing there as slaves, had little if any knowledge of the sea or of the skills necessary to survive in a marine dominated environment. Boatmanship became a virtual 'sine

qua non' for existing on Seychelles, for communicating with the outside world, or for moving between islands of the group, and there was a high priority on good boat-building and general seamanship. Knowledge of craft design derived from several quarters, with some Malagasy natives imparting their knowledge of small canoe/boat design and French carpenters fearlessly tackling construction of quite large boats. In the early days of the colony's administration by the French, pirogues were brought from Mauritius for use in Seychelles, establishing this particular craft as the most popular small boat for use in coastal waters among the islands; a role which it held until it was recently ousted by fibreglass outboard-powered craft, some of which are actually based upon the pirogue design. The availability of plenty of hard wood, suitable for boat construction, on the granitic islands led to the establishment of several ship-building ventures including that owned by Messrs Crook and Naz on Mahe who used to keep a quarter share of the vessels they constructed; one eighth to Thomas Crook and one eighth for Jean Baptiste Naz. In 1834 for example they built the 285 ton Barque "Lancier" with an overall length of 97 feet 2 inches which was unfortunately wrecked off western Australia in 1839. In view of the brief history of settlement in Seychelles, it is almost inevitable that their boats should have been based upon well established designs imported from other countries. While this is fundamentally true, the physical isolation of Seychelles, together with its unique social, economic and environmental conditions have in fact led to an array of craft which may be characterised today as Seychellois.

The first such boat, already mentioned, is the pirogue (Creole: Pirog) whose origins are widely assumed to have been the African dug-out canoe. The Seychelles pirogue was traditionally constructed in three

sections: first each end was hewn from solid tree trunks, and finally the centre section, carved from two pieces of wood, was added with copper strips nailed over the joints. Whilst their length varied considerably, from about 5 metres to as much as 12 metres, the basic shape, with its pronounced sheer and uplifted ends remained constant. Nearly always tarred or painted black with white weatherboards, their exquisite lines bespeak a long period of evolution based upon trial and error. As work-boats they are magnificent craft, ideal for launching off sandy beaches and rowing through surf. As one who is used to seeing the traditional curraghs off the west coast of Ireland, whose origins are also lost in time, I cannot help comparing their lines. Is this an example of convergent evolution, arriving at similar solutions in response to the same design problems, or is it possible that both craft are the result of an early Arabian influence upon coastal communities of both East Africa and the west of Ireland? There are good reasons to believe the latter may in fact be the case. Be that as it may, the Seychelles pirogue remains an exquisitely formed craft, whose confident curves belie it's ancient, some would say primitive, origins. Sadly, these boats are not being built any more, although there are still many in existence, some used for fishing, often as a means of towing a beach seine-net around schools of mackerel or sardines. As a symbol of Seychelles life and traditions the pirogue, pulled up under the shade of Takamaka trees just above high-tide mark, evokes an image with few equals.

The Katyolo (or Catiolo) is similar in shape to the pirogue, with narrow beam, pronounced sheer and long raised curved ends. They are small, shallow draft boats, only about four metres in length, with a one metre beam with the flat bottom formed from three wide boards joined together by rebated battens. The sides are of clinker construction and they are built throughout using local Takamaka, including grown frames. Inside, the undecked craft there are two thwarts with benches

Arrival of a fishing boat ashore is always cause for excitement and a gathering of Seychellois who retain a love of sea-foods and a fascination with the sea. (Vine).

at each end and a very small shelf at the bows for placing the anchoring stone. Unlike the pirogues, the katyola is traditionally brightly painted, often blue with a red gunwhale, and is still in use today throughout the islands.

A craft which derives its origins directly from early Seychelles history is the 'Welbot' known in French as the 'Ballinier' or, more familiarly in English as the 'Whaler'. There is little doubt that this local craft is based directly upon the English whaling craft of bygone days, the original design of which was almost certainly of Norse origin. Approximately nine metres long, with a three to four metre beam, they are today powered by 30 hp diesel inboard engines and used for bottom line fishing. They still carry mast and sails and offer their crews the additional comfort of make-shift sleeping quarters beneath fore and aft decks.

Seychelles 'Schooners' (Fr. Goelette) differ from the internationally recognised, large double masted sailing craft of that name. Here they are smaller, generally about twelve metres long, of carvel construction, with a single mast, and invariably powered by an inboard diesel engine of about 30 horse power. The main craft used for fishing local waters, they carry five or six hands, generally on five or six day trips. Their origins seem to be derived from inshore craft of Brittany or Cornwall.

The larger, clipper bowed, counter stern, two masted motor-sailers one sees at Victoria harbour, or alongside harbour walls on other islands, are true schooners with their main mast taller than the foremast. These elegant craft are used as general cargo trading vessels and as ferries between offshore islands of the group. They are about eighteen metres long, round bilged, carvel constructed using local Takamaka, an ideal material for boat construction. Frequently they undertake round trips in excess of a thousand kilometers, all within the Seychelles EEZ. A trip to Aldabra for example, from Mahe, would be 880 nautical miles in each direction: a major sea journey by any standards, but one regularly plied by these sea-worthy, locally built vessels. No longer reliant entirely on wind, they are powered by diesel engines, generally of 180 horse power, and can carry around 40 tons of cargo plus 55 passengers.

Among the traditional, artisanal hand-crafts of Seychelles, mention must be made (somewhat reluctantly in my case), of the caret, or tortoise-shell industry. Despite its name, tortoise-shell comes not from tortoises, but from Hawksbill turtles, a species whose very survival is now at risk following centuries of slaughter for its ornamental carapace scutes. Despite one's horror at this carnage, it must be stated that Seychelles craftsmen have become truly adept at carving a wide range of items from hawksbill turtle shells, including lady's combs, cigarette cases, mirror surrounds, and a whole host of other items. This activity is a deeply rooted tradition of Seychelles, and one which has been difficult to bring to an end. Today however, there are strict controls in force regarding protection of Hawksbill turtles, and it is to be hoped that the general public will cease to purchase "tortoise-shell" items, thus ending the pressure upon what little remains of the region's Hawksbill population.

Not all of Seychelles' craft industry is based upon tortoise-shell however, and considerable use has been made of other natural resources, in particular the wide range of woods available in the country. Since the days of first settlement, Seychellois have been acutely aware

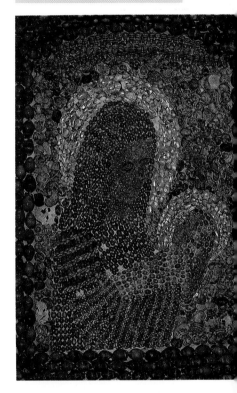

A unique sea-shell mosaic in church at Frigate Island. (Vine).

Construction of scale model craft at La Marine, La Plaine, Mahe. (Harrison).

The corner of Independence Avenue in Victoria is the traditional site for displaying local handcrafts. (Vine).

of the various types of wood grown on the islands and their individual qualities. Today that knowledge is being put to good use in a number of projects creating original furniture, models, toys and other items in natural wood. A major contributor to the Seychelles craft scene has been "4 Degrees South", a design studio and workshop situated at Mont Fleuri. I met there with its coordinator, Jim Warren who is also the artist behind many of the excellent designs created by the workshop. Primary functions of the project are to improve the standards of local handcrafts; expand the production of wood and textile objects to meet local demand; and create an export market for high quality, locally made products. The project's boutique in Camion Hall, Victoria provides a most impressive display of work, all fashioned from local woods. Among the items one may see there, are beautifully carved replica pirogues and miniature thatch cottages in the local style. Another extremely impressive woodwork project is that of 'La Marine', operated by its owner Christine Dias, and situated towards the south of Mahe, at Le Cap. Christine obtains full-scale detailed plans of French wooden sailing craft from the Naval Museum in Paris, and then scales down the plans to produce magnificent, intricate replicas. The work in each model is meticulous and time-consuming with at least a hundred and eighty hours spent to build a fine model of La Marie-Jeanne, a Breton coastal sailing boat of 1908, to ten times that long for the stately French Frigate standing in the centre of her display room, patiently awaiting a purchaser.

Afro-French-Asian influences have combined to create the unassailable art of Seychellois traditional cuisine. Any visitor to Seychelles who fails to sample good, home-style Creole cooking is missing one of the most appealing aspects of these exotic islands, for here one has an opportunity to enjoy the true riches of a tropical paradise where deli-

cious fruits, succulent vegetables, and a mouth-watering array of fresh sea-foods jostle each other for pride of place in a host of delectable dishes. Creole cuisine is, exactly what is says: the ingredients and recipes created by the Creole residents of Seychelles during its quarter millenium of occupied history. In the Creole household the kitchen generally consisted of an outside cooking area where a wood fire or charcoal cooker provided the heat and the old round black cast-iron pot or 'Marmit' held pride of place as a treasured multi-functional utensil, especially for cooking curries or roasts as well as roasting coffee. Other vital pieces of equipment included the pestel and mortar for grinding spices; halves of coco de mer known as 'cocossiers' used as general purpose containers; and the tin coffee pot and filter. While the older Seychellois retain a lingering nostalgia for the unique qualities imparted by their somewhat rustic assemblage of kitchen-ware, the real secret of Creole cooking however lies in the ingredients used, and particularly in the local knowledge of herbs and spices such as thyme, basil chives and mint, parsley, garlic, ginger, tamarind, cotomili, aniseed, peppercorns and allspice. In addition to these, a wide range of aromatic spices are used, including cinnamon, cloves, chilli, nutmeg, turmeric, and vanilla. While the European housewife is already famil-iar with some of these spices, she lacks the advantages of the Seychel-lois for whom they are all locally available as fresh produce.

One of the aspects of Seychelles which will remain vividly in mind, long after the islands' dramatic beaches and majestic mountains have faded from detailed recollection, will be the profusion of it's naturally growing spices. On one of my visits to Praslin my guide, Therese LaBlache, pulled up her redoubtable Miniminor half-way along the road leading over the Vallee de Mai. Opening the driver's side door she leant down and scraped her hand through the dead leaves underneath

Scale model of eighteenth century French Frigate at La Marine work-shop and display room on Mahe. (Vine).

Detail from a scale model con-structed by La Marine. (Harrison).

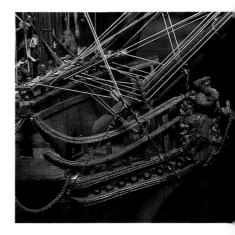

One of the national pastimes for relaxation in Seychelles is dominoes. (Harrison).

A gentle lesson in arithmetic is delivered by purchaser at Victoria's fruit market. (Vine).

The appealing eyes of Seychelles youth, and a free advertisement for Seybrew's soft drinks division! (Vine).

Street cobbler in Victoria. (Vine).

Traditional style snack-shop in Victoria. (Vine).

These two young Seychellois children were caught in the act of lighting a fire underneath their house! Silhouette Island. (Vine).

Two Seychellois girls on beach at Mahe. (Vine).

Market Street is one of the main shopping streets of Victoria, and leads past the Selwyn Clark Market. (Vine).

a tall, mature tree. I had no idea what she was doing until, raising herself back into a driving position, she displayed her catch, a fist-full of ripe deep purple cloves! Therese explained gleefully that there was no need to purchase such spices in Seychelles when they were so freely available and, for the first time, I truly appreciated the delight of collecting one's culinary requirements in nature's own spice-garden! One of the best places to observe local spice-growing is on industrious La Digue, where a wide range of plants are grown in well laid-out plots, and where some of the best vanilla in the world is cultivated!

Creole cooking, like any other national cuisine, has resulted in a some special delicacies such as Tec-Tec and Fish Head Soups; Shark Chutney; Grilled Kingfish; Palmist Salad; Breadfruit and Salted Fish Stew; or Murex Salad. Several of their dishes, such as turtle steaks and fruit bat curry pose problems however for the conservation minded! Whereas bird's egg curry may also alarm nature-lovers, reference to details of experiments carried out on Sooty Tern colonies given on page 136 may help to reassure the reader that carefully managed cropping of Sooty tern eggs is possible without damage to breeding populations. An excellent review of Creole recipes, helping to bring about a revival of this traditional cuisine, has recently been produced by a group of Seychellois chefs, helped and encouraged by the Seychelles Hotel and Tourism Training School. Their book is available in Seychelles bookshops. My personal favourite is tec-tec soup, a recipe for which is given on page 160.

RECIPE FOR TEC-TEC SOUP—CREOLE STYLE.

First stage: Join the ladies collecting Tec-tec at low-tide on one of Mahe's good surf beaches or anywhere else where these tiny bivalves are found. If circumstances should prevent one from such an enjoyable experience, any small, locally abundant intertidal Tellin clam will do, even those found around the shores of Europe!

Ingredients: One Kg of Tec-tec in their shells
1.2 Kg of shelled Tec-tec
100 grms onions
20 grms garlic
10 grms ginger
1 dl oil
50 grms rice
salt, pepper and parsley to taste
3.5 Litres water.

First prepare the vegetables by peeling, washing and slicing onions; chopping parsley; grinding ginger and garlic; and washing the rice. Next soak the Tec-tecs in clean water (ideally sea-water), rinsing them thoroughly. Heat the oil in a saucepan and add chopped onions, frying gently before adding the Tec-tecs, both shelled and unshelled. Now pour in 3 litres of cold water and add rice together with ground ginger and garlic. Sprinkle a light seasoning of salt and pepper into the pan then place a lid on the pot and simmer for about twenty minutes. Serve hot with a sprinkle of chopped parsley.

Sheikh Mohammed Mosque in Victoria serves the Moslem community of Seychelles. (Vine).

Island architecture is still a highly visible traditional aspect of Seychelles life. Here the hand of fate has played its part and, so far at least, the landscape has been saved from the characterless concrete boxes spoiling so many towns, villages and rural scenes in other countries. In Seychelles the family house, whether it is a modest agrarian 'shack' or a much more grandiose old plantation property, possesses its own style and a sense of innate dignity. Whereas early settlers roofed their homes with indigenous palm-thatch, today the corrugated roof has taken over but the elegant shape of the old structures has been miraculously well preserved. Whatever the financial status of its occupants, one can be sure that the Seychellois house will be clean and well kept inside, and its often luxurious gardens will compliment the building, lending a colourful personal touch to the surroundings. One of the most used parts of the house is the verandah where the family often gathers in the early evening for conversation, supper and perhaps a game of cards or dominoes. Whilst housing standards are now being improved, replacing in some cases the quaint traditional over-crowded and inadequately constructed unhealthy dwellings, which tourists often admire for their ethnicity, the sense of design and love for nature has not left the Seychellois, and in many cases the older-style houses are being improved without destroying their pleasing aesthetic qualities.

Traditional style house on La Digue. (Vine).

Traditional planter's house on Mahe. (Vine).

161

Traditions in Seychelles continue to play an important role in people's lives; whether in the way they dress; the manner of their social behaviour; the form of their houses; or in their cultural celebrations. For a nation which has had little more than two hundred years to accrue a style and identity of its own, it's people have made a strong impact, drawing upon varied backgrounds and merging together in a process of natural integration, creating a new society which has spawned its own set of values and customs: the true heritage of Seychelles.

Opposite above
Interior of Catholic Church at Anse Royale. (Vine).

Opposite below
Sport plays an important part in local life. The Seychelles basketball team receives daily training in the grounds adjacent to State House entrance in Victoria. (Vine).

Queen Victoria Clock still functions and no longer chimes twice. (Vine).

162

ART AND ARTISTS

Seychelles has inspired artists, poets and writers ever since Man first discovered these exotic tropical islands. Today a young and vibrant artistic community is actively engaged in creation of original work, depicting various aspects of island-life, including the impact of political and social change. While several very fine artists have settled in Seychelles, and, by their presence, have helped to stimulate a local interest in art, there is also a growing band of Seychellois who have a unique insight and powerful message to communicate in their work. The abundance of nature, particularly the fascinating interplay between luxuriant exotic vegetation and local inhabitants, is a constant source of inspiration. As artists like Gerard Devoud or Christine Harter vividly portray, traditional Seychellois live so close to nature that they merge into the environment, gracefully moving across the vivid multi-hued canvas of real— life. Their images, like those of many other Seychellois artists, evoke a deep appreciation of Seychelles and, perhaps, an increased awareness regarding the value of traditions and a better understanding for the importance of conservation.

Many Seychellois are descendants of Africans, forcibly brought to the islands by late eighteenth and nineteenth century slave-traders. Their lives have passed through periods of turmoil, through experiences of extreme poverty, and through the illusionary process of liberation, only to discover that options for self-help were severely limited. Other Seychellois are descendants of voluntary settlers whose efforts to create new homes were met by continuous challenges and difficulties. A bond, created by mutual efforts to improve their lives, links all Seychellois and their brief, but eventful, history provides an inevitable and important theme for artistic expression.

Some artists draw upon the more immediate subject of Seychelles revolutionary struggle, portraying the popular aspirations for liberty, equality and fraternity, cornerstones of the contemporary political process. Some look also to the international arena and the worldwide struggle against discrimination based on creed, colour or race. Indeed, Seychellois have a vital message to communicate in this sphere, since they have existed, for many years, as a well integrated muti-racial community in which colour or race has no bearing upon rights or social status.

Art in Seychelles has total freedom of expression and is encouraged by the Government through education, training and patronage of Seychellois artists. A central figure in this process is Leon Radegonde, himself an accomplished artist, and Director of the Department of Culture at the Ministry of Education and Information, and chairman of the Seychelles Artist's Association. Leon's acrylic/water colour collages mirror his daily environment: "*the walls of old houses, decorated with photographs from newspapers, weathered roads with changing colours, rusty metal on huts or picturesque Creole houses, street graffiti, small shops in expressive red or green tones*". Leon, who was born on La Digue in 1950 and studied art in Canada and France, creates his eye-catching collages at a studio, not far from his office at the Ministry of Education and Information.

On meeting Seychellois artists one is struck by their youth and great enthusiasm for the creative process. Guided by various influences affecting their own lives, their paintings and sculptures have an originality and freshness rendering a unique quality of dynamism to their work. I am most grateful to them for allowing me to display aspects of their work in this book and hope that the following pages will speak for themselves, communicating the vitality of both art and artists in Seychelles.

Imier Lespoir: "The Struggle" 1986

Leon Radegonde with collage in his studio in 1987

Christine Harter: "M. Rene. Praslin"; Watercolour 1986

Christine Harter: "Old Boat, La Digue", Watercolour 1986

Jacques Vidot: "Fishermen after work"; Watercolour 1987

Donald Adelaide: "Palm Forest"; Watercolour 1987

Julien Brioche: "The Old Windmill"; Acrylic painting 1987

Peter Pierre-Louis: "Symbol of Liberation"; Acrylic on cloth 1987

Pacquerette Lablache: "The Arrival"; Acrylic 1986

170

Marc Luc: "Basketball players"; 1985

Vincent Uzice: "The Front"; Oil and collage on plywood 1985

Myrna Morin: Collage; 1985

Gerard Devoud: "Forest glade"; Watercolour; 1986

Andre Woodcock: "Creole Woman"; 1986

MODERN SEYCHELLES

Seychelles has achieved a great deal since it's emergence, in 1976, from a long period under British colonial government. Presented with a seemingly impossible challenge, the Seychellois have tackled many of the problems facing their country, a difficult task exacerbated by an apparent lack of exploitable natural resources and a daunting isolation from the world's major markets. To the casual visitor or sun-seeking tourist, many of this young nation's accomplishments will be taken for granted or pass unnoticed, but anyone who has been acquainted with Seychelles since the early 1970's or before, will recognise that steady progress has been made in a number of fields, including agriculture; fisheries; rural development; housing; tourism infrastructure and education. The present government has adopted a pragmatic approach to development policies and their successes are enjoyed today by both residents and visitors alike.

I vividly recollect my first visits to Seychelles in the early 1970's when it was still a British Colony. Flying into Mahe on the second commercial flight to land at the newly constructed airport, our plane-load of passengers were greeted by hoards of Seychellois, fascinated by their new link with the rest of the world. Since its first settlement, roughly two hundred years earlier, the only means of travel into or out of the islands had been by lengthy and frequently hazardous sea journeys. Now at last, a jet-age runway enabled the world's major airlines to land here and to use Seychelles as a staging post on flights across the Indian Ocean, between Europe, Arabia or Africa and Asia or perhaps Australia. I was among the first of that new class of visitor to Seychelles, the air-borne tourist, and I found a warm welcome from people who were largely untouched by the stresses and strains of so-called western civilisation. But the excitement engendered by the promise of great benefit flowing from the airport was dulled by the uneasy feeling that life would never be quite the same again. How soon would it be before traditions were swamped by a deluge of tourists and by the inevitable commercialisation which mushrooms in their wake? What about the country's unique wildlife and its superb natural beauty? How long would it take before sky-scrapers dwarfed the picturesque capital of Victoria, or towered over white-sand beaches of Mahe, Praslin, La Digue and the other islands? How would the islanders cope with the inflationary pressures which were bound to come? Would tourism simply increase the gap between rich and poor? All these side-effects had happened in other tropical tourism resorts, why should Seychelles fare any better? Fortunately however, Seychelles was to prove its claim that it is in fact different, and that Seychellois have a genuine love and deep

The main granitic islands of Seychelles are all relatively close together and are dominated by the high cone shaped profile of Silhouette and the long, mountainous image of Mahe, shown in this view from the shore of Anse Lascars on Silhouette.

While many tourist brochures tend to portray Seychelles as a land of sea, sand, sun and little else, I have made a deliberate effort to steer away from this stereotyped and inadequate image of the country. Nevertheless, the country is blessed with some of the most beautiful beaches in the World and its seas offer endless opportunities for enjoyment. (Vine).

An early morning helicopter-eye view of the Northolme Hotel, and adjacent private beach. The Hotel is owned by Seychelles Hotels Corporation and has a long history as one of the island's most popular venues. Marine-life adjacent to the hotel is protected and extremely rich. (Pavard)

appreciation of their enchantingly beautiful island homeland. Seychelles, they declared, would take great care to avoid the pitfalls of basing its entire economy on tourism. The country would remain, as the travel slogan declares, "unique by a thousand miles"!

On my return in 1987, I was more than pleasantly surprised to discover that considerable care had been taken to preserve the natural beauty of the islands, and the approach to touristic development re-

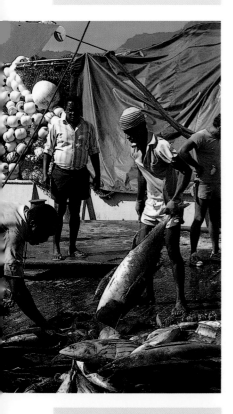

Tuna are offloaded in a frozen condition and either trans-shipped immediately, stored at the port's deep-freeze facility, or sent to the processing factory. (Vine).

mained a cautious one. The government, while recognising the key role of tourism in the country's economy, is determined that the true essence of Seychelles should not be destroyed, and that other aspects should be greatly encouraged, both as a means of creating foreign earnings, and as part of their sustained efforts to achieve self-sufficiency.

For many years planners have been commenting that one thing the Republic of Seychelles has in abundance is a vast area of sea with presumably under-exploited marine resources. Despite various efforts to harness these for the nation's benefit, there had been remarkably little progress in fisheries development until the mid 1980's. It was then the Indian Ocean Tuna fishery selected Mahe as a natural point for transshipment of its catches, and the Seychelles Government established a joint-venture with French partners for a large new state-of-the-art Tuna Processing plant: a project providing two hundred and fifty new jobs. A crucial factor in this development was the creation of a legal framework within which the Government could control fishing activities in Seychelles waters. The 1977 Maritime Zone Act was the first step in this process, followed by the 1978 Exclusive Economic Zone Order and the 1979 Foreign Fishing Vessel and Regulations Decree. Placing one million square kilometers of the Indian Ocean under control of the Republic of Seychelles, these legislative instruments established the Seychelles Exclusive Economic Maritime Zone and made the way clear for much of the economic activity which was to follow.

Tuna vessels operating in the Seychelles EEZ must first seek a licence from the Seychelles Government. In this regard a dominant role has been played by EC member-nations, particularly France and Spain, whose vessels catch Tuna by purse-seining. The facilities at Victoria's fishing port have been greatly improved in order to make Seychelles an attractive venue for Tuna vessels ranging over a vast area of the Indian Ocean, not just within the EEZ, and a capital investment of over $40 million has created the best equipped Tuna port in the Indian Ocean. Fisheries development in Seychelles has thus moved ahead in leaps and bounds since the comparatively relaxed approach of the colonial era.

Development of Tuna fishing in Seychelles waters has been extremely rapid, and the new industry provides employment for an ever increasing numbers of Seychellois. (Vine).

In view of the vital role it plays in the government's economic planning, let us take a somewhat closer look at the overall fishing industry and its future prospects in Seychelles.

FISHERIES OF SEYCHELLES.

The total land-mass of Seychelles' one hundred or so islands is only about 455 sq.kilometers whereas, as we have stated above, Seychelles EEZ covers a million square kilometers of ocean within which the relatively shallow and productive Seychelles Plateau occupies roughly 45,000 sq.kms.—a vast natural resource capable of providing considerable income to the country. Seychellois love fish. As a result, the vast majority of the four thousand or so tons of fish landed each year by the islands' artisanal fishermen are consumed by local people. Tourism has greatly increased the demand for fish however, and has had an inevitable effect upon both prices and availability of fresh-fish. For the fishermen all this is good news since the incentives to catch fish have been increased: no bad thing in the light of the dangers and hardships involved in artisanal fishing.

Visitors to Seychelles will have seen many of the small boats used by traditional fishermen either moored to harbour quaysides or pulled up above high-tide level along the shoreline. Outboard powered craft ranging from five to eight metres together with somewhat larger, inboard powered, open boats fish upto thirty miles offshore from the main islands on the Mahe Plateau. Generally, fish are caught on hand-lines, in traps, or by beach-seining. The majority of the artisanal catch comes from inshore waters and comprises primarily carangids such as *Carangoides gymnostethus* and *Caranx fulvoguttatus*; the brilliantly banded Emperor Red Snapper (*Lutjanus sebae*), the Humphead Snapper (*Lutjanus coccineus*), the Green Jobfish (*Aprion virescens*); various groupers, rabbit fish, lethrinid emperors and the Indian or Gill-raker Mackerel, *Rastrelliger kanagurta*. A more complete list of the artisanal landings is given in table 12).

Fishing Schooners, working further offshore than the small open boats discussed above, generally undertake ten day trips crewed by about half a dozen fishermen and equipped with an insulated hold capable of carrying up to two tons of ice and fish. They fish entirely by hand-lining, usually over banks on the edge of the Mahe and Amirantes Plateau.

A new level of organisation was introduced to traditional fishing in Seychelles by the establishment, in 1984, of the Fish Division of the Seychelles Marketing Board. The Board's prime objective is to secure a steady supply of fish at prices fair to both fishermen and general consumers. Several strategies have been employed to achieve this objective and the Board operates freezing and storage facilities as well as assisting with collection, distribution and marketing of the catch. I was personally impressed at how well this organisation was run and its management's commitment to achieving their objectives.

While traditional fishing methods are well established in Seychelles and have, since the country's earliest settlement, provided an essential source of protein for its inhabitants, there remain natural constraints on development. Set in the midst of a vast ocean, the tiny islands afford limited protection from the effects of weather. There have been numer-

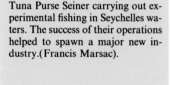

Tuna Purse Seiner carrying out experimental fishing in Seychelles waters. The success of their operations helped to spawn a major new industry.(Francis Marsac).

178

The Tuna catch is concentrated at the side of the vessel before being brailed aboard. (Francis Marsac).

Hand-lining for Red Snapper near Aldabra. (Guy de Moussac).

ous tragedies down through the years and many near disasters in which fishermen have been rescued after long and difficult struggles against the sea. Today's younger population, presented with a wider range of options, tends to be less attracted to the rigours of sea-fishing than were their predecessors, and so the Government has sought to improve conditions in the fishing industry and to provide training and encouragement for young people entering the field. National interests have been protected by preserving the entire Seychelles plateau, and up to five miles beyond its edge (as defined by the 200 metre isobath) for locally owned and registered fishing boats. The Seychelles Polytechnic Maritime Studies Department has established training schemes aimed at imparting practical skills and hands-on experience to the younger generation. National boatyards have concentrated much of their attentions on producing an improved design of decked-in fishing boat ensuring higher standards of comfort and safety for fishermen. At the same time fisheries research work continues, aimed at locating resources suitable for exploitation; carrying out stock assessments on the fishery, and improving techniques for locating and catching fish. Results of some recent studies are worth quoting since there have been several estimates of the quantity of demersal fish living within the area of the Mahe plateau. Estimates, based on catch-effort statistics indicate the total biomass of this important zone is between 42,000 tons (lowest figure proposed by Berkett in 1979) and 80,000 tons (highest estimate, by Tarbit, 1980). The sustainable yield or allowable catch is considered to be around seven thousand tons per year, or roughly two thousand more than present landings. One objective of current development programmes is to increase landings to this level by focusing on underexploited species and by introducing new improvements in catching methods such as bottom-set longlines, fish-locating echo sounders and mechanical reels.

Industrial fishing in Seychelles is a relatively new innovation and has

Table 12

LIST OF COMMERCIALLY IMPORTANT FISH LANDED BY THE ARTISANAL FISHERY

Local Name	English Name	Scientific Name
Caught on Handline:		
Bourgeois	Emperor Red Snapper	*Lutjanus sebae*
Bordemar	Humphead Snapper	*Lutjanus coccineus*
Vieille Maconde	Brownspot Grouper	*Epinephelus chlorostigma*
Vieille Platte	White Blotched Grouper	*Epinephelus multionatatus*
Croissant	Moontail Seabass	*Variola louti*
Vara Vara	Two spot Red Snapper	*Lutjanus bohar*
Job Gris	Green Jobfish	*Aprion virescens*
Job Jaune		*Aphereus rutilans*
Batrican	Bluespot Jobfish	*Pristipomoides filamentosus*
Carangue Balo	Buldger	*Carangoides gymnostethus*
Carangue Platte	Yellow Spotted Trevally	*Carangoides fulvoguttatus*
Thon Jaune	Yellowfin Tuna	*Thunnus albacares*
Bonite	Bonito	*Euthynnus affinis*
Kingfish	Kingfish	*Acanthocybium solandri*
Diable La Voile	Sailfish	*Istiophorus platypterus*
Espadron	Marlin	*Makaira sp.*
Monsieur Hangard	Tomato Hind	*Cephalopholis sonnerati*
Capitaine Blanc	Bluelined Large-eye Bream	*Gymnocranius robinsoni*
Capitaine Rouge	Spangled Emperor	*Lethrinus nebulosus*
Babonne	Spotted Coral-Trout	*Plectropomus maculatus*
Becune	Pickhandle Barracuda	*Sphyraena jello*
Guele Longue	Longface Emperor	*Lethrinus elongatus*
Caught in traps		
Cordonnier Blanc	Shoemaker Spinefoot	*Siganus sutor*
Cordonnier soule-femme	Streamlined Spinefoot	*Siganus argenteus*
Cacatoi Blanc	Yellowscale Parrot	*Scarus ghobban*
Cacatoi Bruno		*Scarus sp.*
Chirurgien	Bleeker's Surgeonfish	*Acanthurus bleekeri*
Rouget Local	Seychelles Goatfish	*Parupeneus seychellensis*
Rouget tache	Dash and Dot Goatfish	*Parupeneus barberinus*
Caught by Net		
Macquereaux Doux	Indian Mackerel	*Rastrelliger kanagurta*
Macquereaux Gros	Big-eye Scad	*Selar crumenopthalmus*

received a considerable impetus from the Government's determination to maximise the return from its oceanic resources. Prior to the mid 1970's, this form of fishing simply did not exist in Seychelles or, if it did, Seychelles received little or no benefit from the scattering of Japanese and South Korean longliners who stalked the Indian Ocean in search of Tuna. According to FAO statistics, two thousand one hundred and thirty tons of Tuna were caught in Seychelles waters in 1976. In the following year the catch increased more than eleven times, to twenty four thousand,one hundred and ninety three tons! In 1984 over ninety eight thousand tons of tuna were landed at Mahe, while the following years the total catch from the Mahe based fleet exceeded one hundred and twenty seven thousand tons! What produced this dramatic escalation? Well, first of all it seems unlikely that there were any major changes in the abundance of Tuna, but the catch effort and efficiency seems to have improved. The first bumper harvest in 1977 focused attention on the necessity for the Seychelles Exclusive Economic Zone, a legal framework for which was provided by the Maritime Zone Act of August 1977 and the Exclusive Economic Zone Order of February 1978. But it was not until the 1980's that real progress took place.

Tuna purse-seining in the Seychelles EEZ began in December 1980 with the arrival of the French vessel "Isle de Seine" basing itself at Port Victoria, and demonstrating a capacity to catch on average about ten tons per day. The French purse seiner "Yves de Kerguelen", a sixty-nine metre, eight hundred ton capacity, modern Tuna catching vessel arrived in November 1981 and fished for just over six months, covering a large area of the Indian Ocean including the Mozambique Channel, the Amirantes Plateau and the North Bank of Saya de Malha and the sea area stretching eastwards towards the Chagos Archipelago. The previously established ten tons per day average catch-rate was maintained with a total harvest, during the period, of one thousand three hundred and seventy tons: a commendable performance when one considers that the vessel lacked the advantages afforded by membership of a fleet in which various ships can communicate their findings.

Experimental tuna purse-seining successes in the Indian Ocean coincided with a dramatic fall-off in catches elsewhere, so that many of the Atlantic fleet of tuna vessels were seeking new hunting grounds. Their response to the pioneering efforts by "Isle de Seine" and "Yves de Kerguelen" were thus immediate and the Seychelles Government negotiated fishing agreements with various fishing companies and national governments. Spain received permission for fifteen purse-seiners to operate while the EEC received agreement for eighteen French vessels to catch tuna in the EEZ. Other agreements were made with different countries such as the Ivory Coast and by December 1984 there were forty-nine vessels catching Tuna in and around the Seychelles EEZ. The contribution of this rapidly developing industry to the local economy has been quite dramatic with 1985 figures showing direct benefits at four million dollars; indirect benefits providing an additional nine million dollars; not to mention the approximately five hundred people employed in fishery-related jobs.

Quick to recognise the need to consolidate on its early success in attracting the Tuna fleet to Mahe, the Seychelles Government has embarked upon a most ambitious plan for harbour improvements, creating in the process a new fishing port, divided into an area set aside for the demersal fishery, with separate berths and land-based facilities for the tuna fishery. The latter include a 90 metre long quay and separate bunkering-pier with depth alongside at least 7.5 m.; new processing plants including blast freezers and a one thousand ton capacity cold-store, together with a state-of-the-art canning factory. General administration of the fishery is the task of Seychelles Fishing Authority

SUBSURFACE STRATIGRAPHY OF SEYCHELLES WELLS

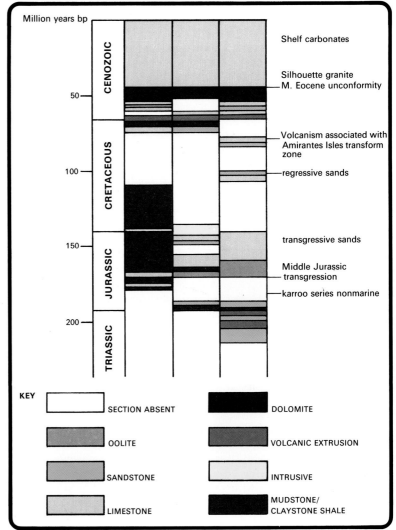

FIGURE 13

whose headquarters are within the new complex. Our visit to the tuna berth took place on a typically busy day during which off-loading of tuna was taking place. Five purse-seiners were tethered to the new wharf and activity on board was focused on making transshipment of their valuable cargoes of frozen Tuna as rapid as possible, thus enabling the vessels to return to the productive fishing grounds encircling Seychelles.

OIL EXPLORATION

I vividly recall meetings attended in the early 1970's when a great deal of cold water was poured on the suggestion that commercial tuna fishing by purse-seining could be successfully established in Seychelles waters; or indeed anywhere else in the western Indian Ocean. There were few people then who believed in such a project and yet today, it is very much a reality and Seychelles is gaining valuable earnings from careful management of this renewable natural resource. At the time of

182

writing, there are new moves afoot to investigate the possibility of discovering commercially viable oil resources on the Seychelles Bank. There are good reasons to suppose that petroleum deposits will be found in the Seychelles EEZ, and exploration work is currently underway. As shown on page 78 Seychelles is situated within what geologists call the Somalia plate. The main tectonic elements in Seychelles territorial waters are shown in figure 5 on page 80 , which indicates a complex pattern of rifting and volcanic activity, resulting in deposition of thick sedimentary columns overlying a basaltic crust. Oil exploration has already been carried out by a number of interested parties, including the French company CGG; Texaco which drilled two wells; Burmah Oil who carried out a seismic survey on the western banks, establishing sedimentary thickness at over six thousand metres; and by the Amoco-Seychelles Petroleum Company. The interesting, and commercially promising profile of subsurface stratigraphy in these Seychelles wells is indicated in figure 13 on page 182 .On studying this picture geologists conclude as follows; "*The definite presence of source, resevoir, cap, and favourable structures makes the Seychelles shelf worth exploring for hydrocarbons*" (Khanna and Pillay, 1986). As the same writers state, the Seychelles basin has been inadequately explored and further exploratory work is now needed. The task of coordinating this exciting aspect of the country's development falls upon the Seychelles National Oil Company whose chairman recently attended the signing of a new exploration agreement with Enterprise Oil Exploration of London. The oil company appears to have selected sites with high potential for success, including the area around Coetivy where surface seeps on the beach in the form of tar balls have provided renewed optimism for a major oil find in the area. As pointed out by Minister Morel however, the area allotted to Enterprise Oil is less that five percent of the country's EEZ, and there is still a large area left for exploration and potential development. There are still plenty of sceptics of course, but the Seychelles Government takes a positive view of prospects for oil discovery and I would not be the least surprised if their efforts, as with those of the tuna fishery, prove fruitful, helping to provide a firmer base for the country's economy and improved living standards for all its people.

COMMERCIAL SECTOR

Coming from Ireland, I was pleasantly surprised to discover that the hallowed beverage Guinness is actually brewed in Seychelles. The story of SEYBREW, commencing production in July 1972, is in fact one of the notable success stories for business ventures in the country and I met with company general manager, Edwin Palmer, to obtain the full story. He explained that the project was established with the technical and commercial participation of Haase-Brauerei GmbH of Hamburg, Germany. Guinness is brewed under a licence agreement issued by Guinness Overseas Ltd. whilst Eku beer is made under licence from Erste Kulmbacher Actienbraueri. Major shareholders in Seybrew are the Haase Brewery company; Guinness Overseas; the German Development Bank; East African Breweries, and over six hundred Seychellois shareholders. The company's products are seen throughout Seychelles and one could not help but remark upon the slight incongruity of seeing crates of Guinness off-loaded from beautiful old wooden sailing schooners tied to picturesque island quays, such as at La Digue.

Seychelles Marketing Board's new administrative headquarters at Victoria. (Vine).

Container ship alongside new deep-water berth at Victoria's new harbour. (Vine).

One of the country's most successful private industrial projects is that of SEYBREW which produces a range of beers and soft drinks. (Vine).

It would be quite wrong however to render the impression that Seybrew's major growth has stemmed from only supplying thirst -quenching beer to islanders and tourists. In fact, much of the company's expansion has been in the soft drinks sector, registering an increase of 150% between 1978 and 1987. With an eye on weight conscious consumers, the company has also produced a range of low calorie drinks and at the time of writing plans are underway to install a new soft drinks line, at a cost of more than ten million rupees. Apart from the company's direct contribution to the economy through employment creation, the Brewery pays over 40 million rupees a year in the form of taxation, a valuable contribution towards the cost of national development.

Other aspects of Seychelles industrial development include SMB's FOODPRO factory at Union Vale; SMB's dairy unit at Pointe Larue; Seychelles Tea and Coffee Company's processing and packaging of various tea and coffee products; Electronique Seychelles' assembly plant for televisions; the PENLAC paint factory; the SODEPAK factory manufacturing soap, detergents and paper packaging products; a cigarette plant; several furniture factories; a pottery works; a number of small clothing plants and other small industries, particularly in the wood-crafts sector. New projects are proposed or planned for milling flour; biscuit making; manufacture of breakfast cereals, confectionery, clothing, artificial marble and glassware. Development projects on outer islands are managed by the Islands Development Company, active on Silhouette, Coetivy, Desroches, Marie Louise, Desnoeufs, Alphonse, Providence, Astove, Cosmoledo, Farquhar and Platte. The land area under its jurisdiction is approximately 50 square kilometres and over five hundred people are employed on projects managed by the organisation. The largest island under company ownership, Silhouette, is currently undergoing several important developments, including operation of a new well-appointed hotel, and construction and management of an extensive livestock farm, rearing poultry, pork, beef, goats, turkey together with an impressive fruit and vegetable growing project. The main natural resources of the outer islands are of course their fishery stocks, still quite under-exploited; coconut plantations yielding 2,500 tons of copra per year; and their natural beauty rendering them attractive as tourism locations, especially for those interested in nature and water-sports such as diving.

AIR TRANSPORT

Tourism in Seychelles could not have experienced the dramatic revival which has taken place in recent years without the help of the National Airline: Air Seychelles, an impressive, modern air-carrier offering regular non-stop flights to Seychelles, and serving an ever expanding selection of international routes.

Established in response to the need for an air-service dedicated to serving the country's needs, Air Seychelles cut its teeth on the inter-island routes, providing short hop flights between Mahe, Praslin, Bird, Denis and Frigate islands and in the process opening up these islands for both tourism and other developments. Their decision to expand to international routings was thrust upon them by a temporary withdrawal of regular flights by Lufthansa and British Airways. Thus, in October 1983 an Air Seychelles DC10 flight, operated by British Caledonian, took off from London's Gatwick airport on the first international flight by the fledgling airline. Flights to Mahe, via Frankfurt, with high passenger loadings soon demonstrated the viability of the national airline's new venture and as tourism figures once more rose in response to the availability of a regular and efficiently operated service, plans were laid to transform the company into a fully fledged international airline, operating more aircraft and serving more transit points. In November 1985 Air Seychelles, proudly displaying its uniquely appealing Fairy Tern motif on its own Airbus A300 aircraft, commenced twice weekly flights between Europe and Seychelles. Developments have been taking place so rapidly since then that this is not the right place to provide an up to the minute account of Air Seychelles activities. Between writing and publication, there is no doubt that further changes will have taken place, to render such an account out of date. Some things have, however, remained constant throughout the company's growth. A determination to provide a high quality of service, on

On Denis Island guests are greeted personally by the island's proprietor, Pierre Burkhardt who insists that one must regard one's visit like that of a house guest, rather than a tourist. The island offers an ideal "get away from it all" atmosphere. (Vine).

a par with that of the world's major airlines, has ensured that the long flight from Europe to these unique Indian Ocean islands remains a pleasant experience for those lucky enough to undertake the journey. A factor in Air Seychelles favour is that they are also, at present, the only airline operating non-stop flights from Europe to Mahe. At the time of writing there are four flights each week, three emanating from London, one each via Zurich, Frankfurt and Rome while the other flight is from Paris via Athens. A direct service between Mahe and Singapore commenced in November 1987. Prior to landing at Mahe, a special inflight film about the islands is screened, providing a useful briefing for maiden-voyagers. A measure of the company's success in becoming universally accepted as the most obvious mode of transport to and from Mahe, is the fact that it has maintained an 85% average loading factor since starting international operations. As one of the first people to have flown into Seychelles on board a new British Airways service in the early 1970's, I am greatly impressed at how far the country has come in the intervening years, consolidating its position and carving out its own niche on the world stage.

An Air Seychelles inter-island flight (Gilbert Pool).

TOURISM: HOTELS

One of the most appealing aspects of tourism in Seychelles is the degree of planning which has taken place in order to preserve the natural environment and minimise the impact of touristic facilities on local scenery. Virtually all hotels are set back from the beach, preserving the natural beauty of the coastline. The long established rule that no hotel building shall rise above coconut tree height has resulted in many unique, and tastefully designed hotels, a welcome contrast to developments at numerous other tropical coastal resorts. Frequently hotels are so well camouflaged by natural features of local landscape and vegetation that they are in fact quite difficult to pick-out from a distance. A classic example is the Northolme Hotel, flagship of Seychelles Hotels Corporation, and favoured resting place for numerous literary and film notables from around the world. On swimming out from the shore, alongside the Northolme, and looking back, the impression is given that some unseen magician has, in the blink of an eye, whisked the hotel away altogether. All one sees are tall swaying coconut palms, and a luscious slope, cloaked by fragrant frangipani, a riotous mass of bouganvillea and a host of other exotic plants. There is no hotel in sight! On turning back to the sea, one is greeted by an underwater world which could have sprung straight from the pages of a Jacques Cousteau book. Here, within less than a hundred metres of the secluded hotel, multitudes of angel-fish, butterflyfish and a host of other marine-life abound. Each hotel, and indeed each island has its own special features, and visitors are well advised to move around in Seychelles, perhaps spending three or four days at each location before sampling new delights. It was with this concept in mind that Seychelles Hotels Corporation introduced their unique "Fun Card" automati-

One of the most impressive hotel entrances in the world must be that of Frigate Island lodge where guests are guided through the gigantic root system of a Banyan tree in order to gain access to the reception lobby. (Vine).

An aerial view of Praslin Beach Hotel, an attractive and popular place to stay on Praslin and a member of Seychelles Hotels group. (C.Pavard).

188

cally issued to guests at any of their hotels, entitling them to inter-
change with other hotels within the group, perhaps in order to enjoy
watersport facilities; or to sample different cuisine; to visit a popular
nightspot; or even to move from one hotel to another. A popular
arrangement is for visitors to spend the first week of their holiday on
Mahe, staying at one of the group's hotels, such as the Northolme; the
comfortable and friendly Vacoa Village; the Reef ; or Beauvallon Bay
Hotel; and then to fly to Praslin where they may stay at the Praslin
Beach Hotel; Flying Dutchman or Cote d'Or Lodge. Seychelles Hotels
are unique in this regard, and do provide flexible and attractively
priced holidays. Much of the enjoyment of a holiday in Seychelles
however does not depend upon lush, modern hotel facilities, but upon
the island environment. Indeed, some of the most beautiful hotels have
maintained an air of the "back-to-nature life-style" attracting many
people to holiday here. Thus, for example, on the low coral sand-
cays of Denis Island and Bird Island, comfortable accommodation
is provided in palm-thatched bungalows, filled with the soothing
sound of the sea, or depending on the season on Bird Island, the
all-night cries of about a million raucous Sooty Terns! Nature is
never far away. Two or three beautiful emerald green geckos will probably share your bedroom, and if you have never fed teeming wild-
birds by hand, this is surely the place to do so. At both of these islands
the visitor is greeted by their respective proprietors and instantly made
to feel at home. Frigate is another small but intriguing island serviced
by Air Seychelles. Here the only accommodation for guests is at the
Plantation House which may be booked at Frigate's Mahe office or
through travel agents such as those listed in the appendix. Frigate
is a fascinating place to stay for a few days, a place where one
may approach within a few feet of one of the world's rarest birds; the

The main-street at Silhouette island
is lined by large Breadfruit trees.
The island provides a unique opportunity for a truly peaceful holiday, together with some energetic
walks and unspoilt endemic vegetation. (Vine).

Thatched guest accommodation on
Denis Island. (Vine).

189

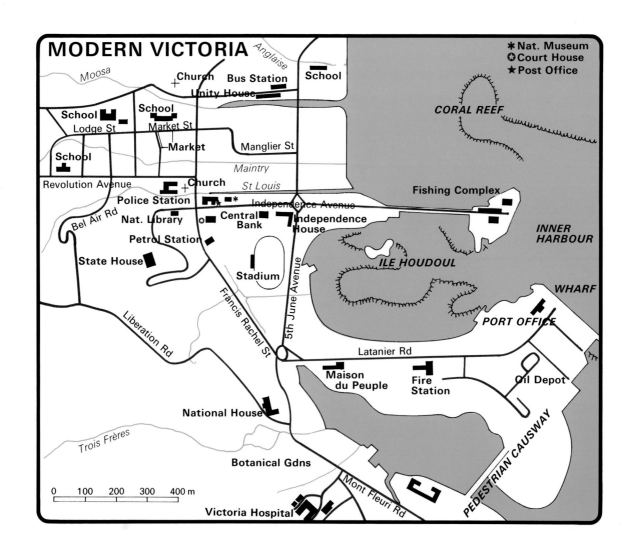

MODERN VICTORIA

Anglaise

Moosa

* Nat. Museum
⊙ Court House
★ Post Office

CORAL REEF

+ Church
Bus Station
Unity House
School

School
Lodge St
School
Market St
Market
Manglier St

School

Maintry

Fishing Complex

INNER HARBOUR

Revolution Avenue
St Louis
+ Church
Police Station
Independence Avenue
Nat. Library
⊙ Central Bank
* Independence House

Petrol Station

ILE HOUDOUL

State House
Stadium

5th June Avenue

WHARF

PORT OFFICE

Bel Air Rd

Liberation Rd

Francis Rachel St

Latanier Rd

Maison du Peuple
Fire Station

Oil Depot

National House

PEDESTRIAN CAUSEWAY

Trois Frères

Botanical Gdns

Mont Fleuri Rd

0 100 200 300 400 m

Victoria Hospital

Magpie Robin, or perhaps live out childhood fantasies of searching for buried pirate treasure. Silhouette Island is approached by sea only, making it even more secluded and special. Bookings for holidays in Seychelles are generally made through travel agents who employ one of the major Seychelles based agents to handle incoming flights, meeting passengers, transferring them to their hotels and taking care of special arrangements during their visit. At the time of writing the three main agents are the Government owned National Travel Agency (NTA), Masons Travel and Travel Services Seychelles. These agents all provide efficient service to tourists and are continually improving the facilities on offer.

AGRICULTURE

The strive for self-sufficiency is nowhere more intense than in the field of agriculture where vigorous efforts have been made to improve efficiency of land-use and to apply modern organisation and technology to crop production and marketing. Regarded as a key sector of the economy, the Government has focused its attention on developing agriculture as a guaranteed food source ; a means of import substitution; a provider of employment and as a means to earn foreign exchange. A key element in its planning has been the Seychelles Marketing Board, whose remit is to seek ways to stimulate production by providing a guaranteed year around market, through establishment of efficient distribution systems, and through participation in processing and preservation projects. Training in agriculture begins in the primary schools and extends right through the education system, into the Polytechnic and to on-site training by agricultural extension officers. One of the problems in this sector has been to control what farmers grow on their land. Success of the Grande Anse Experimental Agricultural Station in identifying high yield tomato, bean and cabbage strains has back-fired to a certain extent with over-production of these crops and a tendency for the market to become flooded with these commodities. It is one of the functions of Seychelles Marketing Board to try to minimise this effect and to encourage production of a wider range of crops for which demand does exist. At the time of writing, a new requirement has been created for cassava and sweet potatoes for use, together with fish-meal from the Tuna Processing plant, as ingredients at an animals feed factory situated in the new port. The feed factory will itself provide valuable food for rearing pork and poultry. Improved methods of fruit growing are also showing results, with the country's first fruit farm being set-up at Beau Vallon in 1980. Visitors to Frigate may well have been impressed by the large quantities of oranges and other fruits there, many of which were (during 1987) left unpicked. While the luscious fruit trees underline the feasibility of growing such crops in Seychelles, they are also a reminder of the inevitable power of market forces. When prices are depressed it can be uneconimical to transport oranges from Frigate to Mahe. Seychelles Marketing Board, acutely aware of the need for farmers to be adequately recompensed for their efforts, is doing its best to tackle this kind of problem. One of several success stories has been in the poultry and meat sector with self-sufficiency in eggs and poultry now established, and production targets for beef and pork being met. With an eye on the high export value of fish, the Government is trying to wean

Victoria still lays claim to being the World's smallest capital city. The town's friendly character and traditional appearance have been preserved, despite the construction of a number of modern buildings in recent years. In 1987 there were still no sky-scrapers in Victoria; long may it remain so!

Opposite
Helicopter-eye view of the harbour at Victoria, showing new deep-water port facility with container vessel alongside, and the new Tuna Fishing port together with large Tuna processing facility. Government planning has emphasised the importance of these modern facilities for the future development of Seychelles. (Vine).

consumers away from very high fish intake, in favour of a greater consumption of pork, poultry and eggs, leaving more fish for export. While western countries are shifting their diets in the opposite direction, i.e. towards eating more fish, it must be stated that the per-capita annual consumption of fish in Seychelles is one of the highest in the world! Other efforts in the agricultural sector worthy of mention here are the trial production of potatoes and onions; the establishment of state-owned farms on Mahe, Praslin and La Digue; and the successful organisation of a number of cooperative farms increasing national production and providing useful employment to many local inhabitants. On La Digue the state-farm at L'Union Estate is successfully reviving production of vanilla, while a Government-backed project at Anse Aux Pins on Mahe is helping to keep the cinnamon industry alive. Both copra and cinnamon have been affected by dramatic falls in world prices and while these two crops once formed the mainstay of Seychelles' agro-economy, they are today somewhat in the background with emphasis being placed on specialised products like cup-copra (for which Seychelles is famous) and hybrid high oil-yielding coconuts suitable for home-production of cream, oil and margarine. While it would be naive and dishonest to state that there are no problems in the agricultural sector, the considerable advances made in the last decade or so, deserve full recognition and encouragement. There is still a long way to travel towards complete self-sufficiency and a healthy food export industry, but there is good cause for optimism about the future.

Modern agricultural irrigation schemes such as this project at Silhouette are transforming the country's food production capacity. (Vine).

CONSERVATION

Among the major achievements of Seychelles internationally has been its firm stand on conservation issues and in particular its insistence that whales in local waters should be fully protected from any form of hunting, whether for so-called scientific purposes or commercially. It has played a key role in guiding through the International Whaling Commission meetings a proposal for a large Indian Ocean sanctuary for all marine mammals. Seychelles is to be highly commended for its principled stand on this issue, made in the face of considerable opposition and pressure from at least one of the world's major nations. The status of whales in local waters was reviewed by the Seychelles representative at the IWC meeting. Despite heavy predation by whaling nations upon the Indian ocean stocks, it is heartening to report that some of the great whales do still visit these warm waters, during their winter migrations away from frozen Antarctic seas. Paragraph sixteen of the submission calling for the whale sanctuary is quoted below:

IWC SUBMISSION BY SEYCHELLES

"The waters around Seychelles are described as being of "intermediate productivity" (Walford, 1958). Baleen whales are occasionally encountered—a few Sei, Bryde's and Humpback are seen from November through March, when the North West Monsoon brings richer waters in from the African coast. A Blue Whale was recorded in

October 1957, North-East of Seychelles (Slijper, 1964). By far the most common great whales however are Sperm Whales, which seem to reach a peak between July and September (during the South East Monsoon) when calves are most commonly seen. These patterns of distribution and migration are directly reflected in Post-War whaling statistics, and may have something to do with the fact that the numbers now appearing in Seychelles seem to have fallen dramatically in the past decade. During the summer months (from November to March) the whaling fleets concentrate on the Antarctic, south of 40 deg. S, and there is no whaling in tropical waters. (All species of baleen whale which occur there are anyway now protected by the Commission). Catches made from Durban showed a high peak of Sperm Whale in May and June and a smaller peak in September, suggesting that it is during these months that the mature males move through the subtropical area on their way to and from the tropical breeding grounds. In recent years the pelagic whaling fleets on their way to the Antarctic in November, and on their way back in March, have been taking an increasing number of Sperm Whales North of 40 deg. S. Most of these are males in transit, channelled by the formation of ocean ridges in the Indian Ocean from all the broad Antarctic base of Areas III and IV between 20 deg. E. and 80 deg. E., up to a narrow apex of their breeding ground on the Seychelles Banks. Every one taken is one less to arrive for breeding in our waters. So, although there is little actual pelagic whaling currently taking place in Seychelles, and there has been no land base there since 1915, the zoogeography and the patterns of whaling in other parts of the Indian Ocean nevertheless have a direct effect on one

Seychelles has called for a zone of Peace in the Indian Ocean. (Vine).

of our principal natural resources.

"*For this historical reason (in addition to others outlined in our Initiative—IWC/31/6), we request that the International Whaling Commission consider the proposal for the establishment of an Indian Ocean Sanctuary, at least in the area of* 40 *deg. S., as a matter of some urgency.*"

Seychelles Government's attitude towards conservation is both pragmatic and reasonable, recognising the need for Man to live alongside nature, and the deleterious impact that development projects can sometimes have on the environment.While seeking to minimise damaging effects in those areas where developments must proceed, the Government has also set aside a number of areas which have been designated as National Parks or Reserves where nature takes precedence over Man's immutable desire to place His own signature on the landscape. The present list of protected areas is given below:

NATIONAL PARKS AND RESERVES OF SEYCHELLES

MORNE SEYCHELLES NATIONAL PARK
PRASLIN NATIONAL PARK
ALDABRA STRICT NATURE RESERVE
ARIDE ISLAND NATURE RESERVE
COUSIN ISLAND NATURE RESERVE
CURIEUSE MARINE NATIONAL PARK
STE. ANNE MARINE NATIONAL PARK
PORT LAUNAY/ BAIE TERNAY MARINE NATIONAL PARK
DESNEUF ISLAND (one-third of which is a Strict Nature Reserve)
LA DIGUE—"RENE PAYET VEUVE RESERVE"
BEACON (OR ILE SECHE)
BOOBY (OR ILE AUX FOUS)
BOUDEUSE
ETOIE
KING ROSS (OR LAMPERIAIRE)
LES MAMELLES
BIRD ISLAND
VACHE MARINE
COCOS: LA FOUCHE AND ILE PLATTE
AFRICAN BANKS AND SURROUNDING REEFS
VALLEE DE MAI (In Praslin National Park)

On June 5th 1977 James Mancham was deposed in a bloodless coup and the government of Albert Rene took over. The date is celebrated as Liberation Day and commemorated in this street name. (Vine).

195

At a cross-roads of cultures, ethnic ties, political ideologies, and international communications routes Seychelles has played an important role in the international sphere where a voice of reason has been raised in various areas including for example, at the International Whaling Commission as well as in the forum of non-aligned states. Decisions regarding the country's course of action are made upon the merits of the issues involved rather than upon a dogmatic ideological basis. This view has been expressed by the country's President, France Albert Rene, as follows:

"*Non-alignment is an expression of our independence and integrity as a nation. It allows us to decide an issue on its own merit and based upon Seychelles' interests. We are not locked into any camp of East or West with a pre-determined view, but free to decide for ourselves, and in allegiance with all those nations struggling for peace, independence, justice and equality. This is why we refer to our stance as positive non-alignment.*"

Seychelles will, in my view, continue to confound its critics by adapting to changing situations and by maintaining steady social and economic progress, despite the difficulties it continues to face. Its brief history, diverse cultural affinities and strong traditional values have helped to create a solid framework around which Seychellois can confidently build their future. I, for one, wish them well in the challenges they face, and hope that this book will help to open many people's eyes to the tremendous natural and human resources which exist in Seychelles—a country which, as the travel brochures proudly proclaim, is truly "unique by a thousand miles"!

Street Poster with a political message in Victoria. August 1987. The struggle for independence, national identity and social change is characterised as the revolution of Seychelles. The transformation from two hundred odd years of colonial rule, to one of self determination has inevitably been accompanied by evolution of new socio-political and economic solutions together with a fair degree of experimentation. There have been many successes, as well as a few failures, but the over-all impression one gains from comparing the country prior to independence with its current status, is that of steady improvements in most aspects. (Vine).

APPENDIX ONE

GENERAL SUMMARY OF INFORMATION

KEY FACTS

Official title: Republic of Seychelles
Area: 455 sq kms.
Population: 65,653 (1986 census)
Capital: Victoria
Official Language: Creole
Other Languages: French, English
Currency: Seychelles Rupee (SR) = 100 cents
Climate: (average 1972-1986)
   Rainfall: 2230mm; Sunshine: 6.9 hrs per day; Mean max.temp.:29.8 deg.C.;
   Mean min. temp. 24.5 deg.C.; Humidity: 80%; Max.gust:60 knots.

Tourism: Visitor arrivals (1986) 66,782.

Agriculture: Cash Crops (tonnes, 1986)
   Copra exports: 2,374
   Cinnamon bark: 1,214
   Tea/green leaf 136
   Fish landed 4,633

Beverages and Tobacco Production:
   Drinks ('000 litres, 1986)
   Soft drinks 3,886
   Beer and Stout 4,148
   Cigarettes (millions)—59.6.

Education:
   Number of students (1987)

Total	21,772
Creche	3,217
Primary 1-9	14,553
Secondary	2,590
Polytechnic	1,412

Number of teachers (1987)

Total	1,199
Creche	134
Primary 1-9	698
Secondary	204
Polytechnic	163
Pupil/teacher ratio	18.2

Health: (1986)

Hospital beds/total	331
Victoria Hospital	249
Medical/dental officers	40

APPENDIX TWO

USEFUL INFORMATION

The following information is reproduced by kind permission of Seychelles Tourist Board.

ACCOMMODATION
All owners and their staff have codes of standards aimed at ensuring a high level of customer satisfaction

AIRLINES
Direct services are provided by Air Seychelles, Air France, British Airways and Kenya Airways covering Europe, Africa, Asia and other Indian Ocean islands. Air Seychelles provides a regular internal service between the major islands.

BANKS
The Seychelles Savings Bank, branches of Barclays Bank International, Banque Francaise Commerciale, Bank of Baroda, Bank of Credit and Commerce, Habib Bank, Standard Bank will exchange foreign currency and travellers cheques. Banks at the airport always open for arrivals and departures of International flights.

CUSTOMS AND EXCISE
The Duty Free Allowances are:
200 gms Cigarettes; 50 gms Cigars; 250 gms Tobacco or any combination of these up to 250 gms.
1 Litre of Spirits and 1 Litre of Wine.
125cc. Perfume and 25cl. Toilet water.
Other dutiable articles up to a value not exceeding SR400/-(adults) and SR200/-(under 18's). The importation of arms, ammunition, drugs and spear guns is prohibited; animals, food, agricultural produce are strictly controlled and subject to licensing.

CURRENCY
The currency unit is the Seychelles Rupee (SR) which is divided into 100 cents. For daily foreign exchange rates consult any local bank.

ENTRY REQUIREMENTS
You must have a valid passport to enter the Seychelles and onward or return tickets, valid travel documents, accommodation and sufficient funds for your stay. Camping is not allowed. Visas are not normally required. A one month visitor's pass is issued by the Immigration Authorities on arrival. This may be renewed for up to three months free of charge.

MEDICAL FACILITIES
Visitors may obtain emergency treatment under the National Medical Service for illness and accident at a basic consultation fee of SR75. Prescribed medicines and drugs can be bought at the hospital pharmacy or some chemists. The main hospital, out-patients clinic and dental clinic are located at Mont Fleuri (near the Botanical gardens). Most other districts also have a clinic.

POSTAL SERVICE
The main post office is in Victoria. Airmail collections are at 3-0pm on Weekdays and at noon on Saturdays.

TELECOMMUNICATIONS
Telephone, telex, and radio links world-wide are operated by Cable & Wireless Ltd. on a 24 hour basis.

TIME DIFFERENCE
The Seychelles is 4 hours ahead of G.M.T. (3 hours ahead of British Summer Time). Or three hours ahead of Central European Time in winter and 2 hours in summer

TIPS
These are not expected in Seychelles. All hotel and restaurant tariffs include service.

TRANSPORT
There is an efficient bus service on Mahe and Praslin from 5-30am to 7-0pm. Cars are easy to hire. Taxis stand at major hotels, the international airport and Victoria's central taxi station. There are also regular ferries between the islands of Mahe, Praslin and La Digue.

VOLTAGES
Electric current is 240 volts A.C. 50Hz. Plugs are square pin, three point.

WEATHER

The climate is tropical—mostly equable as the surrounding ocean has a moderating effect. The Seychelles are outside the cyclone belt so high winds or thunderstorms are rare.

Weather statistics: Monthly Data and Twelve Year Averages 1972-83. Seychelles International Airport. Sea Level.

	Jan	Feb	Mar	Apr	May	Jun	July	Aug	Sept	Oct	Nov	Dec
Rainfall (mm)	405	295	177	203	107	54	65	90	132	212	241	314
Sunshine hrs/day	5.1	6.4	6.9	7.6	8.5	7.9	7.3	7.6	7.6	7.3	6.8	5.3
Mean Maximum Temp. deg.C.	29.8	30.4	30.9	31.3	30.6	29.4	28.5	28.5	29.0	29.6	30.1	29.9
Mean Minimum Temp. deg.C.	24.1	24.7	24.8	25.0	25.6	25.0	24.2	24.1	24.3	24.3	24.0	23.8
Humidity (Average %)	82	80	79	80	78	79	80	79	79	80	80	83

WHAT TO WEAR

Women—light cotton dresses, slacks and shorts at any time of year. Formal dress is seldom worn in the evening.

Men—lightweight slacks or shorts and open neck shirts. Slacks and shirts are fine for the evening. All clothing should be lightweight and washable.

USEFUL ADDRESSES

1. SEYCHELLES TOURIST BOARD AND NATIONAL TRAVEL AGENCY

United Kingdom
50 Conduit Street,
London W1A4PE
Tel. 01 439 9699
Telex 21236 SEYCOM G.

Seychelles
Independence House,
PO Box 92,
Victoria, Mahe.
Tel. 22881
Tlx. 2275 SEYTOB SZ
Fax. 76551

France
53 bis Rue Francois 1er,
Internazionale
5eme etage,
75008 Paris
Tel. (1) 720.37.43
Tlx 649140 SEYPAR

Italy
Centro Cooperazione
P.zza Giulio Cesare 1,
2014 Milan
Tel. (02) 49.85.795/46.92.964
Tlx. 331360 EAFM I.

Federal Republic of Germany
Kleine Boockenheimer Strasse 18A
D-6000 Frankfurt am Main 1,
Tel. (069) 292064
Tlx. 414788 SEY D.

National Travel Agency
PO Box 611,
Victoria, Mahe.
Tel. 21180
Telex: 2356
Fax: 21555

Seychelles
Victoria House,
PO Box 386, Victoria, Mahe.
Tel. 76501 (reservations)
Tlx. 2337 (int. reservations)
Tlx. 2314 (administration)
Fax. 23989

United Kingdom
Kingston House,
Stephenson Way, 3 Bridges
West Sussex RH10 6AA
Tel. 0293 36313
Tlx. 877033 AIRSEY G.
Fax. 0293 562353

PRIVATE TOURIST HANDLING AGENTS/TOUR ORGANISERS

Travel Services (Seychelles) Ltd.
Victoria House, PO Box 356,
Victoria, Mahe
Tel. 22414, Fax. 21366
Tlx. 2234 LINWES SZ.

Masons Travel (PTY)
PO Box 459, Revolution Avenue
Victoria, Mahe.
Tel. 22642, Tlx. 2230
Fax. 21273

APPENDIX THREE

There have been a number of swimming fatalities in Seychelles, many of which could have been avoided if swimmers had been more aware of which beaches are considered dangerous for swimming. The following information, issued by the Tourist Board, is therefore reproduced in this appendix, in the sincere hope that visitors will follow the advice contained here, and that such accidents will be avoided in future.

GRANDE ANSE BEACH: MAHE: Dangerous for swimming. Strong south-easterly winds and powerful currents may be experienced from May 1st to September 30th.

VAL MER: MAHE: Dangerous for swimming. Strong south-easterly winds and powerful currents may be experienced from May 1st to September 30th.

ANSE GAULETTE: MAHE: Dangerous for swimming. Strong south-easterly winds and powerful currents may be experienced from May 1st to September 30th.

TAKAMAKA: MAHE: Dangerous for swimming. Strong south-easterly winds and powerful currents may be experienced from May 1st to September 30th.

INTENDANCE BEACH: MAHE: Dangerous for swimming. Strong south-easterly winds and powerful currents may be experienced from May 1st to September 30th.

ANSE COCO: LA DIGUE: Dangerous for swimming. Strong south-easterly winds and powerful currents may be experienced from May 1st to September 30th.

PETITE ANSE: LA DIGUE: Dangerous for swimming. Strong south-easterly winds and powerful currents may be experienced from May 1st to September 30th.

GRANDE ANSE: LA DIGUE: Dangerous for swimming. Strong south-easterly winds and powerful currents may be experienced from May 1st to September 30th.

ANSE SONGE: LA DIGUE: Dangerous for swimming. Strong south-easterly winds and powerful currents may be experienced from May 1st to September 30th.

ANSE MARRON: LA DIGUE: Dangerous for swimming. Strong south-easterly winds and powerful currents may be experienced from May 1st to September 30th.
ANSE KERLAN: PRASLIN: Dangerous for swimming. Strong north-westerly winds and powerful currents may be experienced during December and January.

FURTHER READING

Aleem, A.A. 1968. Concepts of currents, tides and winds among medieval Arab geographers in the Indian Ocean. *Deep Sea Research 14* 459-463.

Anon. 1982. Histoire des Seychelles. *Ministry of Education and Information.*

Bailey, D. 1971. List of the flowering plants and ferns of seychelles. Government press.

Baker, B.H. Geology and Mineral resources of the Seychelles Archipelago.

Baker, B.H. and **J.A. Miller** 1963. Geology and geochronology of the seychelles islands and structure of the floor of the Arabian Sea. *Nature* 199. 346-348.

Beamish, T. 1981. Birds of Seychelles. Dept. of Agriculture, Seychelles.

Beamish, T. 1970. Aldabra Alone. George Allen and Unwin.

Benedict, B. 1984. The human population of the Seychelles, in Stoddart, D.R. 1984. Biogeography and ecology of the Seychelles Islands. *Monographiae Biologicae* Vol *55*. Dr W. Junk Publishers. The Hague.

Benson, C.W. 1984 Origins of Seychelles land birds, in Stoddart, D.R. 1984. Biogeography and ecology of the Seychelles Islands. *Monographiae Biologicae* Vol *55*. Dr W. Junk Publishers. The Hague.

Bour, R. 1984. Taxonomy, history and geography of Seychelles land Tortoises and freshwater Turtles, in Stoddart, D.R. 1984. Biogeography and ecology of the Seychelles Islands. *Monographiae Biologicae* Vol *55*. Dr W. Junk Publishers. The Hague.

Braithwaite, C.J.R. 1984. Geology of the Seychelles in Stoddart, D.R. 1984. Biogeography and ecology of the Seychelles Islands. *Monographiae Biologicae* Vol *55*. Dr W. Junk Publishers. The Hague.

Bruce, A.J. 1984. Marine caridean shrimps of the Seychelles, in Stoddart, D.R. 1984. Biogeography and ecology of the Seychelles Islands. *Monographiae Biologicae* Vol *55*. Dr W. Junk Publishers. The Hague.

Christensen, C. 1912. On the Ferns of the Seychelles and the Aldabra group. *Trans. Linn. Soc. Ser. 2. vol. vii.* 409-425.

Cheke, A.S. 1984. Lizards of the Seychelles in Stoddart, D.R. 1984. Biogeography and ecology of the Seychelles Islands. *Monographiae Biologicae* Vol *55*. Dr W. Junk Publishers. The Hague.

Clark, A.M. 1984 in Stoddart, D.R. 1984. Biogeography and ecology of the Seychelles Islands. *Monographiae Biologicae* Vol *55*. Dr W. Junk Publishers. The Hague.

Coe, M. and **I.R. Swingland** 1984. Giant tortoises of the Seychelles, in Stoddart, D.R. 1984. Biogeography and ecology of the Seychelles Islands. *Monographiae Biologicae* Vol *55*. Dr W. Junk Publishers. The Hague.

Cogan, B.H. 1984. Origins and affinities of Seychelles insect fauna, in Stoddart, D.R. 1984. Biogeography and ecology of the Seychelles Islands. *Monographiae Biologicae* Vol *55*. Dr W. Junk Publishers. The Hague.

Denis, U. et al 1987. Culinary Delights from the Seychelles. Editions Delroise.

Diamond, A.W. 1984. Biogeography of Seychelles land birds, in Stoddart, D.R. 1984. Biogeography and ecology of the Seychelles Islands. *Monographiae Biologicae* Vol *55.* Dr W. Junk Publishers. The Hague.

Fauvel, A.A. 1909. Republished 1980. Unpublished Documents on the History of the Seychelles anterior to 1810. Originally published by Government Printing Office, Mahe. Republished with collaboration of the Government of Belgium.

Feare, C.J. 1974. Desertion and abnormal development in a colony of Sooty terns, *Sterna fuscata* infested by virus infected ticks. *Ibis. 118*, 112-115.

Feare, C.J. 1975. Post fledging parental care in crested and sooty terns. *Condor 77*, 368-370.

Feare, C.J. 1976. The breeding of the Sooty tern *Sterna fuscata* in the Seychelles and the effects of experimental removal of its eggs. *J.Zool.* Lond. *179*, 317-360.

Feare, C.M. and **J. High** 1977. Migrant shore-birds in the Seychelles. *Ibis. 119*, 323-338.

Feare, C.J. 1984. Seabirds as a resource: Use and management, in Stoddart, D.R. 1984. Biogeography and ecology of the Seychelles Islands. *Monographiae Biologicae* Vol *55.* Dr W. Junk Publishers. The Hague.

Feare, C.J. and **J. Watson** 1984. Occurrence of migrant birds in the Seychelles, in Stoddart, D.R. 1984. Biogeography and ecology of the Seychelles Islands. *Monographiae Biologicae* Vol *55.* Dr W. Junk Publishers. The Hague.

Fosberg, F.R. and **S.A. Renvoize.** The Flora of Aldabra and Neighbouring Islands. Kew Bulletin. Additional Series. VII.

Frazier, J. Marine turtles in the Seychelles and adjacent territories, in Stoddart, D.R. 1984. Biogeography and ecology of the Seychelles Islands. *Monographiae Biologicae* Vol *55.* Dr W. Junk Publishers. The Hague.

Friedman. F. 1986. Flowers and trees of Seychelles. O.R.S.T.O.M.

Fryer, J.C.F. 1910. The Lepidoptera of Seychelles and Aldabra. *Trans. Linn. Soc. ser. 2. Zool. xiii.* 397-404.

Fryer, J.C.F. 1910. Bird and Denis Islands, Seychelles. *Trans. Linn. Soc. 2nd. ser. Zool. xiv (2).* 15-20.

Garth, J.S. 1984. Brachyuran decapod crustaceans of coral reef communities of the Seychelles and Amirantes, in Stoddart, D.R. 1984. Biogeography and ecology of the Seychelles Islands. *Monographiae Biologicae* Vol *55.* Dr W. Junk Publishers. The Hague.

Gaymer, R. et al. 1969. The Endemic Birds of Seychelles. *Ibis 111*, 157-176.

Gerlach, J. The Land Snails of Seychelles. *Justin Gerlach.*

Harris, L. The Stamps and Postal History of Seychelles. *Seychelles Government.*

Haig, J. 1984. Land and freshwater crabs of the Seychelles and neighbouring islands, in Stoddart, D.R. 1984. Biogeography and ecology of the Seychelles Islands. *Monographiae Biologicae* Vol *55.* Dr W. Junk Publishers. The Hague.

Hoogstraal, H. and **C.J. Feare** 1984. Ticks and tickborne viruses, in Stoddart, D.R. 1984. Biogeography and ecology of the Seychelles Islands. *Monographiae Biologicae* Vol *55*. Dr W. Junk Publishers. The Hague.

I.C.B.P. Cousin Island. Leaflet issued to visitors.

Khanna, S.N. and **G. Pillay** 1986. Seychelles: petroleum potential of this Indian Ocean paradise. *Oil and Gas Journal*, 1986.

Lawson, T.A. et al 1986. The western Indian Ocean Tuna Fishery from 1980 to 1985. A summary of data collected by coastal states. *Seychelles Fishing Authority Technical Report*.

Lionnet, G. 1986 Romance of a Palm. Coco de Mer. i'ile aux images.

Lionnet, G. 1972. The Seychelles. David and Charles. UK.

Lionnet, G. 1984. Terrestrial testaceous molluscs of the Seychelles, in Stoddart, D.R. 1984. Biogeography and ecology of the Seychelles Islands. *Monographiae Biologicae* Vol *55*. Dr W. Junk Publishers. The Hague.

Lionnet, G. 1984. Lepidoptera of the Seychelles, in Stoddart, D.R. 1984. Biogeography and ecology of the Seychelles Islands. *Monographiae Biologicae* Vol *55*. Dr W. Junk Publishers. The Hague.

Lionnet, G. 1984. Extinct birds of the Seychelles, in Stoddart, D.R. 1984. Biogeography and ecology of the Seychelles Islands. *Monographiae Biologicae* Vol *55*. Dr W. Junk Publishers. The Hague.

Loustau-Lalanne, P. 1962. Land birds of the granitic islands of the Seychelles. *Seychelles Society* 1.

Michaud, P. and **J.P. Hallier** 1986. Le developpment de la Peche Thoniere dans l'ocean Indien face aux Resources. *Seychelles Fishing Authority Technical Report*.

Mortimer, J.A. 1984. Marine Turtles in the Republic of the Seychelles. Status and Management. *I.U.C.N.* and *W.W.F.*

Moussac, G. de. 1987. Seychelles Artisanal Fisheries Statistics for 1986. *Seychelles Fishing Authority Technical Report*.

Nussbaum, R.A. 1984. Snakes of the Seychelles, in Stoddart, D.R. 1984. Biogeography and ecology of the Seychelles Islands. *Monographiae Biologicae* Vol *55*. Dr W. Junk Publishers. The Hague.

Nussbaum, R.A. 1984. Amphibians of the Seychelles, in Stoddart, D.R. 1984. Biogeography and ecology of the Seychelles Islands. *Monographiae Biologicae* Vol *55*. Dr W. Junk Publishers. The Hague.

Pavard, C. Seychelles, from one island to another. Editions Delrosse.

Polunin, N.V.C. and **F.R.J. Williams** 1977. Coral reef Fishes of Seychelles. *Seychelles Government Report*.

Polunin, N.V.C. 1984. Marine Fishes of the Seychelles, in Stoddart, D.R. 1984. Biogeography and ecology of the Seychelles Islands. *Monographiae Biologicae* Vol *55*. Dr W. Junk Publishers. The Hague.

Procter, J. 1974. The endemic flowering plants of the Seychelles: an annotated list. *Candollea 29*, 345-387.

Procter, J. 1984. Vegetation of the granitic Seychelles, in Stoddart, D.R. 1984. Biogeography and ecology of the Seychelles Islands. *Monographiae Biologicae* Vol 55. Dr W. Junk Publishers. The Hague.

Procter, J. 1984. Floristics of the granitic islands of the Seychelles. Stoddart, D.R. 1984. Biogeography and ecology of the Seychelles Islands. *Monographiae Biologicae* Vol 55. Dr W. Junk Publishers. The Hague.

Pryce-Jones, R.P. and **A.W. Diamond** 1984. Ecology of the land birds of the granitic and coralline islands of the Seychelles, with particular reference to Cousin Island and Aldabra Atoll, in Stoddart, D.R. 1984. Biogeography and ecology of the Seychelles Islands. *Monographiae Biologicae* Vol 55. Dr W. Junk Publishers. The Hague.

Racey, R.A. and **M.E. Nicoll** 1984. Mammals of the Seychelles, in Stoddart, D.R. 1984. Biogeography and ecology of the Seychelles Islands. *Monographiae Biologicae* Vol 55. Dr W. Junk Publishers. The Hague.

Sauer, J.D. 1967. Plants and Man on the Seychelles coast. *University of Wisconsin Press*.

Smith, J.L.B. and **M.M.** 1969. Fishes of Seychelles. *J.L.B. Smith Institute of Icthyology*. S.A.

Stoddart, D.R. 1984. Impact of man in the Seychelles, in Stoddart, D.R. 1984. Biogeography and ecology of the Seychelles Islands. *Monographiae Biologicae* Vol 55. Dr W. Junk Publishers. The Hague.

Stoddart, D.R. 1984. Biogeography and ecology of the Seychelles Islands. *Monographiae Biologicae* Vol 55. Dr W. Junk Publishers. The Hague.

Stoddart, D.R. 1984 Coral reefs of the Seychelles and adjacent regions, in Stoddart, D.R. 1984. Biogeography and ecology of the Seychelles Islands. *Monographiae Biologicae* Vol 55. Dr W. Junk Publishers. The Hague.

Stoddart, D.R. 1984. Scientific studies in Seychelles, in Stoddart, D.R. 1984. Biogeography and ecology of the Seychelles Islands. *Monographiae Biologicae* Vol 55. Dr W. Junk Publishers. The Hague.

Stoddart, D.R. 1984. Breeding seabirds of the Seychelles and adjacent islands, in Stoddart, D.R. 1984. Biogeography and ecology of the Seychelles Islands. *Monographiae Biologicae* Vol 55. Dr W. Junk Publishers. The Hague.

Stoddart, D.R. and **F.R. Fosberg** 1984. Vegetation and floristics of west Indian Ocean coral islands, in Stoddart, D.R. 1984. Biogeography and ecology of the Seychelles Islands. *Monographiae Biologicae* Vol 55. Dr W. Junk Publishers. The Hague.

Travis, W. 1959. Beyond the Reefs. George Allen and Unwin.

Vine, P.J. 1972. Life on Coral Reefs in Seychelles. Seychelles Government.

Walsh, R.P.D. 1984 Climate of the Seychelles, in Stoddart, D.R. 1984. Biogeography and ecology of the Seychelles Islands. *Monographiae Biologicae* Vol 55. Dr W. Junk Publishers. The Hague.

Warren, B.A. 1966. Medieval Arab references to the seasonally reversing currents of the north Indian Ocean. *Deep Sea Research 13*, 167-171.

Watson, J. 1984. Land birds: Endangered species of the granitic Seychelles, in Stoddart, D.R. 1984. Biogeography and ecology of the Seychelles Islands. *Monographiae Biologicae* Vol *55*. Dr W. Junk Publishers. The Hague.

Webb, A.W.T. and **H.J. MacGaw** 1987. Inventaire des Archives Nationales Des Seychelles. Published by National Archives Seychelles.

ACKNOWLEDGEMENTS

During the preparation of this book I received help from numerous individuals and organisations, all of whom were most gracious in their cooperation and made my own work an entirely pleasant experience. The Minister of Tourism and Transport, and the Minister of Education, Information and Youth both took a deep interest in my work and I am grateful to them for the encouragement I received, both directly and through their respective staff. In this regard I should like to pay special tribute to Captain Sam Andrade, Director of Port and Marine Services Division, who was extremely helpful in coordinating assistance for the project, and also to Maurice Loustau-Lalanne, previously Chairman and Chief Executive of Air Seychelles, and presently Director General of Civil Aviation and Tourism. Sadly, space does not allow me to list the many ways in which these people and their staff assisted me in my work in Seychelles. I might add however, that it was not just the fact that I received considerable help, but also the fact that this was offered most graciously, in a true spirit of cooperation and hospitality. It was this, more than anything else, which made my work on this book so personally rewarding and enjoyable.

Among the first contacts I met, when preparing to write this book, was Liz Naya, Manager of Seychelles Tourist Board office in London. Liz was most helpful in steering me in the right direction, and in coordinating support for my work. I owe her a special vote of thanks for, without her initial encouragement, it is true to say that the book may never have happened! Air Seychelles were most generous in their assistance and I have nothing but praise for their extremely high standard of service. The national airline remains the most convenient means and a superbly comfortable way to travel to Mahe from Europe or the Middle East. I should like to offer my sincere thanks to the airline, as well as to its managerial staff in Mahe and London, for their enthusiastic support for my work. Once on the islands, I was accommodated by Seychelles Hotels Corporation who provided me with the opportunity to stay at nearly all their hotels on Mahe and Praslin. These are managed to a uniformly high standard and while, each hotel had its special characteristics, likely to appeal to different people, the group has the unique advantage of offering a flexible holiday with accommodation alterable at short notice to other venues within the organisation. I am most grateful to Seychelles Hotels for their support, and to Rose-Marie Hoareau, Therese Blanc and Derek Savy, for their kindness and hospitality. On the subject of transport and accommodation, I should also like to record my thanks to the National Travel Agency (NTA) who provided me with land transport; and to Mr and Mrs Pierre Burkhardt of Denis Island; Mr and Mrs Guy Savy of Bird Island and Mr and Mrs Mason of Masons Travel, all of whom arranged for me to visit their respective projects, and who each briefed me upon interesting aspects of local history and wildlife. Particular memories I shall treasure for many years are my SCUBA dive off Denis Island together with the superb hospitality (and French cooking!) I enjoyed there; being greeted by the birds of Bird Island, not to mention its friendly human inhabitants; searching for pirate's treasure on Frigate Island and for ancient sites on Silhouette (both courtesy of Masons Travel); and an extremely enjoyable day snorkelling in Ste Anne's Marine Park, guided by Alan Mason, a most competent and pleasant companion.

In my search for information on Seychelles' past, I was drawn first to the National Museum in Victoria, and then to the National Archive Centre at La Bastille. I was very happy indeed to renew my acquaintance with Henri McGaw, director of these projects, who worked assiduously to create an efficient document centre on Mahe. It is an invaluable facility for the serious researcher and Henri McGaw was most accommodating in his assistance, and free with his advice. In this regard I should also like to record my gratitude to Guy Lionnet, who has written at length on many aspects of Seychelles and is a mine of information on cultural, historical and natural aspects of the islands. He was most courteous and kind in his advice to me while researching this book and I have in several places referred to published works by him. Another legendary source of Seychelles history is Kantilal Jivan Shah, an old friend from my earlier visits to Seychelles. I was pleased to discover that Kanti, as he is widely known, has not changed in the intervening years, and is still imbued with enthusiasm for Seychelles and for the pursuit of knowledge on all aspects of its heritage: a love which he has passed on to his son Nimo. For her contribution of historic postcards I am grateful to Mrs Susan Hopson of the Indian Ocean Studies Group. The chapter on art and artists could not have been prepared without the support of Leon Radegonde, Chairman of Seychelles Artists Society and of the individual artists who kindly agreed to allow their works to be displayed in the book. Guy de Moussac was most helpful with providing information on the artisanal fishery and a number of unique photographs, and I wish to thank Francis Marsac of ORSTOM for his own data on the tuna fishery. Following completion of the text I returned to Seychelles in February 1989 and on this visit I was pleased to meet with Minister of Education, Information and Youth, James Michel, who showed a great personal interest in my work and facilitated me by arranging a meeting with Director General of the Information and Telecommunications Division, Patrick Nanty. Patrick is a keen historian of Seychelles and as such was able to advise me on certain aspects of the text. I am most grateful for his careful and constructive approach to this task.

I should also like to thank Lindsay Chongseng for checking the natural history text and for taking me up MtBernica to see the 'jellyfish trees' which survive there.

Individual photographers are separately credited, both with the respective captions, and at the front of this book. I should like here to thank in particular Susanna Harrison who spent several weeks taking pictures for this book.

Finally, I am indebted to my wife, Paula for her research, writing assistance and editing of this book.

INDEX